A Boy and his Bear

A Boy and his Bear

A MEMOIR

Gregory Ladner

Hardie Grant

BOOKS

Published in 2022 by Hardie Grant Books an imprint of Hardie Grant Publishing

Hardie Grant Books (Melbourne)
Ground Floor, Building 1, 658 Church Street
Richmond VIC 3121, Australia

Hardie Grant Books (London)
5th and 6th Floors,52–54 Southwark Street
London SE1 1UN

www.hardiegrant.com.au

Hardie Grant acknowledges the Traditional Owners of the country on which we work,
the Wurundjeri people of the Kulin nation and the Gadigal people of the Eora nation, and
recognises their continuing connection to the land, waters and culture. We pay our respects to
their Elders past and present.

 A catalogue record for this
book is available from the
National Library of Australia

A Boy and His Bear
ISBN 9781743798959

Publication commissioned by Courtney Nicholls
Publication managed by Hannah Louey
Edited by Sally Moss
Design by Kate Slattery
Back cover photograph by Eryca Green
Printed in Australia by Ovato

To Susie Holt, Stephen Maclean and
Terry Cutler, whose encouragement
over the years has got me here.

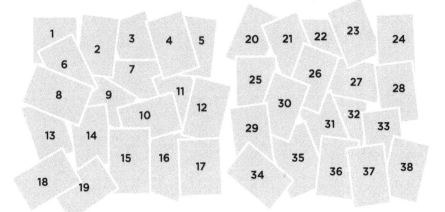

Contents

CONTENTS

Foreword

I first saw Gregory Ladner standing in our street, supervising an odd activity: a mobile crane was conveying heavy boulders high over a tall wall and into specific places in the rock garden he was designing for his newly acquired property.

He was our new neighbour, replacing a church. My wife, Ann, and I had been accustomed to hearing, next door, the sound of the elderly worshippers singing on Christmas Eve or at funerals, but the congregation waned, and we were amongst those invited to the final religious service. And now, a few years later, Greg's boulders and tallish trees finally stood where the congregation once had sat.

In the course of some thirty years we had come to appreciate our neighbours, Greg Ladner and his partner, Mark, but we knew little about Greg's bohemian apprenticeship and exotic life until we read this story. It is so frank that it might not have been permitted to see the light of day sixty years ago.

A rural childhood is the setting for many autobiographies, but less common is an observant story beginning in "the western suburbs" of Melbourne. Even rarer is the story of a creative life in the fiercely competitive and theatrical realm of high fashion.

A "skinny" child, reared in the 1950s in what he thinks was a depressing neighbourhood (his family home was too close to a tannery), Greg cloaks his childhood with magic and awe, and just a dash of grievance. His possessions then included a teddy bear, a red billycart, a kitten called Ciss Puss, and the imitation feathers with which he loved to decorate himself. Of all Nature's creatures, "I love sparrows the most", he declares. He was also devoted to his grandmother, his Nanna, who ran a little shop opposite a Footscray school, while his own mother baked the meat pies, sausage rolls and lamingtons that the children bought at lunchtime.

Greg observes that, "in the eyes of a child, everything is enormous". Momentous were his first visits to a beach on Port Phillip Bay. The sand dunes concealed thousands of tiny bivalves that could be threaded together, and "I would spend hours making ropes of necklaces and wear them around my neck, wrists and ankles and on my head." After he was piggy- backed by his policeman father onto a shallow sandbar and allowed to stand there, still and silent, he gained a feeling of serenity. "No wonder Jesus loved the Sea of Galilee," he writes, though in other chapters he conveys the impression that he himself is not religious in an orthodox sense. To be orthodox in any activity was never his goal.

Entering the fashion industry in inner Melbourne as a talented teenage designer, he was soon creating and fitting the most expensive wedding clothes, though he was initially assigned to the bridesmaids' dresses and the wedding outfit of the bride's future mother-in-law; these items belonged to the "second league", in football nomenclature. All kinds of outfits and adornments challenged him, and he responded with creativity and high confidence: "I only made mistakes when I allowed others to influence my decisions."

He learned how to combine or contrast different materials and colours in daring ways; and colleagues and rivals recognised his versatility long before women's hats of his making were admired on Melbourne Cup Day, and before he himself was a celebrity amongst well-dressed women. Impressive is the way he makes his profession seem intelligible and often fascinating.

That he is gay is a strong strand in his memoir, and he praises his partner, Mark – of Armenian descent, and a contrast in personality: "We have successfully woven a life together that has enriched us emotionally, physically and financially." Near the close of the book, Greg wished to make a forthright detour, but female friends, of whom he has many, apparently advised him to delete this. Instead – offering the option to readers who have come this far – he provides clues that will enable them to decide whether or not to read the last chapter. Now old, I took the easy option, but young and middle-aged readers may well ask what the fuss is about.

Having chanced to chair various literature and arts boards, I hope I have normally backed the individual's reasonable right to free expression. Hardie Grant, the book's publisher, agrees with the principle. Authors of autobiographies and memoirs definitely gain from such liberty, as do their readers.

This book's pen portraits of Greg's mother, father and other relatives are arresting. We hardly know of their eccentricities, virtues and failings until late in the story when they are variously revealed either with tender affection or some exasperation. His Nanna – born in Manchester and retaining well into her nineties her rose-red cheeks and her intense monarchical loyalties – would, if she came alive and read this book, feel proud of her high-flying sparrow.

Geoffrey Blainey
East Melbourne, 2022

Introduction

I was at the checkout in the lingerie department of David Jones, buying some cotton nightgowns for my mother, Celia, for Christmas.

"You're Gregory Ladner!" The lady at the cash register was so excited when she saw my credit card. I could have been Tom Cruise, by the way she broadcast my name.

"No, I'm not!" was my immediate response. She must mean someone else.

She checked the name again, then looked me up and down. A frown clouded her brow as she reached for the scissors, about to destroy this imposter's stolen credit card.

"No, no!" I exclaimed. "I am, I am."

It was the first time that it struck home. Thanks to the sheer number of "Gregory Ladner" labels branding every single item I had produced over the years, it occurred to me that I was a household name.

She said she had a wardrobe full of my scarves. Oh, she loved my jewellery and race wear. She proudly showed me the earrings she was wearing – cubic zirconia and pearl drops more suited to an evening on the town than behind a register at DJs. She fumbled around under the till for her iPhone to show me a photo she had taken at that year's Melbourne Cup. Indeed, there she was, centre left in a group selfie of

blousy, inebriated girlfriends, balancing one of my fascinators over her right eye.

A cash and wrap to remember. I was genuinely thrilled to be Gregory Ladner in person, brightening up her dreary day. How did I get to a point of modest celebrity in the eyes of this woman who couldn't stop shopping? Was it good luck, karma or just plain hard work? Had I been spurred on by a driving ambition to escape to a fantasy life as seen on the silver screen as a child? Was it an accident that turned out rather well in the end?

This memoir is not going to answer life's great philosophical questions but it may give a clue to the odd path taken by a boy and his teddy bear from a working-class background in Footscray to the periphery of the upper echelons of Melbourne society.

I hope you have as much fun reading about Teddy and me as I have had clocking up our stories. The journey is a reminder that life is not over yet! As Judy Garland sang,

> *Some people can be content*
> *Playing bingo and paying rent.*
> *That's peachy for some people,*
> *For some humdrum people to be,*
> *But some people ain't me.*

The Best Seven Years

I once went to a clairvoyant in Moorabbin, a bayside suburb of Melbourne. Moorabbin's only saving grace at that time was a vast IKEA store. A great Sunday afternoon's excursion was to drive down there and push a trolley around the store for an hour or so, filling it up with all sorts of can't-live-without, must-have things. Approaching the cash and wrap, you would suddenly come to your senses and realise that you only really wanted the two packets of paper napkins. Should any IKEA sales assistant be reading this, I apologise for that mysterious trolley found regularly abandoned, dumped and hidden behind the foldaway patio chairs groaning with "Bergsbo" bookshelves, "Basisk" desk lamps, colour-coded chopping boards, and coffee mugs (six for $10). It was me!

A very dear friend prompted this rare "sans IKEA" excursion to Moorabbin. She had been to the psychic the week before and had been told some startling things. One was that she saw two girls. This news had hit her like a sledgehammer. The previous year, circumstances had forced her to choose an abortion – unbeknown to the psychic, she had been carrying two female foetuses. So, she was convinced of the psychic's powers, and I was more than a little intrigued.

I don't remember much about the experience. Did the psychic read my palm? Lay hands on me? Hold an object? I do remember wrenching my mother's wedding ring from my finger. My parents had divorced some time before. Celia had given me the ring and I had worn it ever since. I also remember what the psychic told me, and an unexpected, uncontrollable flurry of tears as she dug up things I had secreted away in my mind – things I had buried, hoping they would never surface again. Many of the things the psychic told me have since come true, and some things still might.

She told me that I would never be really rich but that I would never have to worry about money. From that day on, I never gave money a second thought, and she was right – somehow, at the darkest moment when the wolf was at the door, money would come from nowhere. After all these years, you would think I would wake up and stop buying lottery tickets. However, habits are hard to break, and I've stuck to the possibility that she could be wrong, and that untold riches await me next Saturday night, slim though that possibility may be.

"You've got to be in it to win it!"

The other thing she told me was that one's life goes in seven-year cycles and that the best cycle of my own life happened from when I was born up until the age of seven! My first reaction was, "Well, why bother to go on? I am never going to be rich, and it's downhill all the way."

The worst thing about the first seven years is that you don't remember all that much. I was born in 1950 in a private hospital in the working-class suburb of Yarraville in Melbourne's west. Nothing traumatic happened in my childhood, neither was there anything spectacular. I felt secure and loved, and the memories and people I draw upon are all treasured and have formed the character that I am today.

My grandmother (Nanna) owned a milk bar in Wingfield Street, Footscray, which my mother helped her run. We all lived behind the shop. Nanna always lived with us, or we with her, and because my mother always worked, my younger brother and I spent most of our formative years under Nanna's care.

The milk bar was directly opposite a Catholic school. "Position, Position, Position." The playtime and lunchtime trade and the after-school lolly rush were a goldmine. I can still hear the sound of the crisp, shiny white paper bags as they filled up with assorted lollies. A penny's worth of freckles, the same of chocolate bullets, false teeth, bananas and clinkers, all topped off with a musk stick. Everything else that was for sale in the shop was made by my mother. She baked all the pies, sausage rolls, pasties and cakes. Fairy cakes, lamingtons, Swiss rolls and – my favourite – apple cakes. She put a squeeze of lemon in the icing, which took some of the sweetness away and left a delicious tang lingering on your tongue. When I see apple cakes to this day, I buy them in the vain hope of recapturing that long-gone childhood experience. Unfortunately, they usually go straight into the rubbish bin after one bite. It's a peculiar thing about those elusive tastes and aromas from the past. They are always lurking somewhere at the back of the throat, between the taste buds and the mind, but not quite retrievable.

Aromas we had plenty of – there was a malodorous tannery at the bottom of our street, and we were slap bang in the middle of a lot of factories. There were only three houses near us – one right next door, one about six lots away, and the house that belonged to the tannery. The security guard lived in the third, and for a while I was friendly with his son, Ricky, who was a couple of years older than me. There was a scarcity of children in the area when school had finished for the day. Pickings were slim, and I guess I was better than nothing for him.

The tannery was strictly prohibited, but Ricky would sneak us in after the troglodytes had gone home. It was the Harry Potter scenario of its day – all locked up and hauntingly dark, a realm full of imagined dangers, a spooky and terrifying place. I thought evil wizards and demons lived there and that the huge bubbling vats (which I now realise were for boiling down creatures past their use-by date) were full of magic sap that was halfway to becoming gold. I loved it. Everything was multi-tones of browns, gold and rust. The dribbles would glisten as they oozed their way down the vats and congealed on the floor. The all-pervading pong inside the tannery didn't daunt me at all – I just loved it, the stench being an integral part of this enchanting forbidden world.

Other neighbourhood whiffs, though, would sometimes be too much for me, especially on the train trip to the city, passing by the local abattoirs, although not fast enough for my liking. I always asked my mother for her handkerchief to cover my nose as a way of diffusing the smell. She would usually pass me her best finely embroidered, perfume-daubed hankie until we safely passed. On one such trip, as we approached that particular stretch of track, she couldn't lay her hand on a handkerchief, so she gave me one of her new gloves. Without any hesitation, I promptly used to it blow my nose. It was one of her favourite stories about me, the telling of which over the years always brought on an embarrassed flush.

In the house right next-door to ours lived an extended family of Yugoslavs, as they were known then. I was besotted with the old grandmother, who in turn doted on me. She was a tiny bundle of black skirts, cardigans, aprons, wool stockings, shawls and headscarves. I can't remember if you could distinguish any features at all under that aura of blackness, although I can visualise a warm, wide, kind, toothless grin and wizened, tiny, white hands. Speaking not a word of English, she would take my tiny white hands in hers and off we would go down to the river to collect briquettes. (For those unfamiliar with briquettes, they are little bricks of compressed black coal used as a cheap source of domestic fuel.)

A train like a black dream would regularly shunt alongside the banks of the Maribyrnong River at the bottom of Wingfield Street. It carried briquettes from a factory to the nearby dock for dispatch. We would head off, pushing a shabby old shopping trolley with mismatched wobbly wheels, and collect any briquettes that had fallen off the train. I loved these excursions with the old woman. I would depart a snowy-haired angel and return looking like the chimney sweep straight out of

Oliver Twist. My mother must have sanctioned these forays into the soot as I can remember many such outings.

I think my enduring admiration of classical architecture stems from this period. One year, there was a huge traditional Yugoslavian wedding in the family. The next day my Babushka presented me with a large folded damask napkin. She pressed one finger to her toothless smile, and I understood that it was to be a secret between the two of us. I could hardly wait to unwrap my present and see what it could possibly be. To my delight, it was all the decorations from the multi-tiered wedding cake. There were bows, lovers' knots, roses and butterflies; but what impressed me most were the dozens of Greco–Roman pillars. It didn't take me long to discover that they were all made of icing sugar. The roses and butterflies were easy to demolish, but the Corinthian columns were another matter altogether.

Many childhood memories are not, in fact, memories at all, but things you have been told. In my case, there are stories about how I was so skinny and ugly as a baby, having been born bright yellow with jaundice, that my mother would travel only by the back lanes when taking me out in the pram and would cross the street if she saw someone she knew approaching. Then there was the time she went to the butcher's and returned home alone, leaving me sitting outside the shop for a considerable length of time before she missed me. Or the fact that I didn't walk until I was nearly two. I would sit motionless and observe the world passing by (some things never change). One day I simply stood up and took off. No crawling, no toddling – I just started with a dash.

My father pinned my nappy to my dick once, and on another occasion my mother lifted me out of my bath in the kitchen sink and sat me down on a still glowing hot plate on the kitchen stove. Of these two incidents, which I am sure were painful at the time, no memory exists Thanks to my father, I could probably wear a silver stud in my penis, should I embrace the current craze for body piercing, but I have no psychological scars from what must have been traumatic events for new parents.

A favourite reminiscence of my own probably explains my passion for sparrows. Of all God's creatures on earth, I love sparrows the most. Donkeys run a close second – something to do with their colour.

The occasion was a school play. It was a forest scene, and you were either a sparrow or a tree. I was lucky enough to be chosen to play a sparrow. We sparrows had beautiful costumes made out of crêpe paper, with wings that covered your arms with hundreds of crêpe-paper feathers. These fluttered and made a crisp noise as we swept and plummeted around the trees. The trees were quite pretty, but they were anchored to one spot and were only allowed to gently sway from side to side. While the trees offered no avenue for artistic expression, the sparrows had enormous scope to display their talents – to show off, basically.

After the performance, we each got to keep our costume, and one of my most vivid recollections is of standing in Wingfield Street, a tiny sparrow all alone, watching and waiting for a friend of Nanna's, Mrs Whitney, to visit so I could show her my beautiful costume. Our shop was at the top of the street, which was on the crest of what I thought at the time was the biggest hill in the world. The sky was clouding over, and a wind had sprung up, ruffling my feathers just a little. A few drops of rain should have warned me; my paper wings shrivelled up at the first drop.

Finally, Mrs Whitney appeared
at the bottom of the hill and
I burst into full flight. Down
the hill I danced in ever-widening
circles, dipping and swooping
faster and faster as I ran to greet her.
I wasn't fast enough, though, and the few
raindrops soon became a heavy shower.
Before I could reach her, all of my glorious
plumage had stuck to my skinny little
arms, and its colour had drained away.
I must have looked more like a drowned
rodent than the gorgeous sparrow I had
been at the start of my flight. Mrs Whitney
clutched me to herself under her umbrella
and gave me a big kiss. She told me I was
the best sparrow she had ever seen, which is
all I needed to hear. I often wonder: If it hadn't
rained that day, would I still have that costume packed away
in a box somewhere? I expect I would.

It must have been about this time that I got a kitten. She was grey with
white markings and quite petite. My mother called her a silly puss, but
I couldn't say it correctly, so she became Ciss Puss. My first memory of
Ciss Puss is of her climbing up a solitary gladiolus growing in the tiny
patch of garden we had at the back of the shop. As she climbed to the
top, the gladiolus buckled under her weight, and she just hung there like
an animated Christmas decoration, swaying to and fro. I would have
Ciss Puss for twenty-one years.

Next to the outhouse stood another of my favourite spots, the laundry,
which was always full of lovely, fresh, soapy smells. I loved to help
with the washing, a laborious chore that lost its appeal over the years.
(I have never rediscovered the pleasures of putting on a load of whites;
luckily I have always had someone close in my life who adores washing.)

The laundry had a large copper tub, which was built in to the corner. It gleamed and changed colour when the fire was lit underneath it to heat the water. Next to it stood two concrete tubs. The washing would be rinsed in the first tub after coming out of the boiling copper.

I loved the big wooden stick that was used to stir the clothes in the copper. I imbued this stick with all sorts of magical qualities. It was a wonderful shade of grey at one end, which was all shiny and smooth. The other end, which was boiled to death, was almost white and sort of fuzzy. I was always taking this stick and playing with it, so when the time came to do the washing, it could never be found. From the first tub, the washing would pass through a hand-cranked wringer into the next tub for a final rinse and then back again. I loved helping to do this last stage, but I was only good for hankies and tea towels as it was hard work and I took too long. Instead, for all the years Nanna lived with us, I would help her take the sheets from the line, and we would fold them, fold and stretch, fold, stretch and fold again. In reflecting on this time-honoured ritual, I was always reminded of a minuet and I thought it should have been set to music.

Directly behind the shop was a small furniture factory, and for a while I had a friend whose mother worked in the office there. One of our favourite pastimes was to make confetti with the office hole puncher. Unfortunately, one day, we ran out of waste paper, and I thought nothing of using all the paper lying around on her desk. We made tons of confetti that day but it was terribly bad luck that the papers were last month's invoices and next month's orders. I was banned from the office and that friendship, but I would sneak into the factory to play by myself whenever I got the chance. Then I was barred forever after being Sir Edmund Hillary one day. I was climbing up the mountains of timber stacked to the roof when I slipped and fell, catching and opening up my leg on a protruding nail on my descent from Everest. I still have a faint reminder in the form of the scar on my left leg.

Billycarts were the big thing at the time, especially for boys, and kids from all around would come to Wingfield Street to race down the world's biggest hill. I took a drive not long ago to visit the places where I lived as a child. Wingfield Street looked like it had been deflated. What I remembered at the age of six as a death-defying plunge to hell is just a gentle slope.

The average billycart was a rough and ready affair, a knocked-together arrangement of fruit boxes on ball-bearing wheels. They made a lot of noise! It was on my sixth birthday that I got my own. My father had made it with much love and care. Compared with all the other billycarts, mine was a Rolls-Royce. It was glossy, fire-engine red with a white interior and fat rubber tyres on white, moulded-plastic wheels, which were deadly silent. My initial pride and joy soon changed to mortification as they laughed and poked fun at me and my new speed machine. The fact that it was much faster than any other billycart, so I would win every race, became just another factor working against me. Soon I was excluded from all the races.

It is not much fun to be by yourself in a billycart. After all, you need someone to push you at the start. On my own, however, I started creating a fantasy world in which to escape the real world of snotty-nosed boys and their fruit boxes on wheels.

About this time, Nanna sold the milk bar, and we moved to Hobbs Street, Seddon. It was one stop down the train line and one step up the social ladder.

2

Hobbs Street

Hobbs Street, Seddon, was so pretty the year we moved to number 13. Plane trees lined both sides of the road and formed a magnificent arched colonnade. Viewed from the bottom of the street, it had the semblance of an ancient cathedral, the trunks being massive pillars with soaring Gothic branches supporting a lofty green ceiling. The trees were the street! With a leafy green roof of tranquillity and security hovering above, the ordinariness of the houses was lost in the splendour.

We had the pleasure of this holy setting for some time before the council decided that the roots of the cathedral were playing havoc with the gutters, and our sacred trees would have to go. In the meantime, I loved our trees. They provided shade in the summer; glorious mounds of fallen, coloured leaves in the autumn; and wicked, prickly pom-poms in the winter. The pom-poms were fabulous for crushing and putting down the backs of girls' school uniforms. Instant torture! This despicable act ensured reciprocal games of retaliation and revenge for weeks on end.

The council came every so often to "trim" the branches when they threatened to interfere with the powerlines. With no art direction, sense of proportion or style, they hacked away at our beautiful cathedral. Our street took on an architectural transformation from the Christian Gothic to something more Middle Eastern, as the freshly butchered trees assumed the iconic shape of the Muslim crescent. I remember making harem pants for Teddy from an orange chiffon scarf that the wind had released from someone's outfit, only to be caught in the exposed branches and later offered up.

We kids swooped on the prunings after the chop, as they made superior swords for duelling when we imitated our favourite five o'clock television show, *Zorro*. I recall the sounds of the whooshing and the occasional whelp and cry of pain as a branch would connect with your opponent or, if misjudged, yourself.

Many sounds such as these link the tastes and smells of my childhood memories. One of my favourite sounds, rivalling walking to school with a stick rattling along neighbourhood front fences, was the noise made when you attached a discarded cigarette packet to the rear wheel of your bicycle with a clothes peg. Not only did this sound great, but it also seemed to help enormously with acceleration.

Dressing Teddy was my major childhood preoccupation, and the plane tree outside our house didn't escape playing a part in my constant quest for fashion excellence. I would spend hours of delight peeling away the bark, turning one piece into a stunning handbag for him. It had a hole just perfect for his hand. By the time I had decorated it, it looked like a precursor of one of Judith Leiber's beaded collectables. I was a bowerbird as a child, garnering anything that shone or sparkled. Glitter, odd beads, broken jewellery, tinsel, gold and silver foil from chocolates – all were waiting for me to embellish any lacklustre object that would come my way.

It was a nasty shock when the council announced they were going to remove our trees. I was extremely upset at the news and even hatched a plan to chain Teddy and me to ours, even if it meant martyrdom for two dedicated, young fashionistas. However, one day I came home from school to find it was all over. The trees were gone. The whole street was devastated. No more sword fights, no more pom-poms, no more mountains of leaves to crash through as they piled up in the gutters, twisted and contorted. No more sweeping and raking into piles. No more burning off, the smell of smoke a pleasure to warm the crisp autumn air, another sensory memory to be fondly recalled.

This was in the days before we were aware of imposing damage on our fragile environment. I saw nothing wrong with the twisted and buckled drains. When it rained, I loved to smash through the dams that the fallen leaves would form along the course of this imaginary water world. I would set off a paper boat at the top of the street, plot its course and navigate an epic journey with the help of a big branch. Speed was an essential element as the fragile craft raced through the various seas, lakes, rapids and waterfalls towards ultimate destruction in the big stormwater drain that disappeared under the railway line at the bottom of the street.

When the trees came down, you noticed the houses for the first time. The trees had softened the streetscape and formed a strong visual link. After they were gone, what remained was ugly urban blight. Architecturally speaking, our street was a judicial dissection of the social strata: we had everything from an imposing mansion to derelict timber cottages and the whole shebang in between.

To me, number 13, our modernist/Victorian renovation, was the obvious jewel in the crown. I thought the previous owners had done a great job worthy of a *Home Beautiful* cover. To add her signature, my mother planted a silver birch tree in the pocket-handkerchief-size front garden, causing quite a stir in the street where the norm was set by the ubiquitous standard rose bush, a Princess Elizabeth being the most popular. To this day, I still think Mum's single silver birch was a very stylish planting.

My father had a few improvements of his own in mind. Our side driveway to the garage was only just wide enough for our old Dodge to navigate. He decided to get it concreted and always boasted that he gave Bruno Grollo – today a well-known property developer – his first job.

The previous owners had installed a huge picture window in the lounge. Now, I'm a great devotee of "let there be light", but this window's only outlook was onto the driveway and the shabby neighbouring fence. Bleak, to say the least. There wasn't a skerrick of soil available to plant a creeper, nor even room for a pot plant. So Dad decided to update the fence with a new one that would have white-painted caps, a definite improvement. It was my job to split the old fence planks for kindling and I delighted in the ping sound as they shot off like arrows. I also loved finding a few fossilised grubs in them. Should someone from the Department of Health, Safety and Child Labour be reading this, I'm sure the statute of limitations has well passed.

Hobbs Street's own mansion was a large bluestone Victorian house with a return iron-lace veranda. It was most likely the oldest house on the street and had probably been on a much larger plot originally, the other houses encroaching on it over the years. Seeing it today, it is not nearly as large or grand as I remember; in the eyes of a child, everything is enormous. It certainly made a big impression on me when we moved to Hobbs Street.

Mrs Weigard, a widow of independent means, owned the big house. We kids thought she was really rich. We thought her name was really rich as well, and we got a lot of mileage out of sniggering behind our hands whenever we heard or spoke it. "Mrs Wee Wee Piddle in Your Pants." She didn't appear all that often, but when she did she was always immaculately groomed, not a hair out of place. The reason she looked like she had just been to the hairdressers was that she *had*.

Mrs Weigard had a daughter and two grandchildren who lived in Balwyn, a much posher suburb. They would visit once a month, driving up in a big, pale-green Humber sedan. The grandchildren, who were similar ages to us, would arrive all dressed to the nines, the boy in a bow tie and the missy in puffed embroidered organza. They would play with us, but you always got the impression that they had instructions not to get too close.

Ma Ma, as Mrs Weigard was more affectionately known, had a boarder,

"Uncle Len". He supposedly had a bungalow out the back, but you could often see him through the front screen door coming out of Ma Ma's large front bedroom in a Chesty Bond singlet and pyjama bottoms. Looking back, I think a bit of drinking went on in the mansion. Sometimes Uncle Len would stagger out in his striped pyjama bottoms and move us further up the road when our games became a bit rowdy. In all the years I lived in Hobbs Street, I never stepped past the two big lions that guarded the steps leading up from the garden path.

Every year, Ma Ma treated all the kids in the street, – up to twenty sometimes – to a Christmas excursion. It was usually a trip to the pantomime at the Tivoli Theatre. I adored these theatrical excursions to the magic world of panto. For me, the colourful sets and glittering costumes were pure enchantment. The live orchestra in the pit, the racket of the kids, the laughter, the stamping of hundreds of feet to sing-along sing-songs – all a magical annual treat. On stage, we were treated to everything from old-fashioned slapstick to gooey romance. When attention might be waning, there would be the scary bits. The wicked queen (usually some notorious old Melbourne queen) would creep up behind the innocent ingenue with dastardly intent. We would scream, "Behind you, behind you" until we were blue in the face.

All would turn out well in the end. The wicked queen would repent and see the error of his ways. The handsome prince (always played by a young lassy) would claim his sweetheart, his heart's desire, and live happily ever after. The reformed queen would dig into a bottomless purse and reward all the good boys and girls by hurling purple-and-gold wrapped Cadbury chocolates into the auditorium. I always thought it "common" to scramble to get one of these chocolates and never caught one. The only time I ever had one was when Ma Ma gave me one on the way home on the train – the one she had caught.

My most unforgettable Christmas excursion was a visit to Melbourne Zoo. The elephant that took kiddies for a gentle stroll went berserk. I just happened to be strapped onboard its full howdah, and I can still see the terrified faces of distraught mothers as they watched in horror

the rampaging pachyderm belt around in a huge cloud of dust with its frantic trainer in hot pursuit. I don't remember how it finished up, except that I lived to tell the tale. I remember the jostling about and I have a hazy memory that the poor old elephant was put down, but that could have been something I made up. I was prone to exaggeration when I was a child. I think I told the school it was shot from underneath us and did a triple roll before at least a dozen bullets silenced its last mutinous protests. Knowing me at the time, old Dumbo probably just broke into a canter nearing the home stretch. But those mothers' faces stay with me to this day. Ma Ma remained serene.

When I mentioned the ordinariness and splendour of the houses and that there wasn't a factory in sight, it wasn't just another lie. There was a factory in our street, but you couldn't see it. It was some kind of foundry and was up a small lane, about halfway along the street. Directly in front of the factory was a row of four small Edwardian workers' cottages, the slums of Hobbs Street. They were like abandoned children's playhouses and could have had only two or three rooms at the most.

Amazingly, when I walked past these houses, everything seemed to change – the colour and aura around the houses seemed to drain away. In retrospect, it felt as though you had been transported back to the pages of a Charles Dickens novel – although, at that stage, the magic of such words had not yet revealed themselves to me. These tiny, dilapidated cottages were timber. They were a dirty brown and looked like they had never seen a coat of paint. Where everyone else had a lawn, they had a brown patch of dust. They were set back only a metre or so from the street, and the patch of dust was barely distinguishable from the very low timber veranda, its twisted and buckled boards the same brown as the façade.

The fences and gates were a peculiar type of twisted wire, also brown with rust. The letterboxes were hanging off or tied on with a different kind of wire or string. The only colour I remember about those cottages was the vivid green of the weeds growing in the rusted gutterings, which even I could reach and hang onto with a single jump. On my visits to metro Manila nowadays, I always think of this tiny row of terraces when I pass the cardboard and flotsam shanties that are so abundant throughout that city.

I hated going past the lane next to these houses on my own, as the factory had a guard dog, a large German Shepherd, which was often off its chain. Once, it took me by the wrist and led me right up the lane and into the foundry. I was sure this wolf was going to gobble me up without my even getting to wear the red cape with the celebrated hood. Inside the foundry was very quiet and dark, and I remember the rusty iron sawdust that lay in piles after a busy day. Even in such dire peril, my eyes cast on a discarded band of bright metal rings that I thought would make a perfect tiara for Teddy. Eventually Hans released his grip and gave me an affectionate lick. I grabbed the silver rings and went on my way.

A childless older couple, Mr and Mrs Ryan, lived at number 37, next to the lane leading to the foundry. When television came to Australia in 1956, they were the first in the street to own a set, a highly polished mahogany Pye 21-inch-screen model with gold-tipped legs. The Ryans took great delight in issuing an open invitation every night at 5 o'clock for all the kids in the street to watch the popular shows of the day. Somehow our secular divisions would be put aside, and we would sit in a large half-circle, glued to the tiny, black-and-white screen, watching *Tarzan*, *Zorro*, or *Jungle Jim*. To this day, I still have a fear of quicksand. Turning any corner, I watch out for a lurking pit. Unlike Jungle Jim, I have never had a Tamba to fetch me a stick when waist deep and sinking fast.

Shortly afterwards, we got our own Pye television, just in time for the Olympic Games in Melbourne. Not only did we get to see the spectacle on the flickering screen, but we actually got to go one day. In fact, it was the day Betty Cuthbert made history and became Australia's "golden girl". I have a vivid memory of sitting in the upper reaches of a newly built stadium. It was dark and cold, and I was given a beautiful flag. Sitting on my father's shoulders, I waved it like a maniac, carried away by the euphoria of the crowd; I had no idea why.

I adored that flag. Made from white silk and simply decorated – just five rings in the Olympic colours – it inspired a turning point in my

life. Up to this point, every dress I had made for Teddy was folded, knotted or pinned using my mother's treasured hatpin or one of Nanna's brooches. After our trip to the Olympics, I took the flag, cut out two of the rings for armholes and cut a strip to fold around the neck and shoulders. For the first time ever, I had taken an idea and created an item of clothing from scratch.

Directly next door to us, at number 11, was a tiny bluestone cottage right on the street. It could have been older than the big house or served as an out-building of the original property if you took away all the other houses built since; its distance and position in relation to the big house made that theory plausible. The Pilkingtons lived there. Although the house was tiny, it was on a massive block of land and opened up from the narrow span at the front to extend to the width of the rear of the adjoining house.

Two giant peppercorn trees overshadowed the whole plot, so nothing else would grow. One had a long, thick horizontal branch that, with a little imagination, morphed into a pirate ship or a Roman galley. This set the stage for many fierce sea battles. We had a network of ropes, and we would swing from one tree to the other, shouting and brandishing swords and deadly sharpened spears made from a massive stand of bamboo that grew in the corner of the yard. It's a wonder no one suffered more than the occasional scratch, although I nearly lost an eye once when the misdirection of my attack sent me straight into a branch I wasn't expecting.

Chooks scratched away at the dirt all day, and we would torment them by following them around and prodding their bottoms with a long branch. This would either bring on a poo or an egg, much to our delight. Glen Pilkington had a very scientific bent and, apart from torturing the chooks, he would conduct many different scientific experiments, some on me. He would bury things in the ground and compare them at regular intervals to observe the force of pressure and ground movement. I would be his assistant and follow him around making notes. He went on to be a successful scientist and was instrumental in the breakthroughs made in AIDS research.

Sometimes we would join a group of the older boys and play across the road in yet another of my favourite backyards. It was also a dustbowl. (I think we were the only house that had any green.) It was built up in several levels, and we had fashioned a series of mountains and valleys crisscrossed by a multiple system of highways and byways. We motored all over this terrain with Kevin's huge collection of Dinky Toy cars. I could only maintain my interest if I was allowed to play with (wouldn't you know it) the pink convertible Cadillac.

Opposite us in Hobbs Street was a beautiful timber, double-fronted house with a sagging, low-slung return veranda. It was set well back from the street and had a very old, slightly neglected garden. It was full of gone-to-seed hollyhocks, rusty hydrangeas, snail-ravaged agapanthus, heady gardenias, overblown roses, lilacs and snowball trees. The garden's main attraction, however, was the pair of colossal mulberry trees that dominated the front. These made the owner, old Mrs Smith, very popular during silkworm experiments at school. Her son and daughter-in-law lived next door to her, in a 1940s chocolate-brick villa with a curved window, and a magnolia tree as the feature in a very well-groomed, formal garden.

Mrs Richards lived on their left and although she hardly ever went out, she was constantly watching. All you ever saw of her was her hand as it adjusted the Holland blind to get a better look at the comings and goings of the neighbours. I suppose she had agoraphobia in the days when little was known of such illnesses and there was no help available for such a wretched life. Mind you, we made her life hell – no wonder she was loath to venture out. We would taunt her, yell out terrible names, leave horrible things on her doorstep, and blow up her letterbox on Guy Fawkes night. Just awful things. Mind you, when I say "we", I don't mean to include me; it was the older kids who were the perpetrators. But I remember being a witness and thinking what fun it all was. I am sure the adults, too, must have disliked her; otherwise surely our parents would have put a stop to this disgraceful behaviour.

The Crowders lived at number 7, a substantial Edwardian double-fronted red-brick house with a wrought-iron-lace veranda. With a hedge of Lorraine Lee roses across the front, it was a picture of solid respectability. Rose Crowder could talk (and bore the leg off a chair) while Alf, her husband, was affably resigned to this. Alf was a butcher by trade and the smartest, neatest dresser I ever saw. No matter what time of the day, he always looked fresh and immaculate. His hair was beautifully groomed and glistened from "A little dab'll do ya" Brylcreem, the choice of every well-groomed gentleman at that time.

When the Crowders won the Tattersalls lottery and did up their house, they did over their backyard as well. Their idea of gardening was to concrete their backyard from edge to edge and paint it green. They put in a new trellis and thought it the ant's pants – well, I guess it was low maintenance. Alf Crowder gave every kid in the street a 10-shilling note. I think I spent mine on *Richie Rich* comic books.

Tragically, Alf succumbed to Alzheimer's disease late in his life. He became unrecognisable – barely distinguishable from the wild man of Borneo. Rose and Alf had been beautiful ballroom dancers in their day. A touching story tells of Rose visiting this absent, hostile man with shoulder-length, unkempt hair and long scruffy nails at the home where he had been placed in care. They were having a day of light musical entertainment. At the sound of a two-step being played, Alf took Rose in his arms and glided her around the room as if transported back to the golden days of their youth at the Trocadero Ballroom.

Next door to the Crowders, at number 5, lived the Flannagans – Vinnie and Helen. Their house took the prize for the ugliest in the street. It had such a depressing aura that I reckon it must have been built during that time of general financial hardship, the Great Depression. Built right up to the street, it had three massive inverted obelisk-shaped columns holding up a skimpy little veranda. An ashtray-like arrangement was supposed to hold a garden planting, but the Flannagans seemed to have taken gardening tips from the slums up the road – they had gone with dust as well, while incorporating cigarette butts and assorted rubbish to highlight the effect. Their house was finished in a rough-pebbledash stucco, originally painted white, with small groups of glazed and embossed bricks exposed every now and then as a design feature. The place exuded a war-like sensibility. Its front window, which was long and narrow, looked more like a slit from some sort of bunker. You could imagine a canon swinging out from it at the first sniff of an attack.

Vinnie Flannagan's mother lived next door to us, at number 11. Her house was a Californian bungalow and would have taken out tidy town prize had it been a town, not a house. It was spotless inside and out. Old Mrs Flannagan was often to be seen on her hands and knees in the front garden with nail scissors, trimming any rebellious blade of grass that showed lofty ambitions. She would take a damp cloth to the front fence after a strong wind might stir the dust. She proudly owned an amazing set of clackers (dentures), which were always in a perpetually wide grin. Old Mrs Flannagan was as blind as a bat, and when you addressed her, she would throw her head back. Her glazed expression would aim at you but miss by a couple of inches, and the clackers would beam.

If you thought the outside of old Mrs Flannagan's house was well-manicured and spotless, that paled into insignificance when you stepped inside. I had never seen so much gleaming stuff. I could never quite believe she was really blind, as there were more things to look at than in any museum. There were couches and armchairs with crocheted antimacassars, rocking chairs and slipper chairs, poufs and footstools, coffee tables, side tables, nests of tables covered with doilies, sideboards, buffets, crystal cabinets, shadowboxes, bookcases, camphor chests, shelves and picture rails. From the latter hung many paintings, mainly of a religious nature as she was a devout Catholic.

There were dozens of Our Lord Jesus, the Virgin Mary and various saints and popes. These all seemed to glow as if lit from behind, with almost phosphorescent halos and bleeding hearts that were so lifelike, you could practically hear them beating. There were quite a few crucifixes too. These were attached directly to the walls, and every room had at least one. The one hanging over her bed was a beauty – it was made of highly polished carved wood, and the tears were so convincing that I almost expected the beautifully starched Cluny lace pillows underneath to be damp. There were statuettes on just about every surface – highly coloured plaster figures of the Holy Mother beckoning you to repent and come to her for absolution. Not a speck of dust was to be found on any surface or heavenly forehead, and on every surface that didn't hold a holy figurine, there was a crystal vase full of plastic roses. There were also peculiar half-vases on the walls, blooming with cascading roses augmented with real wandering jew to trick you into thinking the rest of the arrangement was real.

At floor level, the house was an absolute obstacle course. Not only did one have to navigate the furniture, but the floor also had rugs upon carpets upon dangerously highly polished linoleum with a few mats thrown in for good measure. How the old dear never tripped and broke a hip is beyond me.

Down the backyard, she had a bungalow, which a legit boarder occupied at one time. I remember watching him through a hole in our fence one day. He was lying on his bed with the door wide open. A shaft of sunlight lit up enough of the darkened room to expose him with his trousers around his ankles, playing with a half-hearted erection. Along came old Mrs Flannagan, on her way to the clothesline. "Now," I thought. "This will be a test if she really is blind." I am still not sure, but, as she passed back by the open door after hanging out the washing, I might just have detected her grin full of clackers growing even wider.

Postscript: TV

From that early introduction to the telly, I became, and am to this day, a TV addict. I used to rush home from school to catch Denise Drysdale go-go dancing on Kommotion. *Then, years later, whether you were picnicking in the Dandenongs or down at the beach, there would be a mad Sunday afternoon dash home to catch Molly Meldrum on* Countdown; *you could not miss it. The years of Joan Collins and* Dynasty *were the acme of my addiction. We would have dinner parties and dress accordingly to celebrate the latest catfight between Alexis and Krystle. Shoulder pads and Champagne. I have never detoxed from my TV habits, and I am probably worse today; what with Stan, Netflix, Apple TV, Britbox … you name it, I stream it. And I still adore Denise – or Ding Dong, as she is affectionately known to this day.*

3

Hyde Street School

For me, the best thing about school was that it was within easy walking distance of home. When I got to Hyde Street School on my first day, I found that I had somehow lost my packed lunch. I burst into tears and ran from the classroom, heading home. Halfway there, I found my lunch: the paper bag had been ripped open, and some very happy sparrows were enjoying a free-for-all. Nanna didn't give in to my pleas for sanctuary and sent me back with lunch money for the tuckshop. But now I had my first experience of being late for school.

With today's helicopter parenting, I doubt that six- and seven-year-old kids would have the freedom we were granted at that age. I walked to and from school and home for lunch every day. I don't remember ever being shown the way – the sense of direction seemed in-born. When we were a bit older, our path to school was along the railway track in the long grass, which sometimes grew over our heads. I don't think our parents knew about our secret safari track, although a few must have had an inkling because some kids would never follow us – to them, the railway line was strictly taboo. It was an adventure and terrific fun. We would dig around

in the long grass, find all sorts of abandoned ephemera, poke at it with sticks and fling it over our heads. Lace panties with funny stains, men's underpants with very recognisable stains, mini balloons half full of gooey fluids, and sometimes pairs of trousers and brassieres. All of this being unfailing evidence of another sort of life, which we were convinced was extra-terrestrial. There was further proof – little pockets of thrashed-out grass-like crop circles that these creatures from outer space inhabited at night when the sun went to bed and the shadows crept in.

When the long grass was too wet, we would walk along the railway track, always watchful of the city-bound train. A favourite game was to place a penny on the track in the path of an approaching train and see who could find the twisted, buckled head of Her Majesty after it had spun off into the grass. Mind you, we didn't play that game all that often, as a penny was still a penny, and it bought two clinkers or six freckles.

The things that impressed me the most on my first day of school (after I had recovered from the lost lunch incident) were the blackboards that lined the four walls of the assembly hall in the junior school. All of the classrooms opened off this cavernous space. Sometimes concerts were held here, and indoor sports, callisthenics and other gymnastic tortures were discharged several times during the week. Those blackboards were masterpieces of the highest artistic achievement. Around the borders, there were splendid depictions of favourite fairy stories and fables, replete with magical goblins and fairies, dragons, handsome princes and damsels in distress. One frieze would flutter with butterflies and dragonflies, their sparkling wings bejewelled with morning dew. Another would show every animal in the zoo, every bird in the sky. One always had glorious examples of the calligrapher's skill, with the alphabet in a myriad of different characters. They were all done in coloured chalks and would change every now and then. Although a favourite story would disappear, it would be replaced by something equally wondrous.

It doesn't occur to a child to question something as fabulous as these blackboards. At the time I wondered many things about them. Who did them? Did someone go around all the schools in the state and repeat these exquisite drawings? Who rubbed them off? Were there transfers that had little dots to help the artist along? Was it like painting with numbers? Back then I didn't ask.

In my very first class, we sat on the floor, and I remember that the boy next to me wet his pants. A small stream trickled down the floor towards the teacher, who didn't show any kindness to the distressed chap – he was told to stop snivelling and a newspaper was placed underneath him. "Hmm! Don't do that!" my tiny brain must have registered. To this day, I can hang on for hours after the call of nature has rung.

Everything had to have a name tag, but that didn't stop me from frequently losing things. As part of the kit we had to take home for our mothers to sew name tags in was a terrible cushion – the most miserable cushion in the world. Covered in blue vinyl and with absolutely no stuffing worth mentioning, mine gave no comfort to my skinny little bottom. We seemed to spend an inordinate amount of time sitting on our cushions on the floor in those early years, so to this day I have an aversion to cushions and I guess it stems from that time.

Hyde Street progressed scholastically from the "Bubbs", which I skipped, right through to forms one and two. These elder statesmen of the school had a uniform. For some strange reason, my mother got it into her head to dress me the same way from about grade three. It was also too big for a couple of years as she wanted me to grow into it. Just another obstacle to overcome as I was constantly being tortured for this fact.

We were very much a working-class school, and most kids were ragamuffins – except me. I was this pseudo-English prince in a stuffy, grey-serge suit and polished shoes. For someone with a passion for shoes, I must admit that I have always hated cleaning them. My father, being a policeman, put me off with his police-academy drilling on spit and polish.

My mother obviously had a method to her madness because whenever I lost an article of clothing everyone in my grade knew it was mine, as I was the only one wearing the school uniform. Like a bloody boomerang, that jumper just kept coming back.

The most horrible thing about school was the government-issue bottles of warm milk that we were obliged to drink at morning playtime. Now, if it had been *meant* to be warm milk, with maybe a spoonful of chocolate in it, it would have been perfectly acceptable. But, no, this was warm milk, which had been sitting in the sun on the front steps in the old bluestone part of the school since 8 am. The very thought of it still makes me gag. However, it didn't take me long to figure out a way around this daily ordeal. I was the first with my hand up to volunteer to be a milk monitor. That task not only gave you a few extra minutes to fool around in the schoolyard but was also a perfect opportunity to empty one of the half-pint bottles just before it was about to go off and pretend to have guzzled it down.

The other dreadful thing about school was the constant amount of gravel that Celia would have to remove from my knees. This was a weekly occurrence for years, even later on when I graduated to long pants. There seemed to be acres of gravel, and I was constantly coming a cropper and transporting vast amounts of it home to Hobbs Street just under the surface of my knees. I often wonder what I was doing to be so accident-prone, but I have an awful feeling I was being chased.

Hyde Street was an architectural hodgepodge of buildings. The oldest part, dating from 1887, was a beautiful bluestone building with sandstone trimmings, which someone had unfortunately painted with white, high-gloss paint. Forms one and two of the senior school were housed in this handsome edifice.

The junior school was built in the 1930s. It was red brick and had a Dutch colonial feel to it, with lots of gables and imitation dormer windows.

The fifth and sixth grades were housed in modern prefabricated classrooms, which were in this far-flung corner of the school's domain – another world away from the Bubs, which occupied the original building. After I had given Nanna rave reviews of the Four'N Twenty sausage rolls, I was allowed to buy my lunch every Monday. I would love to linger under the sprawling branches of a school-ground tree and watch the older boys play and push each other about; I was always mad about older men. There were always seasonal games: hula hoops, jacks and yo-yos one month, marbles the next.

Marbles were all the go, and on one occasion the sixth graders asked me to join in but I was promptly told to piss off when it was discovered that I didn't own any marbles. I was shattered as I had thought this was my one big break to be welcomed into the big boys' clique. On hearing my tale of woe, Nanna went off to her room and returned with a big suede pouch. It was full of my grandfather's marbles – an exquisite collection of all sizes and colours and a myriad of designs, many over sixty years old. My first thought was how to *wear* them, but I soon abandoned that and invented a wonderful fantasy involving pirates, buried treasure and shipwrecked damsels. I was Olivia de Havilland playing to an imaginary Errol Flynn.

The next day I went off proudly to school with my pouch of Spanish jewels. Like a lamb to the slaughter, without so much as one lesson or an understanding of the basic rules, I took up the invitation to join in the older boys' lunchtime game. Of course, all I returned home with that afternoon was an empty suede pouch and very red eyes. On hearing my story, Nanna shed a few tears with me but she didn't admonish me or make me feel guilty. Instead she gave me a big cuddle, and we cried out our remaining tears together. No wonder I didn't like boys.

The one good thing to come out of this unfortunate incident was a very chic sleeveless sheath with a plunging neckline. It featured a geometric border that I executed in Quink ink, highlighting the shredded fringe hem. Teddy had a natural feeling for suede.

Interlude: Teddy's Frocks

Teddy has been my fashion inspiration and muse for my whole life. He's having a bit of a rest lately, as he has devoted his entire life to being tortured by my flights of fancy. He recently had a spell in the toy hospital for new hands and feet as I had worn them out. Here are just a few of the many frocks he had over the years.

1. *The first actual wedding dress. This featured Mum's diamanté cuff bracelet as the bodice, with a skirt made from the paper doily in which the icing sugar treats from the big Yugoslav wedding came wrapped. Icing sugar roses from the cake stand – also from the bonbonniere – held the tulle veil.*

2. *Culturally appropriated, Native American–inspired suede shift made from the pouch that once held my grandfather's marbles. The Navajo design was etched in Quink ink.*

3. *An Indian maharani's outfit, which I made by cutting up Dad's Masonic scarf, held and fashioned by the prized pearl hatpin and Nanna's pearls.*

4. *A medieval gown made from an elaborate Easter egg box. The underskirt was made from the red-and-purple foil. The dress was made from the ribbon around the box and its satin lining with Mum's diamanté earrings and matching bracelet around the waist.*

5. *A more recent creation featuring black velvet leaves and ostrich feathers. Featured are vintage cascade earrings, bought for him in Los Angeles, that cost $250. Nothing but the best for Teddy.*

Magnificent peppercorn trees shaded the playground of the junior school. As they became impenetrable castles or pirate ships like the ones in the Pilkingtons' backyard, we would lauch assaults on them. There never seemed to be any teachers supervising the playground, as I am positive they would not have let us scale the highest branches' dizzying heights.

There was one tree that I would climb to the very end of its extended branch where I would assume a pose very much like Kate Winslet in *Titanic* or, more likely, Greta Garbo in *Queen Christina*. I would pretend to be standing on the bow of a magical vessel as it plied its way to a new world far away.

I loved the emperor gum caterpillars that lived in these trees and I would collect their cocoons and hang them on my bedroom curtains. Then I would watch them carefully until the moths emerged and crashed around my bedroom, desperate to escape and live the brief life that nature had destined for them. I also adored collecting the bunches of peppercorns – or pink pearls, as I perceived them – that adorned the branches. From them I made elaborate headdresses and festoons of necklaces to add to Teddy's extensive collection of jewels. In my rampant imagination, Teddy's jewels rivalled those of the Duchess of Windsor.

I was never much interested in the actual lessons at school. There was always something more interesting out the window or in the margin of my textbook where I would draw, involuntarily expressing the fantasy realm of glamour and beauty that filled my head. I created my own beauties to rival those on exhibit in the Myer Mural Hall, although it was from them that I got my inspiration. I didn't mind history, as that would inspire column drawings of medieval damsels or Spanish queens, and there was always Cleopatra. I didn't mind geography, as I liked shading in the ocean around the edges of maps. I hated Australian history – nothing but dusty fools who were always getting lost while exploring our vast and wonderful land (so we were told).

I got into a lot of trouble myself while dreaming of an exotic land. In senior school, I developed an obsession with Egypt and Cleopatra.

I executed a fabulous charcoal sketch of Cleopatra wearing little more than a jewelled snake brassiere, very much inspired by Claudette Colbert's portrayal of my favourite queen that I had seen in a midday movie several times. I have to admit that it did look a lot like Alison McMinn, a classmate who had developed very early on. She was a beautiful girl, and the brassiere of twisted snakes certainly was her size, a double C cup. I don't know how her mother got to see it or hear about it, but there was all hell to pay. I can still recall Mrs McMinn's tirade and threats. Poor Alison was banned from my company after school for some time.

When I wasn't drawing beauties, it was ladies' high-heel shoes. Hundreds and hundreds of pairs of high heels would fill the pages that should have had long division, short division and something called logarithms, the concept of which eludes me to this day. I really wasn't very good at anything if it didn't interest me.

I did like English, as I enjoyed reading, but I always got appalling marks because of my spelling. I remember one teacher almost in tears as she handed back our compositions. She said she loved my stories, but I was always in the red by the time she had taken off half a point for every spelling mistake.

Art was my best subject, and I always topped the class. I suppose it was because I got so much practice, drawing all day as I did. I looked forward to art classes all week. Encouraged by our art teacher, Mr Irvine, I sent one of my paintings to the *Herald Sun* art prize and won in my age group. The prize was a staggering £2, but it still wasn't enough to afford the whole shebang of Derwent pencils, so I finished up buying some quite unsuitable prissy watercolours. They came in a spectrum of colours but in tiny tubes. I used up all of my favourite colours on the first painting; the rest went unused.

My mother always loved that painting, and my stepfather still has it. I didn't like it much at the time because I had to change it. It was a jungle scene in the moonlight, and the subject was a damsel about to be raped by a gorilla (I had a rather vivid imagination). Mr Irvine made me paint out the gorilla, so there is this rather strange, frenzied woman in silhouette fighting off nothing. He changed the title from "Show me your tits" to "Lost" and it took the prize. I can still see the gorilla when I look at the painting. If I had painted it today, I would have been put into therapy or on medication!

After winning the prize, I reached semi-celebrity status and became almost acceptable among my peers. As a reward, I was commissioned to paint a mural. I was excited for exactly two minutes. It was to be on the sports cupboard doors, and the subject was – you guessed it – "Sport in our school". Try as I might, I couldn't get excited about the job, and the result was awful, to say the least. I decided to do it in shades of mauve, hardly the right choice for such a robust theme. This must have been about 1962. The composition was geometric, and nobody really could see what I was trying to convey.

"It's a football, stupid."

"Because I like that colour."

"No, he is taking a mark."

"No, that isn't a football; that's his head."

Nevertheless, there was an official unveiling by the headmaster. I was mortified and sulked for weeks. Sometimes, I wake up in the middle of the night with the terrifying thought that it might still be there. I hope I didn't sign it!

I had set the standard that first day when I was late for school. I was late the entire time I attended Hyde Street – in fact, forever after.

We took morning assembly outside and would have to do a lot of shuffling around and measuring arms' distances to form perfect ranks. No one would ever let me sneak in late, so I would stand out like dog's balls, ruining the formation. I think we still sang *God Save the Queen* in those days, and on Mondays we took an oath of allegiance. After some uninspiring drivel by the headmaster and much suppressed giggling, we would then march around the quadrangle and spin off in our various directions, with me dangling along behind. To this day, I am haunted by the sound of a desultory kettledrum.

Quite often, I was even late twice in a day. When I went home for lunch I would watch the midday movie. I saw all the great stars and films of the 1930s and 40s, giving me years of the most fabulous Hollywood education. Unfortunately, the movies were longer than lunchtime, and I would be so engrossed that I wouldn't even hear Nanna's anguished pleas for me to go back to school. After a while, she just gave up.

Nanna made me delicious lunches, my favourite being pancakes with lemon and sugar. I ate them as fast as she made them, putting away at least half a dozen, until I couldn't eat any more. There were other delights – homemade egg-and-bacon pies, hearty soups in the winter, my favourite salmon points, potato scones straight from the oven dripping in butter, and bubble and squeak when there were leftovers. But the best thing about lunchtime was definitely the movies. I think I had seen all of Greta Garbo's films before the age of twelve. She still is my ultimate beauty.

My teachers probably gave up on me as I don't recall getting into much trouble after the first year or two. They must have been an uninspiring bunch. Other than Mr Irvine, on whom I had a serious crush, only two – Miss Spence, and Mr Aldwich – stand out in my recollections. I think the reason Miss Spence stands out, even though she hated me and whacked me about, was because she shared my passion for Egypt, so I adored her. She knew Howard Carter, who had discovered Tutankhamun's tomb.

Miss Spence looked so old that sometimes I think Mr Carter must have dug her up with the tomb. She had a personally inscribed first edition of the book Carter wrote. She lent it to me, so she couldn't have been all that bad. I loved that book, reading it from cover to cover several times and poring over the photographs as though transported back in time. I dissolved into those pages, discovering the treasures myself.

The most awkward time for us boys was when we were in senior school and the onset of puberty saw involuntary erections – or, in our case, *didn't* see as they were hidden by books. You never saw a boy, at any time of the day, not carrying a stack of books just in case a stiffy should pop up. One boy, Neil, had a permanent erection, reputed to be a whopper. Kids used to hide behind my sporting doors and take turns looking at it. As the one person who would have really liked to see it, I was never part of the push that was allowed to.

With long pants and a protruding zipper pointing the way to better things, my era at Hyde Street came to an end, and I traded in my hated school uniform for another – at Williamstown High.

4

Willy High

My new uniform was not much of an improvement on the last, about the only difference being the colour of the stripes in the tie and the ribbed band around the V-neck of the jumper. Even before I had embarked on a legitimate career in fashion, I could pick a good fabric a mile away, and something told me that the bird's-eye serge of my new suit would not rank too highly on Jermyn Street or Savile Row.

Williamstown was five stops down the railway track – about fifteen minutes away on an old red rattler. So I could no longer walk to school, and my lunchtime classic movie education came to an end. I was on time for a while, as the trains were usually late, but then I adjusted my natural time clock and started missing them. I would thunder down the ramp of the overhead crossing just in time to see the smile on the attendant's face as he would slam the gate in my face, step forward with his whistle, and signal the driver to be on his way. I didn't mind this time alone as it meant I didn't have to put up with the nonsense and hoo-ha of all the other students. I liked being aloof, not running with the pack. When I did manage to catch the train, I would get in the girls' end – which was a punishable breach of the school's code of conduct. Maybe the powers that be knew I was not likely to – or inclined to – inseminate a Willy High vestal virgin on the short journey to school.

Sometimes Ron James, one of my tormentors, would miss the train, and we would travel together. Alone with me, he was as friendly as could be. It was only in the peer pack that he would taunt and tease me with names and sniggering innuendo. A few years back, he rang to invite me to a school reunion, and I have to admit I was rather rude to him, bluntly asking why I would want to see the bunch of yobs that tormented me and made my life hell at school all those years before.

A while ago, I saw him in person. It turns out that he drives a truck for the company that shifts the majority of our deliveries and he had asked to see the boss. Greeting me like a long-lost brother, he had apparently forgotten how vicious I had been to him on the phone. I, too, was kind at first, professing some interest in his life. I tarried with him for a while and then really stuck the knife in. I reminded him how we would groom our Beatles fringes while waiting for the train. Mine had been the best head of hair in the school, and my fringe far superior to his. We had both been blond and would rinse our hair in lemon juice to bleach it. He was constantly combing his fringe, giving it a little flip-up like a rip curl. Perhaps he combed it a bit too much, as now he was as bald as a badger. I still have a good mop of hair, so I gave him a farewell toss of it, leaving him to load up a ton of boxes emblazoned with my name.

It was strange entering Willy High School at form three. We were not raw novices from primary school, like the first-formers, but we were rookies nevertheless. There was a noticeable animosity in the first few days, everyone circling and bristling like a pack of dogs sniffing bumholes.

I found an immediate camaraderie with the odd bods, misfits and nerds, who naturally gravitated to each other, so it wasn't long before I settled in to a new gang. My gang was made up mainly of the brains trust, the ones who always got top marks in the exams. I don't know how I was embraced by this clique, as I was not exactly academically inclined. I would barely scrape through in Mathematics and Science, my average mark being 26 out of 100 for those subjects. Perceived as a bunch of nerds who would rather pass around a book than a football, they were nevertheless lots of fun. To the onlooker, these odd bods might have given the impression of being a dull bunch, but they were hilarious. We would joke and mess around all week from the moment we grouped at assembly. More than once, we were hauled out of that Monday morning ritual.

In my second year at Willy High, our team scored a real coup with Ray Star. He shone, as his name suggested. He was scholarly and a top sportsman, and I thought he was about the most handsome boy in the school. He had something exotic in his make-up, Indian perhaps – the epitome of tall, dark and handsome. My best friendship, with Stephen, also developed during this Willy High period, although I only knocked about with him outside our motley crew – he wasn't interested in belonging to a gang.

While I had a massive crush on Ray and knew I was gay, high school nevertheless saw me with a succession of girlfriends, sometimes several at once. (June Moody emerged triumphant and remains a dear friend to this day.) I had an aversion to anything that involved a ball – tennis, football, cricket, basketball, ping-pong. All our gang, except for Ray, were similarly inclined. For a couple of years, we had the most fabulous sports master. He would line us up in the afternoon on Wednesdays (sports day) and, with his whistle at the ready, shout, "Right boys, it's a cross-country run ... Ready ... Set ... Go!" At the blast of the whistle, off we would bolt for the railway station. Sometimes, we would buy fish and chips and sit in a long row in the gutter with the newspaper packages steaming on our laps, waiting for the Freedom Express to whip us off to the city for some light shoplifting. I think my sports uniform and runners were in their original pristine condition when I left school three years later. I wonder why Celia never twigged to the reason she never had to wash them.

Art was my best and favourite subject, and I decided I would become a painter. My father could relate to being a house painter or even a signwriter, but being an artist was not an acceptable option. My mother always encouraged me, but she thought it best not to say anything, and just to wait and see. Derwent pencils were still the status symbol. I never did upgrade, but colouring in the margins of my textbooks still occupied an inordinate amount of my time.

In those days segregation wasn't limited to the train. Boys and girls sat on different sides of the classroom. June and I managed to sit together on an aisle so we could talk, draw clothes and plan wardrobes instead of concentrating on the current lecture. We were exceptionally badly behaved in Geography and spent more time exiled in the library than in that particular class. For the school dance one year, we configured a fabulous micro mini dress for her in a wild psychedelic print, with a matching tie for me. Teddy was put aside for the next few years while June replaced him as my inspiration – and became, in fact, my living, walking dress-up doll.

There are not many memorable highlights from my years at Willy High; the best things I took with me when I graduated were my friendships. Apart from June, there was Stephen. He had bulleted past me in the first week, impressing me with his beautiful sheet of black, silky hair, which was much longer than the rules dictated. I was jealous – that's how I wanted mine to be. He also wore his standard-issue black school shoes like scuffs, with the heel under his foot. It wasn't a fashion statement – he had outgrown them, as I later found out, and his family couldn't afford a new pair. He wore them with such flair and abandon that I didn't consider such a possibility – I thought it was so chic. I tried to imitate the look, but my shoes were brand new and resisted any attempt to adapt to this style.

Stephen was so flamboyant and extroverted. He wasn't drawn to any clique, but we had gravitated to one another. I was putty in his hands and absorbed everything he introduced to me like a new sponge. "Put your head in this oven." I'd never heard of Judy Garland before he brainwashed me into the fan club. We both loved the glamour of Hollywood and show business; he had already started his immense vinyl collection (mostly shoplifted) and ended up acquiring a mastermind perspective on mid-century popular music.

Stephen was always wagging school. One of his lurks was playing a dead body being carried from the crime scene on *Homicide*, a popular police TV drama at the time. Ironically, he eventually got a job at Crawford Productions (which produced *Homicide*), and he asked me to do a huge psychedelic painting for a discotheque murder scene. I worked at it solidly for a week and thought my striking image in collage and mixed media was a masterpiece. After the scene was filmed, I expected some sort of acknowledgement or thanks, but nothing was forthcoming. Finally, I asked him how it went and when could I have it back as no remuneration had been offered. "Oh!" he said. "I've painted over it and used it for something else. By the way, it looked great!"

Stephen directed a couple of films that became cult favourites and then went off to Hollywood, where he had some success as a screenwriter. We lost contact. Then, one night, I watched a marvellous documentary about the Australian singer /songwriter Peter Allen and noticed that Stephen MacLean was credited as the director. "That has to be my Stephen," I thought. So, I made contact, and we resumed where we had left off. We wrote to each other for years. His letters were brilliant. I often dine out on a story about him meeting the famed writer Patrick White at a luncheon soon after White had published his letters. Mr White was a close friend of another recipient of Stephen's correspondence, which he often read.

During lunch, Patrick White leaned towards Stephen and said, "Your letters are wonderful. I enjoy them immensely."

"Sorry, I can't say the same about yours," replied Stephen.

Silence fell upon the table!

Having written *Peter Allen: The Boy from Oz*, which formed the basis for the Tony Award–winning Broadway musical hit, he invited me to the New York premiere, where I was seated next to one of my favourite musical stars, Barbara Cook. At one point, Stephen turned to me and whispered, "Not bad for two boys from Willy High."

Indeed, Willy High was far from the pinnacle for me, and my time there was certainly not something I would want to relive. Obviously, the person who coined the phrase about high school being "the best years of your life" was someone who never peaked higher than in those supposedly carefree days before graduating into the real world.

I always managed to be a year younger than most of my classmates. When fifth form and the Leaving Certificate came, I was fifteen. I passed, if not exactly with flying colours, but nevertheless with high enough grades to apply to go to art school. Subject to a presentable folio of work, which I didn't see as a problem, I was, at last, going down a path of my own choosing.

5

Childhood Backyards

My childhood home at number 13 Hobbs Street was a perfect example of Queen Anne front and Mary Anne back. The modernist transformation stopped abruptly at the backdoor, leaving the backyard in its original condition. Two rows of abandoned and neglected chook pens ran the whole depth of the backyard. It was like a little village, as each hen house had a different character and ambience. The overall picture was one of corrugated iron and whitewash, the only vegetation being an old, gnarled apple tree clinging close to a bungalow. Although ours was only a narrow block of land, it was extremely deep and, when the poultry shantytown was demolished, it was quite large.

This was in the days when the plethora of reality TV shows like *Backyard Blitz* was unheard of. Tuscan-inspired feature water walls were not even dreamt about, not even in Tuscany. Instead of a nineteenth-century oil jar painted azure blue with a gushing gurgle, the focal point of our backyard was the very newest Hills Hoist clothesline. Dad had been so inspired by Bruno Grollo's concreting work on the side drive that he decided to try his hand at replacing the path that split the

yard into two symmetrical oblong blocks. It led up to and around the Hills Hoist and continued on to the new chook house that he built behind a discreetly high tea-tree fence right at the bottom of the backyard. A Hills Hoist was not the most attractive feature, but I loved it because you could take a running leap at it and hang on while it spun you around like on a carnival ride. This is why no Hills Hoist ever looked new for long. I don't ever remember seeing one that didn't have a nasty tilt.

Dad was very proud of his chooks, and one of my jobs was to collect the eggs. On one wall, you could lift a long lid on the section where they nested, slip your hands underneath the startled occupant and steal off with the warm excretion, usually an egg.

Overcoming his pride, Dad would occasionally sacrifice one of the chooks. For me, the killing of a chicken was a special event. I used to like to watch the axe fall, but only from a suitable distance. I would run off to the safety of the bungalow and yell out to the executioner to let the guillotine fall. Dad would release the headless Marie Antoinette, which would run around the yard flapping her wings and spurting blood. I would watch with fascination and horror. Dad would hang her from the apple tree to drain the blood, and I recall bumping into an Anne Boleyn on more than one occasion. But worse was to come: the plucking. First, the sacrificial offering would have to be scalded to release the feathers. This I found the most unpleasant procedure and I would run a mile rather than assist. The smell was disgusting.

We would occasionally eat a duly prepared chook for Sunday lunch as a treat. I remember hoping to get a slice of the breast, which was my favourite portion. Mum seemed to carve forever, and a chicken at that time seemed to go so much further than it does today.

Right on the back fence of our place was an ancient privet hedge. It was actually five big bushes that had joined to form a visually solid block about 10 feet tall and 6 feet deep (3 by 1.8 metres). At the back of the neighbour's property was another hedge, a mirror of ours, with similar dimensions although slightly deeper. These hedges formed an enormous mass of no man's land and provided a natural adventure playground for our gang. The fence between the two properties had disintegrated long ago, and there were just a few stumps left to delineate one plot from the other. We devised a fearful initiation ceremony to induct new members into the various secret societies we formed over the years. The hedge was of such dense old growth that we could walk across the top of it, knowing exactly where the weak spots were: where the bushes met. We would demonstrate the initiation test to the unsuspecting prospective new member of our gang by walking the breadth of the hedge. When it came their turn, they would, of course, disappear down the gaps into the bowels of the abyss. We would find this hilarious and rush under the hedge to see the poor helpless victim suspended in a tangle of twisted, contorted and spiked branches.

Girls were particularly good victims, as they would be suspended in limbo, unable to move, usually with their dresses way above their heads. Extricating the poor soul from this tangle was much more complicated than tricking them into it. The newly inducted member often bolted for home looking like they had fallen into a combine harvester – clothes in shreds, and arms, legs and face cut to ribbons. Children can be so cruel!

When I was about eleven, I formed a very close relationship with one of Nanna's friends, Miss New. She was a spinster, a bit older than Nanna. I had met her through our church, St John's, and my friendship with her is a memory that I will always treasure. She mended umbrellas as a supplement to her pension. She lived behind a very old weatherboard house, in a dilapidated double bungalow in the depths of one of the most enchanted backyards I had ever seen. One room was her living-area-cum-workroom and was jammed full of beautiful old furniture, books and knick-knacks. Piles of sheet music – from Edwardian music-hall favourites to vaudeville and 1940s boogie woogie – sat atop an upright piano on which two very ornate brass candleholders clung on for dear life. She had a couple of enormous grey cats that were very old and hardly stirred from the ancient side chairs that had become their beds over the years.

Miss New's books were all Victorian and Edwardian tomes in handsome leather bindings with gold embossing. I think my initial fascination with Egypt may have started in this room, as one of my favourite books was full of engravings from Napoleon's folly in that ancient land. A layer of translucent waxy paper introduced each page, so you would always get a tantalising hint of what was to come. I would pore over those books for hours on end.

The backyard was so beautiful. It was totally overgrown, and a myriad of garden paths wove in and out, some leading nowhere but each one revealing some secret. A hidden rose arbour, a sundial, a pond, a broken statue of Diana the huntress, an aviary with a cockatoo that was even older than Miss New, a love seat, a swing … and the highlight: a dilapidated rusted-out wreck of a Model T Ford motor car. It had become a living sculpture, being utterly overgrown with the vines of an outrageously contorted wisteria. To see this Model T in full flower in early spring was something to behold. It was like a piece from a Jeff Koons exhibition. Every spring, Miss New would get a shovel and together we would dig up the two tortoises that had buried themselves to hibernate during the winter months – she always knew exactly where they were.

There was something outstanding in every season to amaze and bewitch you. Be it the old-fashioned roses at the height of summer, the perfume of which was intoxicating. Or the equally inebriating fragrance of the freesias, daffodils and hyacinths of early spring. Then there were the rusts, reds and golds of the primarily English trees in autumn. And the hauntingly bare and twisted branches of winter, some adorned with jewel-like berries.

I gradually became distracted from this friendship when I started art school. I heard that Miss New went into an Anglican nursing home, and I will never forgive myself for not visiting her before she passed away not long after.

6

Nanna

Nanna was the quintessential Englishwoman. This was not surprising given her background (staunchly English), her upbringing (strictly English), and her inclination (resolutely English). Added to this were her fervent monarchist loyalties. Despite all her years in the harsh Australian bush, she maintained a beautiful English-rose complexion, and when she died she looked many years younger than her ninety-four years.

Orphaned at the age of eleven, Celia (after whom my mother was named) was nearly cast out on the street with her young baby sister, Ada. Like an episode in a Victorian melodrama, they were taken in by their estranged maternal grandmother, Grandma Webster. A chance meeting in a shop when she was about sixteen saw an enhancement in her circumstances and a change of destiny. She was wearing an unusual brooch, one of the only mementos of her late mother. Dating back to my great-grandfather's time in India, the brooch had been the reward, the story goes, for his act of bravery in saving the life of the maharaja's son. As the brooch is rather modest, the potentate must have been either down on his luck, a cheapskate or not particularly fond of that son. I have it today. It is an owl's head carved from a tiger's eye gemstone, inset with ruby eyes.

"Where did you get that brooch, young lady?" demanded a looming and formidable figure, in a voice both threatening and suspicious. Mrs Fanshaw's terrifying demeanour softened when hearing the girl's explanation. The Fanshaws, old friends of Celia's parents, then arranged for her to leave Grandma Webster's care and come to live with them. She became a companion and a substitute daughter while they took care of her schooling and finishing, grooming her for a suitable marriage.

I regret not having been more forceful in cajoling Nanna to talk about her early years. Maybe she didn't have many memories. If she did, she was never forthcoming with them. However, she did recall standing in a crowded Manchester street with a flag when she was really little, waving at a passing black cloud that she was told was Queen Victoria. She also told me with great affection about a giant stuffed brown bear that stood on the top landing of their four-storey townhouse. Her father would lift her up to place an orange in its mouth before she would go to bed of a night. It was always gone in the morning. She remembered her father's manservant, a dark-skinned man, perhaps an Indian, who was horrible to the other servants out of his master's sight. He always carried a crop and lorded over the poor maids as they scrubbed and washed floors repeatedly until the result met with his approval. Because her tales were so far and few between, I never doubted their veracity. If they had been fabrications of imagination, surely there would have been many more memories.

During the First World War, Celia was a society nurse – not qualified to do anything more than cheer up the sick and wounded by being a pretty face, writing letters back home for them and sharing some idle chat. It was on her rounds that she first saw my grandfather. She thought he was an Arab at first. He was heavily bandaged, and all she could see was a pair of piercing black eyes. He had been shot through

the cheek at Gallipoli, the bullet passing through and removing his top lip and smashing his teeth. Every photograph I have of him shows him sporting a spectacular moustache. He couldn't speak for months, but the two fell in love with their eyes. So much for her being groomed for a suitable marriage – when he recovered and could speak, he proposed, and they tied the knot with the Fanshaws' blessing. My mother had a lovely letter that Mr Fanshaw wrote to my grandparents while they were on their honeymoon at St Anne's, where he imagined them with arms around each other, sitting on the sand with Celia's head on "Jack's chest, gazing up with sparkling eyes". Jack was shipped back to the trenches in France until the end of the war, and when peace was declared he was repatriated to Australia.

In 1919, Celia left England on the steamship *The Osterley*, bound for Melbourne via the Cape to start their married life. I am sure she had no idea what she was in for. Jack came down to Melbourne to meet her and take her home to Portland. His family, the Baileys, had come to Portland with the first settlers. "Gracious Bailey", as Jack's grandfather was known, was the Henty family's stonemason, building the first houses in Victoria (Portland having been settled before Melbourne). His work included the tiny bluestone cottage where Jack was taking his Celia home to start their life together and raise a family. It must have been used as a pub or an inn at some stage; years later, while Jack was renovating it, several gold sovereigns were found among other coins under the floorboards.

Portland was a real backwater then, and Nanna stood out with her fancy clothes and city ways. It was a long time before she was fully accepted as a local. She was lucky she could wear her London clothes for years, as it took forever for the fashions to catch up. I have a favourite photograph from that time, taken at a picnic. Nanna is sitting in the middle of a paddock, looking like a fashion model. She is wearing a cloche hat and fur-collared wrap jacket so typical of the style of the early 1920s. Surrounding her is a panoply of real country bumpkins.

My mother describes life with little in the way of material comforts but laughter and love in abundance. For a young woman who had grown up with servants and knew nothing of domestic chores, it would have been an enormous culture shock for Nanna. She started a new family just when the Great Depression hit. Although times were extremely difficult, they never went hungry. My grandfather would fish, and they kept chickens and grew vegetables on their small plot of land, which was enough to sustain them and share with some of those less fortunate in the town. Many a passing stranger was made welcome at their humble table before he went on his way with something in his swag for the futile journey ahead, searching for work.

When the Second World War broke out, my mother and her sister, Auntie Norma, moved to Melbourne to look for work. My mother lied about her age and got a job working in a munitions factory, where her contribution towards the war effort was very well rewarded. After a few months, my grandfather came down to check up on his daughters and didn't like what he found. In his opinion, they were not eating correctly and looking after themselves, so he decided to move to Melbourne, where he could keep an eye on them. My grandmother was always a strict taskmaster. My mother would hand over her pay packet without question and receive £1 a week to live on. In later years, she would muse over the naivete of that decision and feel some regret, but it was just accepted at the time.

Soon my grandmother had enough money to purchase the milk-bar business in Wingfield Street. My grandfather died not long after, at the age of sixty-two. His widow was still a handsome woman. She was only fifty-one, but her life stopped as if thrown into a time warp. Embracing the idea of widowhood, she suddenly turned into Nanna.

I wasn't her favourite grandchild by any means. My cousin John was number one and Susan number two. Their early deaths shook her terribly, and, try as hard as I did, I could never fill the gap. Not that she didn't love me – I know she did. I loved her to distraction, and her influence still dictates my tastes and choices to this day.

My funny Anglophile predilections are the direct result of her active or subliminal tutelage. I think I must have been the very last person who stood up for *God Save the Queen* at the pictures, and I would often be hit on the back of the neck with a half-sucked Fantale. Nanna and I celebrated every royal occasion, from the trooping of the colours to the Christmas message. We shared every birth, christening and bereavement, and we especially loved a wedding.

For many years she would buy her clothes from a travelling salesman, Mr Peters. He was the archetypal middle-European (am I allowed to say) Jew. *Fiddler on the Roof* had not yet been written, but I swear I remember hearing him humming "Yiddle diddle diddle dum" as he opened up his suitcase and displayed his schmutter wares. There was one particular suit from him that I loved. It was a black silk dupione dress and matching jacket, the lining of which (white crêpe de chine with cerise and red roses) matched the bodice of the dress. I can't tell you how many times I made that ensemble in one form or another over the years when I was sewing couture clothes.

Nanna had her own suitcase "shop". It was under the bed and was filled to the brim with every birthday and Christmas present she had ever received. When I was making clothes, I took great delight in creating dresses for her, as I knew she couldn't pack them up and shove them under the bed into the suitcase shop. Of the beautiful dresses I made for her over the years, one of my favourites was made from a fabric sample card that included dozens of large swatches of a heavy wool jersey in a huge rainbow of colours. I chose a base colour and made a stunning patchwork design. She loved it.

Although I would never say she was a big woman, it was the done thing for women of that era to wear foundation garments. She had an armoury of these corsets and continued to wear them for many years. When she got older, and her health started to deteriorate, she lost an enormous amount of weight but would armour up every day in the same battledress she had worn forever. I would help her sometimes with the hundreds of hooks and eyes and I was highly amused by the sight. These testaments to figure control would just swing and hang loose on her sadly shrinking person. Sometimes, when I see myself in a photo nowadays, I wish I had kept one!

When Celia met her knight in shining armour and remarried, she and Duncan went to live in Bahrain. Nanna went for a while to live with my aunt and uncle, Elene and Brian, in Ferntree Gully. When Elene and Brian went on an extended holiday, she moved to a nursing home, Amaroo, not far from their house. When they returned from their grey nomad tour around Australia, she decided to stay at Amaroo. I visited her almost every week, hardly missing one. What I would talk about, I have no idea, but she was used to my prattle after all those years. When Celia returned to Australia, Nanna didn't want to move back in with her and was quite happy to stay put, although she did come home for her holidays and the occasional weekend stay. She wasn't at all surprised that I was gay as I think she had an inkling of my midnight callers and was delighted when I met Mark, who became my life partner. "Such a delightful young man," she would say. "But why does he always shout at me?"

In the same way that he adopts a particular language and manner when addressing some people (particularly of an Asian persuasion), he somehow assumed that Nanna was a bit hard of hearing.

I cannot remember Nanna having anything more to drink than an Advocat and cherry brandy on a special occasion, but she enjoyed a tipple in the last few years of her life. I always made sure there was a bottle of brandy in the bottom of her wardrobe.

One of the last things I made for her was a comfy dressing gown trimmed with lace at the neck and cuffs. I never saw her wear it. I looked under her bed for a suitcase, thinking she was saving it, but the "shop" had long been abandoned. The Yardley talc and eau-de-cologne sets must have gone under someone else's bed.

Nanna was always a bit of a snob, and she wasn't too mad about many of the other residents at Amaroo. She did have one close friend, however: a lady she always called Madam. Madam was French, and French in the same way that Nanna was English. Madam liked a brandy as well.

I couldn't swear to the fact, but I thought I saw something like the lace on the robe I had made Nanna sticking out of Madam's wardrobe. I do hope so.

7

Auntie Ada

As well as Nanna's younger sister, Ada, there was also a third sister, Lillian, who was born in India and died in infancy. They had been in India while their father was doing a tour of duty with his regiment. He also died there of typhoid and, on returning home, their mother succumbed to the same disease. As I have mentioned, they were orphaned. Their parents' union had not been blessed by my great-grandfather's family, feeling that their son had married far below him, so these two daughters of the regiment were not recognised, were disinherited and were abandoned to their fate. Fortunately, their future was in the solid form of their maternal grandmother, Nanna Webster, who owned a public housel.

My Nanna Celia was always sketchy on details. Like in all oral histories, tales emerge of escaping through the snow with diamonds and rubies being sewn into the hem of a threadbare coat and later lost. Celia's take on the family history was fascinating if it was true. There were allusions to distant South African diamond mines and a flourishing business in Manchester involving haberdashery and millinery – an uncanny coincidence in that millinery would play such an important part of my life.

Celia was nine years senior to Ada, so narrative dictated that their paths diverged, but Celia never forgot her little sister. When she had settled in Australia, she sent for Ada; the year was 1926. They were quite different not only in looks but also in manner. Nanna's years with the Fanshaws had given her an edge of gentility, whereas Ada had a more basic upbringing with Nanna Webster in the pub. Nanna was always very proper, almost dour; Ada had more spark and a sense of fun. Auntie Ada had glorious long hair, which she plaited into two buns worn over the ears, very *Star Wars* (Princess Leia) style. She kept it like that for many years longer than was fashionable. Every time Celia listened to her radio headphones, she said she thought of Auntie Ada. She fell in love with a local man, Bob Edridge, and planned to be engaged, but old Mrs Edridge forbade the marriage. Bob went away shearing, and Ada was heartbroken. In her vulnerability, she succumbed to the charms of the local Lothario and became one of three Portland belles to be struck pregnant by the same gong at the same time. "A Flash Harry", my mother called him as she remembered Nanna hurling a frying pan of sizzling bacon and eggs at him. He apparently was very handsome: Portland's answer to Leslie Howard, a Hollywood heartthrob of the time. Flash Harry abandoned all three women and took off with a poor thing who was another relation of ours, a young cousin of my grandfather.

Ada was shipped off to Melbourne, and when her baby, a girl, was born my grandfather decided that he and Nanna would bring her back to Portland and raise the baby as their own. This was my auntie Elene. He put her in a pram and, with Nanna by his side, marched down the main street of Portland with chin up, announcing to any challenger that this was their new baby. He loved Elene as much as, if not more than, Celia and Norma. Ada was there on the sidelines and much loved by everyone. When Elene discovered, through the spite of a vengeful child, that Nanna was not, in fact, her real mother, Ada remained as she had always been: "Auntie Ada". She told Elene that Nanna had brought her up and she should look on her as her real mother.

I always thought (as I didn't find out about the shameful secret until Auntie had passed away) that it was sad that she didn't have any family. But she did, although in the shadows. Bob returned after years away and stood up to the old bitch of a mother who had denied him. He eventually married Auntie as he had wanted to, and they had a few happy years together. He died about eight years after they wed.

My memories of Auntie are in the following years when she would come up to Melbourne every Christmas and stay with us and then with Elene and my cousins Pam, Susan and Mark (who I didn't know were her grandchildren). I absolutely adored Auntie Ada with a passion. I don't know why – she was never lavish with presents or playful or willingly affectionate – but I looked forward to her visit with eager anticipation. We had a funny fold-out single bed that emerged from an equally funny one-and-a-half-person armchair/ sofa. Today, it would be highly sought after as an Art Deco gem, but it was ugly, bulky, and covered in an unpleasant green tapestry. I don't know where it lived most of the year, as I had banished it from the living room, but when Auntie came to stay, I insisted that it be put in my room, where we could barely squeeze it in. Poor old Auntie would be exhausted, but I would make her talk to me and tell me stories for hours and hours, even when the lights were finally turned out. She must have been glad when it was time to go and visit Elene for a bit of a break; I just never let her alone.

Although she was years younger than her sister Celia, Ada looked older. She was as blind as a bat and had the thickest spectacles (Coke-bottle bottoms). I remember trying to put a slice of bread back on an empty plate, which she was trying butter; she had no idea that she had miscalculated her aim. Her glorious golden hair was now short, steely grey and incredibly wiry, and she always had a bit of a bristle on the chin and that faint old lady air, but to me, she was divine. I couldn't get enough kisses and hugs and cuddles from her.

You had to be very careful with her and just couldn't launch yourself

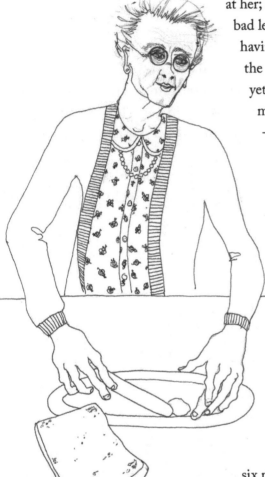

at her; she was fragile. She had always had bad legs; Elene cannot remember her not having them fully bandaged because the slightest knock would result in yet another painful ulcer. Nanna maintained that these afflictions – the eyes and the legs – resulted from her always reading and from standing too close to the fire.

Those happy times dwindled away, and Ada stopped coming to our place. She had a very bad heart condition and became too sick to make the trip. After years of Elene and her husband, Brian, trying to convince Ada to come to live in Melbourne, she finally agreed, but her condition had deteriorated seriously, and she was hospitalised and died within six months. Although she didn't get the chance to live the last few years of her life in the bosom of her real family, she still lives deep in the hearts of those who remember her so fondly.

In a classic case of history repeating itself, my cousin Pam, Ada's granddaughter, found herself in the same delicate situation as her grandmother. Someone decided that the shock of hearing of this situation would "kill" Nanna, and Pam was shipped off to Perth in secret to deliver her indiscretion. I was delighted with the situation as I got to mind her Volkswagen for the confinement. Pam had a little boy, and Nanna found out about it about an hour later. Not only did it *not* kill her, but she took it in her stride as she did most things we tried to hide from her.

Although I can't say life was an easy haul for Pam in the following years, she has emerged through it all and is an example of a strong and proud woman who faced the consequences of her decisions without regret. We have come a long way since the days of Ada's decision to give up the care of her child for the sake of respectability and to step back into the shadowy role of auntie. I hope the regrets that she had didn't cloud the love she was given regardless by Elene and her family and a pesky little me.

8

Childhood Holidays

I can't remember a year as a child when we didn't have a family holiday. I am sure there were years when my parents would have had to stretch the household budget, but we always went somewhere for two weeks at Christmas time.

In my memory bank, I have a foggy image of a heavy, red-brick balcony and some steep steps with two big bushes on each side. My mother said it sounds like the place where they stayed in Sydney the year I was born but that I couldn't possibly remember that, my first holiday at three months of age. Until I was six, we always went to Seaford, then an outer bayside village of Melbourne. (Seaford has since been absorbed into the substantial suburban sprawl that the city has become.) A funny old guest house provided our holiday digs. It was right on the Nepean Highway, just opposite the buffer zone of sand dunes and tea trees that separated it from the beach. Mine Hosts were Mr and Mrs Fox, a genteel couple most likely in their late sixties.

Mr Fox was balding and had a patchy red complexion. In fact, he looked like a highly waxed, polished and distressed Pink Lady apple.

Although that sounds awful, it wasn't. In fact, he had a most attractive glow about him. His pleasant countenance and gentle smile far outshone any physical imperfections. He was the first man I remember that tried to coax the few thin wisps of snowy white hair from behind the left ear and cover his naked dome in an attempt to reach the right ear. If it didn't fool a four-year-old, then any observer could tell that it wasn't a full head of hair. Even on the hottest of summer days, he wore a woollen cardigan, a starched striped shirt and a bow tie.

Mrs Fox had that magic old-lady hair that sometimes turned purple when she returned from the hairdressers on Wednesday afternoons. I later found out this was called "a pensioner special". To protect her coiffure, she would wear one of those gauzy nylon headscarves that resemble pressed cobwebs. They were usually shocking pink, orange or turquoise and often hovered above the coiffure for several days. These scarves were in sharp contrast to her general palette. She always wore washed-out prints and faded pastel-coloured twin sets. Her jewellery was always colour coordinated. I was particularly fond of a matching set of ice-green pearls: triple strands around her neck, earrings, and a huge brooch that looked like it had been run over by a steamroller.

Mr and Mrs Fox moved silently and spoke in whispers. Looking back, in all probability, I think they were ghosts. They

offered a full board – breakfast, lunch and dinner. The food had a haunted aura about it as well. Boiled eggs and toast soldiers were standard fare. You couldn't go wrong with those for breakfast. On the sideboard, there would be side dishes of bacon, sausages and grilled tomatoes, with the cereal offered being Rice Bubbles if you so wished. Lunch could be sandwiches with the crusts cut off or a salad. The salad was a formal arrangement of shredded lettuce, tomatoes and onion rings in vinegar, sliced beetroot, hard-boiled eggs, some grated carrot, cubed cheese, and sometimes a cold chicken leg, but always luncheon meat rolled around a gherkin and speared with a toothpick. Mrs Fox always served afternoon tea, which we often missed as we spent the whole day at the beach. She was famous for her date scones. On my childhood palette, these rivalled my mother's apple cakes. For dinner, some things appeared in ghoulish white sauces, but more often than not Dad preferred to take us to the Frankston pub for a counter tea. Mr and Mrs Fox ran a dry establishment, and Dad enjoyed a beer.

I adored the beach at Seaford, as the sand had that not-quite-finished coarse texture, about a number four on a grade of ten (imagine pulsing shells in a Magimix for three minutes or so). There were thousands of half and intact little bivalves among the mixture, and many had holes so that you could thread them together. I would spend hours making ropes of necklaces and wear them around my neck, wrists and ankles and on my head. If I couldn't get my hands on Mrs Fox's green pearls, I'd go one better.

The dunes between the highway and the beach were an eerie no man's land. It was so silent and cool and it held a primal attraction for me. The first time I ever heard the word *poofter* was in those dunes one day when Dad took off yelling. He was in pursuit of someone lurking in the darker realms of the tea trees.

Being in the shelter of Port Phillip Bay, the water at Seaford was as smooth as glass. The calmness at the water's edge was also helped by a complex of large sandbars about 30 metres offshore. Dad piggybacked me out there to play in the ankle-deep water as I didn't swim at that age.

It was a wonderful feeling to be surrounded by all that water. No wonder Jesus loved the Sea of Galilee.

When I was about nine, we bought a camping spot from some friends at Torquay. They had been going there for years, and it was their permanent site. There was a built-in old wood stove in the garden, tables built around trees, and a tea-tree fence covered in climbing geraniums. We had spent a couple of weeks there one year and loved it. It was so different from becalmed Seaford, Torquay being a rough and wild surf beach. When they offered to sell it, we were only too happy to keep it in the family (so to speak).

We took it over lock, stock and barrel – the tent, the bunks, the hodgepodge of collected odds and ends, cutlery, crockery, pots and pans, sheets, towels and my favourite things of all time – the Tilley lamps. Their brilliance came from the exquisitely delicate bulb which was like a crocheted baby's bootie. I could hardly wait for it to get dark so I could watch Dad go through the motions of pumping and adjusting to get the lamps aglow. I would also love waking up in the morning. I had a top bunk, and the first thing I would see was the silhouettes of early-morning birds as they walked all over the green canvas roof of our tent. Being so close to the top, you could give them a terrible fright by tickling their little feet with a finger.

Over the years, Dad made "improvements": a concrete floor, carpet, electricity, a refrigerator and fluorescent light. We even had a fly-wire front door. We set it up in late spring and kept it up sometimes well into autumn. It was always a big party day when we set up and took down the tent, as the friends who would also use it during the summer would all come and help. It had become a whopping job, thanks to Dad making our summer home-away-from-home more sophisticated.

I can't imagine where everyone slept, but often there seemed to be dozens of people staying for the weekend or for a couple of days during the week. Dad would take us down before Christmas and stay a couple of weeks before returning to work; then, he would come down for the weekends. We often would spend six weeks of glorious summer there.

My cousins John and Richard would be included and often spent the whole summer with us. Sometimes Auntie Elene and Uncle Brian would come with my other cousins – Pam, Susan and Mark. We had lots of lovely times.

The beach at Torquay was so different from Seaford. The surf beach was near us at the camping ground, but there was also a more sheltered beach in the English style, with lawns, a promenade and giant Norfolk pines. On weekends, large families of Greeks and Italians would picnic under the shade of those magnificent trees. The men wore handkerchiefs knotted at the corners on their heads, and the women often carried small umbrellas – quite a contrast to the mad Aussies on the surf beach around the bluff where we were all oiled up and spit roasting.

There were fantastic rock pools on the point, and Mum and I spent most of our time exploring these sheltered aquariums. At low tide, they were exposed for hours at a time and they would be replenished every day with new supplies of sea urchins, cowrie shells, fish, crabs and crayfish. There were pools of all dimensions – from the size of a bucket to the big one right on the point, which had a large rock in the middle of it and was as big as a suburban swimming pool. Mum taught me the finer points of swimming in this pool. It was exciting when the tide came in, as we would try to stay as long as possible until it became too dangerous. The encroaching sea would send huge crashing waves over our heads as we scurried away with our buckets brimming with King Neptune's bounty.

Torquay offered me a wealth of activities to do over the holiday period, including the blossoming of my awakening sexuality. There was a huge sand dune around the bluff at the next beach, Jan Juc, and this was fabulous for tobogganing down on a rusty sheet of corrugated iron. I will never know how we didn't ever come to a sticky end with severed limbs or gangrenous gashes. We knew no fear, but I shudder as I think today about some of the spills we had. The dune was also great for a roll – you would close your eyes and mouth as tightly as you could and let go, picking up ever-increasing momentum until you reached the bottom.

This was also dangerous, as the dune ended in a rather nasty drop over a ledge of volcanic rocks.

We often had a winter holiday as well. One year, we had a snow trip planned. Dad knew the owner of a caravan hire firm and promised us our first caravan adventure. Mum and I were excited at the prospect and eagerly awaited Dad's return after he went off to collect our dream home on wheels. We nearly died when we saw him pull up outside number 13. Instead of the slick aluminium Franklin deluxe six-berth dream van we expected, he had come home with a dilapidated relic. It looked as though some displaced Romany gypsies had abandoned it after failing to sell it because even *they* were ashamed of its sad, neglected persona.

It was made out of a three-ply marine board that was peeling and coming apart at the seams. It didn't have windows as such – the glass apertures that let in what light and air they could were so tiny that to call them windows was a stretch of the most generous imagination.

I will never forget the look of disappointment on Mum's face, but it was nothing compared with her horror when we opened the door to have a look inside. The smell sent you reeling. From the state of the outside, you wouldn't imagine that anyone would *want* to take a look inside, and

I don't think anyone had for many years. I took off to my bungalow with acute embarrassment and swore I wouldn't go away if we were expected to go in *that*. Mum, her usual indomitable self, got buckets of boiling soapy water and donned rubber gloves. Dad didn't see what the fuss was all about as it seemed perfectly all right to him. Mum scrubbed away for hours and disinfected every surface until it shone. and some essence of the van's faded glory was restored.

I was persuaded to come out of my room and cajoled into joining the rest of the family for the planned excursion. I agreed that it had scrubbed up all right, Mum and I nicknamed her Violet (the colour of her peeling paint), and off we set. We stayed in a caravan park in the beautiful small country town of Bright, at the foot of Mount Buffalo, and had a wonderful time. We grew to love Violet and look back on that holiday with fond memories.

The last few years were troubled, with my parents' marriage falling apart. Mum was completely shattered as she loved my father desperately. One day when she and I were lying together on the beach, I noticed a look of total nothingness on her usually animated face. She got up without saying anything and went for a swim. For some reason I watched her. An outstanding swimmer, she went out much further than the line where the big breakers started, and I thought, "She doesn't intend coming back." I decided to take off after her. I was quite a good swimmer, as she had taught me, but I was not that strong. By the time I reached her, I was about to drown. Luckily for me, her mothering instincts kicked in, and *she* had to save *me*, dragging me back to the shore. We never discussed it, but that was the end of Torquay and that whole happy period of my growing up and my parents' marriage.

9

The Deep End

Before I smashed my collarbone, I swam a lot. I was swimming fifty laps of a 50 metre pool every day at one stage, with little effort and much pleasure. At times since, I doubt that I could have managed a lap of a blow-up Mickey Mouse wader, but the Esther Williams in me always manages to resurface, and I still love it. I find swimming transcendental, my mind slipping off into another world where contemplation and problem-solving make sense of the world and one's life in general.

For those not familiar with the name, Esther was a big box-office draw for MGM films in the 1940s. Her movies and style were, shall we say, "mellifluous". My mother was a big fan of the aquatic romantic comedies that she starred in. They featured big production numbers with hundreds of nubile mermaids in extravagant water ballets, with Esther at the centre of everything – twirling from ropes, diving through flaming hoops, and swimming into the hearts of many an impressionable young girl – all underwater without seeming to take a breath. Esther was a direct influence on my style and ability.

The compulsory swimming lessons run by the school ignored the fact that I could already swim, and my teachers didn't think too much of my Hollywood affectations. Their standards required a lot of splashing and thrashing. My way was frowned upon, even though I would glide past the other kids easily while they nearly drowned in their frenzy. Try as my teachers may, I refused to surrender my style to theirs.

I have never had a sense of competition in the sporting arena and would always dip out when athletic events were looming. After getting my first Herald Learn to Swim Certificate for swimming 25 yards (22 metres) across the pool, I lost interest in visible signs of merit, such as certificates and medals. Maybe if they had made them more attractive – perhaps with more gold or some diamantés – I would have shown greater interest.

I also hated Footscray Swimming Pool, where we went for lessons. You had to walk through a shallow trough and under a few sprouting showerheads to attempt to rinse off offending bodies before they hit the water proper. I hated wading through this bit, as there was invariably a floating ice cream wrapper or an abandoned band-aid floating around. No matter how carefully or speedily you made your exit, one or the other would somehow stick to your ankle or lodge between your toes.

Often we went to this same pool for a social outing. Pat Crowder would cajole me into going with her, then abandon me the moment we arrived in order to flirt with the older boys. All the girls would swan around the deep end, watching these older boys showing off on the diving board. Even at such an early age, I must admit it was an activity that I enthusiastically shared with the girls.

Not all the girls were blessed with Nature's charms as Alison McMinn was. I remember one girl emerging from the water with her cottonball-enhanced bosoms not only drifting in different directions but also shrinking into hard little lumps. Meanwhile, I would keep a careful eye on the boys' Speedos to see if any likely enhancements were shifting and getting hard and lumpy.

Hyde Street School did have its own pool, but it was too little for serious swimming. Occasionally, small groups would be allowed to go in, but purely for mucking about. Much as I hated Footscray Pool, it wasn't nearly as dreaded as this one. It was ancient and looked filthy – the concrete around the edges was a slimy green, and you had to be careful not to slip. Because it was surrounded by a very high corrugated iron fence, it was dark and gloomy even on the hottest day – no sun ever reached it. The only attraction was that my art teacher, Mr Irvine, would take us on these afternoons. I had a serious crush on him for a couple of years, so I never objected to any chance to be near him or see him change into his well-filled Speedos

My father, ever hopeful that he could turn me into an Olympian athlete, decided to encourage my only vaguely sporting predilection with professional training, and I started swimming lessons at the City Baths.

About this time, I was in Miss Spence's class. I was a great chatterer, and she would constantly move me around the classroom, hoping to place me next to someone I wouldn't want to talk to. She told my mother that I was a "flibbertigibbet", something Celia kept from me for many years.

One day, I was jabbering away to someone when Miss Spence came up behind me and whacked me across the back of the neck with a yardstick ruler. Although it hurt like buggery, it was the shock and embarrassment that caused the most pain. I remember crying, which annoyed her even more, and she banished me into the corridor, where the headmaster found me. On questioning me, he promptly took me off to his office and gave me six of his best to seal the deal. Anyway, what my beloved Miss Spence had done was crack my eardrum.

All of a sudden, my swimming became torture. Whenever my ear came into contact with water, I would suffer excruciating pain in the inner ear. My father didn't believe me, nor did my trainer. They both thought I was trying it on. They would make me swim lap after lap underwater until, one night, I couldn't stand it any longer and climbed out of the pool in tears. I took off down Swanson Street via the centre of the tram tracks, dripping all the way, determined to get as far away as possible from water.

My father took a long time to catch up with me, as I was pretty fast

on land as well. That's when he finally believed me, as it was too dramatic a show to be an act. The doctors confirmed the damage, although I never confessed to the cause. Even though Miss Spence continued to abuse me, I was still mad about her and didn't dob her in. Today you could sue for millions, but I am sure my experience was not uncommon in those days. I had to give up swimming for the rest of the year. Drops administered daily eventually fixed the problem, although I have to wear earplugs to this day. I wonder what happened to that old bitch.

I very nearly drowned once, which surprised me at the time, as I was a confident swimmer and thought I would never find myself in that situation. I was in my early twenties and was on holiday with my friend Veronica at Club Med in Tahiti. We had enjoyed our fourteen days there, but the airlines went on strike near the end of our stay, leaving us stuck for at least another week. We decided to do all the things that we had deleted from our busy social calendar, one of them being the barbecue picnic on a romantic deserted island. This was a big mistake.

We found ourselves trapped with all the people we had been avoiding during the previous fortnight. The only way back to the main island was via the boat that had brought us over, and it wasn't due to depart until 5 pm. Sitting as far away from this merry band of revellers as we could, I caught sight of the main village just over the whitecaps of the sea. It felt like you could almost touch our burro. A fellow desperado decided he had had enough and started swimming back, so I thought I would follow him. He was built like the proverbial brick shithouse, but I was confident that my swimming prowess would see me keep up with him.

The water was not as deep as I had thought. I caught my hand on the coral after several strokes of freestyle, so changed to breaststroke, not my most vigorous style. I kept my eye on my trailblazer, trying to keep up with him. Suddenly he was gone. Where? I stopped and trod water, trying to see where he had disappeared. Then I saw him quite some distance to the left of where we needed to go. It was obvious that he was in trouble and had been caught a rip.

Halfway to my goal, I tried to turn back, but it was too late. I could feel the rip sweeping me away too. My first thought was, "Don't Panic". I remembered from somewhere that the best approach is to stop swimming and go with the rip. However, the thought of being swept way out to sea changed my mind, as I now found myself even further out than the brick shithouse. I started to swim across the rip. I could see the beach, and it didn't seem too far away. I don't think I have ever swum with such strength. Somehow, I made it to the shore, miles from where I had intended and with many cuts from the coral, but alive. Exhausted, I just lay on the sand, gasping for breath like a shipwrecked castaway. When I had recovered, I made my way back to the village, pretending nothing had happened.

Later that night, as we made our way down to the communal dining experience, I looked out for my rip buddy, hoping to feel some special bond through our experience. But I didn't see him then, or for the rest of our stay. Maybe he didn't make it. It didn't occur to me at the time to enquire. I am sure someone would have noticed.

Lucky to be alive, I enjoyed the rest of our bonus Tahitian idyll, never straying far from the pool. The currency at Club Med used to be popette beads that you would wear around your neck. You could always gather at least enough for a gin and tonic from the lost beads floating around.

When I returned home, I was disappointed to learn that I had just missed out on something special. At the time, I was hand-painting the wedding gown for the daughter of a prominent Melbourne industrialist. Had the strike gone on one more day, he was going to send his private jet to bring me back! I finished the dress on time, and she divorced a few years later. All that work!

My Tahiti experience left me wary of the ocean. Nowadays, I much prefer a pool and have built a spectacular one at our house in Queensland. Esther is back to fifty laps.

10

Art School

To apply for admission to art school, my Leaving Certificate in hand, I had to present a folio. I had a few old paintings hanging around, and I did a special one, an oil on masonite. Because I was currently in love with the musical *Man of La Mancha*, the subject was Don Quixote. Thinking it was rather good at the time, I submitted it to the Prahran Institute of Technology in pursuit of my next period of transition. My brother still has it.

I was accepted and I found myself back on the train, heading in the opposite direction to the one I used to catch to Willy High. Past the Footscray abattoirs, too old for Mum's perfumed hankie now, I would stop and change at Flinder Street Station for Prahran. For the first time ever, I was free of a school uniform. On the opposite side of the platform, I could see those kids who were going on to do their matriculation year. Their uniforms were really shabby by now. There was no sense in replacing them with only one year left, even though some boys showed more than a couple of inches of ankle.

Mum started me off rather neatly, but it didn't take long for me to

embrace the spirit of the times, the Age of Aquarius. By my second year, Mum would actually weep as I went off to art school, especially in the summer when I would wear almost nothing. I had trained a pair of jeans until all that was left of the crotch were two rows of stitching. There was a dangerously thin patch over my bits, which I embroidered with a bright yellow sunflower – X marks the spot – which I found to be a marvellous marketing device.

I had very good legs, long and brown, with a fine covering of sparkling golden hair. My nickname at art school was Legs Ladner. I had a pair of brown leather sandals that crisscrossed right up my legs to my thighs. These I teamed with an almost-sheer Indian shirt, heavily embroidered with bells and mirrors.

I got even more outrageous as the years went on. On the morning train to her work, Pat, my childhood friend, would be desperate to avoid me. She had a very respectable job at a city bank, and I seemed to embarrass her somewhat. The whole length of the carriage would lean sideways to see what I was wearing and Pat would turn a deep shade of beetroot. I, of course, thought I was fabulous.

That first year, I was like a prisoner serving a life sentence who had been suddenly set free. Classes were all general subjects, so that everyone got a feeling for what they might elect to take as their majors for the following three years of the diploma course. I loved life Drawing and General Drawing, and I consistently scored top marks. In fact, I scored well in all subjects except Painting. I hated the teacher, Alun Leach-Jones, who went on to be quite famous. He wanted everyone to paint in his style, which I found hideous. He allowed no room for any creative expression. As someone who had hoped to be a painter, I found this a great disillusionment. Consequently, I never went to his Painting classes. Instead, I could be found every Wednesday afternoon at the Regent Theatre. A ticket to the front stalls cost 60 cents. I think I must have seen every film made in 1967. If I was wearing my sunflower shorts, I seemed to get extra attention from the men in raincoats.

I did finally present a Painting folio. However, the hastily attached note, "Be Careful – Wet", might have influenced Mr Leach-Jones's decision to give me the lowest possible mark.

His subject wasn't the only one I had left to the last minute. I thought I would fail everything and prepared myself for that scenario, scouring the employment pages and trying to think what my next career move could be.

After my first year at art school, having done nothing but have a good time, I thought I should be prepared for the worst and have a job waiting in the wings. My first interview was for a photographer's assistant. I walked in and sat down in the prospective employer's chair, behind his desk. I guess he thought I had ambition. The second interview was for a first-year hairdresser's apprentice. Being such a natural with hair, I thought this one would be a cinch. The job caught my eye because it was at the city salon of Rene Henri, a famous name for many years in the world of haute coiffure.

My mother would often return from a visit to his salon with her hair piled high with "dog-shit curls" – a vividly descriptive, if somewhat distasteful nickname to give a style of hair adorning a lady's head. Once, she came home with a semi-permanent colour, "plum". My father hated it. He didn't even like my mother to wear make-up, so this blatant exhibition of artificiality caused quite a ruckus. She never gave in to him, however; she continued to experiment with all the latest looks and keep herself in tune with the fashions of the day.

My first impressions of the salon hardly augured a career in hairdressing, with Monsieur Henri's glory days clearly a dim memory. A rope of crystal had come adrift from the chandelier, and it had not just happened that morning; it seemed to be hanging on with the help of a spider's web. Cobwebs also featured on the large vase of faded silk flowers that dominated the foyer. These sat on a tiny half-circle marble-and-gilt console, which was in turn held on to a wall of bronze mirror tiles by a poor, tired gold cherub with a chipped nose.

Without warning I was swept away in what was almost a pas de deux, out of the foyer and into a dark, cramped room which, from the pungent

smell, I gathered must have been the colour mixing room. I presume the ballet master was Monsieur Henri himself. He took my hands in his and pressed himself against me, whispering, "Marvellous, when can you start?"

"Monday," I squeaked and fled, never to return.

That Monday, the results came out, and I passed with flying colours. No one was more surprised than me. Now, I only had to worry about a holiday job. My father always arranged my holiday jobs, and I would just meekly turn up at the appointed time, at the designated place. Looking back, I think he deliberately went out of his way to get me the most terrible jobs imaginable. That year, it was working for a house-wrecking company. They would place a sledgehammer in my hand and point to a shed, or something or other, and – with a smirk behind their hands – instruct me to knock it down, which I would do. Visualising the shed as my father always got the job done in no time. I will never forget the look on their faces when I loaded a huge truck with bricks in the blazing sun before joining them,, in the only patch of shade to have lunch.

"Whatcha gonna buy with ya DOSH, MATE?"

I wistfully glanced somewhere behind their heads, averting my eyes from the odd strangulated testicle trying to escape from a pair of navy-blue King Gees (workmen's shorts).

I proudly announced, "I have my heart set on the latest Elna zigzag sewing machine! It has a free arm and an electronic foot ..." On I droned about all its marvellous attachments. Had they ever seen an invisible zip? That shut them up for a while. I hardly remember having to talk to them at lunchtime for the rest of my tenure. I must admit that the money was good. I bought the Elna zigzag machine, which went on to make hundreds of dresses and a lot of money. It still sews like a dream. Although it's not used much any more, it is still the best machine I have ever used.

Having passed my first year at art school quite well, I had to elect a major for the following year.

The stalemate with my father continued, but he could see a commercial rainbow on the horizon in the possibility of my becoming a fashion designer. This decision was influenced by my Auntie Lorna (a second cousin, I think). I admired her enormously. She was so stylish and sophisticated. Lorna was the head designer for Norman Hartnell in Melbourne, having worked for the grand old couturier in London. She had done terribly well as far as Dad could see and she drove a very racy orange sports car.

Lorna took out "Gown of the Year", which at that stage was a very prestigious award. Her entry was a fabulous white lace creation that was shorter at the front and dipped to a train at the back. An off-the-shoulder coffee-coloured taffeta coat contrasted with the texture and purity of the white lace. It was crowned with a white rose fascinator, the influence of which served me well and would make me a lot of money in my later career. I was so excited when we watched it on the telly. After Lorna won, I made Teddy a copy of her gown from a doily the very next day. So, fashion was in the blood, I suppose, and I was thrilled at the prospect of becoming Australia's answer to YSL.

That time, before all such ambitions and dreams were knocked out of one, was truly wonderful. We had touched on fashion in our first year, and I had been very happy spending time with the teachers from that department. I had been particularly drawn to one of them, Margaret Hatherly, who would go on to become my second mum. She had a stunning five-carat diamond ring, and she often let me wear it during classes.

I was raring to go when we started back in the new year. There were fifty-four students in our class that first year of Fashion but only four of us would finish. The second year was great fun, and you could tell that natural attrition would level out the talent – not that there wasn't an abundance of it. I had to work very hard to ensure a week wouldn't go by without my designs being pinned up on the board. Maree Menzel and I always seemed to have our design drawings featured side by side, and a gentle friendship/rivalry developed between us. She and I remained good friends.

Maree was a Catholic boarding-school girl from the country and still lived with nuns in East Melbourne. When we had night classes, I would walk her home from Flinders Street Station. We would always pass by Hillier's, the chocolatier in Collins Street and invariably ordered the same thing – a "chocolate frosted". This was a chocolate malted milkshake poured into a long glass into which a stream of hot marshmallow had been swirled.

Hillier's was a relic from the 1930s. I think the staff were as original as the Art Deco fittings. One lady sat in a lofty, pulpit-like structure. Her hair was a spun confection in itself and looked like she was balancing a plate of meringues on her head. Her job was to take the money from the man who "harmonised" the goodies. He was bald and short, so he had to stretch up while she leant down. It was a poetic moment when their heads sometimes touched as she dispensed the small change. It didn't seem to be an efficient arrangement. I was never happy because, when he poured the chocolate malted milk into the marshmallow swirl, he would always look into the aluminium beaker before whisking it away, and you just knew there was still good slosh remaining.

Sometimes, I would deposit Maree on her doorstep and run all the way back, hoping to catch them before they closed and indulge in a second one. There was never anything that replaced that elusive, never-quite-enough, chocolate-frosted taste.

Lunch at Prahran Tech offered a million possibilities. The most popular eating spot was directly opposite – Mrs Macs, a milk bar not unlike my Nanna's, except for the fact that the food was one stop short of poison. I only ate something from there the one time. I remember describing whatever I bought as a "Staphylococcus Surprise". We were very close to the multicultural offerings of cosmopolitan Chapel Street. Italian, Chinese, Turkish, Greek – you name it, it was on offer. I have to confess that my favourite haunt was the good old Aussie cakeshop Pattersons. They specialised in party food, so you could have anything from a pie to a cocktail version of pig-in-a-blanket. I would often order a selection that included party-size versions of a pie, a pastie, a sausage roll, a quiche and an egg-and-bacon slice. When you had savoured the last bite and swept away all traces of crumbs, the moment would arrive to open that last white, shiny paper bag hiding a Melba, which was a delightful choux pastry filled with strawberry cream. It was a wonder I didn't explode years before I did!

Because most of my fellow students were much older, an inordinate amount of my social life was spent at the pub. A counter lunch was only a couple of dollars and, although I was never that partial to beer, I could keep up by adding a dash of lime. Once, rolling out of the pub, I was egged on to swipe a slab of beer from the delivery truck. OMG, a policeman's son! I still feel guilty!

Some clever, smarmy entrepreneur opened a lunchtime disco at one stage, and we thought it terribly decadent to drink beer and dance morbidly around to my absolute most hated song of all time, Procol Harum's *A Whiter Shade of Pale*. Janis Joplin was also very popular in those days. When we would go to parties, the first thing I would do was find her album and hide it under a couch. The whole night, all you could hear were plaintive cries of "Where's *Pearl*?"

It wasn't all fun and games. We were expected to work, but it wasn't like work. It was a marvellous time. Looking back, I regret that I didn't take full advantage of it, but I was actually too young. We had an exciting head of our fashion department, Rowena Clark. She was English and slightly eccentric, but she was a stimulating teacher, and classes were never dull.

I found the curriculum not challenging enough in the third and fourth years, so I went on my merry way, designing and sewing outside of school while still keeping up. Not only did this improve my skills; it also made me some extra money on the side. In our final year, we had to produce only three garments for submission. I think I must have made about thirty.

We also continued with our General Drawing and Life Drawing classes. I loved life drawing and not only because I was mad about a particular male model. He worked as a hooker as well, and we used to joke with him.

"How much did you earn last night, Garth?"

"Fourteen dollars and 50 cents."

"And who gave you the 50 cents?"

"They all did."

Hilarious!

I would have gladly given him all my spare change to kiss those lips.

I adored the Life Drawing teacher, Miss Hallandal. She loved my work and would spend at least half an hour huffing and puffing, scratching and gesturing at my drawings, rubbing little bits out, adding other little bits. I never understood a single thing she was talking about. I would agree and nod and look understanding and then just go on regardless. I always got high distinctions, so obviously she thought she was getting through to me.

Fashion did grab my imagination. I loved what I was doing and had celestial illusions as to what I would achieve and where I would go. In our final year, we were encouraged to enter the "Gown of the Year" competition ourselves. I can't remember how it panned out, but only three of us – Avril Hunnybun, a heartfelt young girl called Marilyn, and I – finished up making entries. I remember designing mine one morning on the racing page of *The Sun* newspaper with a blue biro while on the train to school. I usually tried to do something to occupy my thoughts, as I always had a strange compulsion to throw myself off the train as it crossed the Yarra River.

With a design in mind, I had to find a sponsor and organise a model. I was totally besotted with Dawn Scott, who was undoubtedly Australia's top photographic and catwalk model. "Nothing but the best" had always been my motto. I rang Dawn. She wasn't so keen, as the models were not paid, but I was so insistent she reluctantly agreed to see me.

I think she deliberately went out of her way to look as awful as she could on the night I called to see her. She had greasy hair, a bad cold and a red runny nose – far from the great beauty I had idolised. I had placed her on a pedestal next to Greta Garbo in my lexicon of beauty but she was merely mortal. I wasn't to be put off, however, and she graciously agreed to model my entry. Among three student entries, I received one of the top ten Designer Awards and was thrilled to bits. The pleasure was somewhat tarnished as there was quite a hullabaloo in the next few days from disgruntled designers who exposed the winning entry as Vogue Pattern 2856.

I was extremely proud of my final-year examination gown. It was a champagne organdie evening dress with ruffles wherever I could put them. It had a tight waistcoat, which, with June's help, I covered all over with gold, diamond and pearl beads in a paisley pattern. For the finale, I also made a mini jumpsuit in lilac lace set off by an organdie top with giant puff sleeves. The lace hotpants were beaded, and the top was see-through. I was pressured to put a lining in the bodice, as it was thought to be far too risqué. That ultimatum saw the fringe flick and the door slam with extra dramatic impact. Still sporting the five-carat diamond.

One of the other final garments we had to make was a simple cotton casual dress. I could never do things in a simple way. Mine had a 10 foot–long train, and a bare midriff, executed in lilac gingham fabric. (My favourite colour again.) I was mad for ruffles, and the skirt also featured that design element all around the train. An awful amount of gingham was required. Well, my thought process was, "Casual says picnic, picnic says gingham, and picnic rug says 10 foot train. Saves packing one!"

We had a gala parade as the finale to our four years' work. Other departments became involved, and Paul Cox (who later became a famous director) made a two-minute film to open the show. We opened the parade with some fantasy garments in fluorescent fabrics that were shown under ultraviolet light. Very dramatic. After showing our other work, we finished up with our evening wear and "Gown of the Year" entries. We thought it was so glamorous. A precursor of what our life ahead would be.

It was going to be a pushover with that diploma under our arm. YSL, watch out! The world was our oyster.

11

The Beauty Arts

As a child, my opportunities for experimenting with the beauty arts were limited to those times when no one else was home. I loved being in the house alone. Apart from beauty training, I could dress up in my mother's or Nanna's clothes and clop around the house in high heels. My favourite pair was snakeskin with platform soles and ankle straps. They would have dated back to the time before my mother was married, circa 1945, and had no doubt done the circuit of many a dance hall. They invited you to put them on and dance, so I would. (I remember the fashion critics panning one of John Galliano's fashion extravaganzas in Paris because they didn't understand what he was trying to say. He had models wearing giant high-heel shoes, swimming in old-fashioned corsets and oversized jumpers draped and tied around them like evening gowns. Watching the show unfold was like seeing a chapter of my own life pass me by. He obviously couldn't wait for his parents to go out for an hour or so as well.)

Sometimes, eyeshadow would be involved, but I soon learnt that removing thickly applied Cleopatra eyes wasn't as easy as drowning my

new curls with a splash of cold water. I only had a few minutes between hearing the old Dodge purr up the drive and hearing Mum make the not-too-welcome announcement that they were home.

Once, on the cover of English *Woman's Own*, there was a giveaway wand of glitter eyeshadow. Somehow, I swiped one from the magazine section at the local milk bar, and it was my very own. The colours were fabulous: turquoise, silver, gold, violet and a peculiar green not unlike British racing. Traces remain to this day around Teddy's eyes, as he was the primary recipient of the magic of its touch. If I thought I could get a good hour or so to myself, the magic wand would be used to transport me into another world altogether. Even when I had plenty of time to remove it, I could never quite get rid of all traces of its colourful allure. Sometimes, days later as I looked in the mirror, there would be the revealing blue smudge, sparkle of gold or ugly violet glob in the corner of my eye.

My other favourite thing to do when left to my own devices was to go through my mother's drawers. At the bottom of one drawer, I found a pair of curling tongs from the 1930s. I loved to retrieve these, for they were ideal for achieving a perfect imperial Roman fringe. During my serious Roman period, I would transform into Julius Caesar with the swish of an old chenille curtain as a toga and gold-painted ivy leaves fashioned into an imperial laurel wreath around my head. The curling tongs would be heated under some boiling water, and I would finish off with a touch of gold eyeshadow.

"Watch out senators. Big Julie's in town."

Smack in the heart of the city, there was an old draper's shop called Job Warehouse. You could go there and find fabulous fabrics and haberdashery. From there, I bought great hanks of jet-black raffia, and I went through a stage of making fantastic Egyptian wigs. I made four of them, one very formal, with gold and jewel decorations. I would assume one of these wigs and dream away in my Cleopatra-styled bungalow, imagining my purple-draped bed was a barge drifting down the ancient Nile.

Even now, I still cringe at a vivid memory of my first theatrical production, which I staged at my fourteenth birthday party. I was obsessed with Cleopatra, and, much to my father's horror, I devised a musical entertainment that would feature these marvellous wigs, the burgundy chenille curtain and a few other treasures that I had been accumulating.

Double glass sliding doors separated our living and dining rooms – this was my proscenium arch. Unfortunately, once in the living room, the poor audience was trapped and had to endure the whole performance – which, even at the time, I thought dragged on.

Although I was perfect for the title role, I realised my father did have a bursting point, so I gave the role of Cleopatra to my cousin, Pam. I was Julius Caesar. I built the drama around several of the day's top pop tunes, from *I Will Follow Him* (when I dump the Egyptian queen and return to Rome) to *It's My Party And I'll Cry If I Want To* (for the dramatic ending when Cleopatra plunges the asp to her bosom).

12

Goin' to Town

Got a pair of new shoes, polished up and paid for
Honey, they were made for goin' to town.
— Judy Garland

There was nothing I loved more than a trip to town, especially if it resulted in the acquisition of a new pair of shoes. Once past the abattoirs – when you could breathe again – the train trip was full of excitement and anticipation.

I particularly liked it when Nanna took me because we always had lunch at the Myer Mural Hall. These luncheon treats directly inspired my fashion bent. As its name suggests, the grand dining room was (and still is) famous for its series of murals, which had been painted in 1935 by Mervyn Napier Waller. The subjects of the fabulous, huge paintings were women and their achievements throughout history in art, opera, literature, dance, sport and fashion.

I absolutely adored going there and would ask Nanna to try and get a seat at different tables each time so I could observe at close range the

individual paintings of women bejewelled and bedecked in the fashions of their day. I was captivated by these magnificent testaments to women and their grace, beauty and style. Sometimes, I would wander off in the middle of my lunch and be found gazing up at some famous figure from the past. More often than not, it was Cleopatra, my favourite. We never seemed to be seated near her, much to my consternation. The Mural Hall was very formal. Starched damask set the scene, and comparable behaviour was expected of the staff and patrons. The ladies who seated you were very crisp: you sat where you were sat.

I have always wolfed down my food but at the Mural Hall I soon learnt how to prolong lunch. Otherwise it would be an unsatisfying short affair: the moment you had finished, the bill would be presented. Before you knew it, you were up and out, having been replaced by someone at the head of the long queue waiting at the door. I would nibble like a mouse on my sandwich points and only *pretend* to drink my malted milk. I would draw in through the straw, swirl the milk around my mouth, and then pass it back into the glass – making a terrible sound and bubbles that would sometimes get out of hand. A chocolate stain on the double damask would draw a withering glance from the creature assigned to our table, but I would still linger as long as possible.

I always had the same thing to eat in all the years I went there – even in later years when its decline saw trays introduced and a self-serve, canteen-style of dining replaced the brisk table service by the ladies in starched pink. My choice was the six-points-of-salmon sandwich and a chocolate malted milkshake.

I don't know what it was about that train trip to town. When you boarded at Seddon, you were perfect. But "you could grow potatoes in your ears" by the time you reached the city. Just before arrival, out would come the same hankie that I had used to diffuse the smell of the abattoirs. Celia would spit on it and dig for potatoes like it was the Irish famine all over again. When Celia and I went to town, we would get off the train and go directly to Ball & Welch – she was very much a Ball & Welch customer. From there, we would weave through the various arcades that form a labyrinth throughout the city, heading towards Buckley & Nunn. Her timing was always perfect. We would pass the Royal Arcade just in time to hear Mog & Magog chime the hour.

Celia didn't much care for lunch at the Mural Hall. We always had lunch at the Hotel Australia in the Silver Grill. There I had my first Italian tartufo, a delicious chocolate ice-cream confection, like a cricket ball with glacé fruit in the centre. The very first one was a challenge.

It shot off the table into the path of a passing drinks waiter. Avoiding the chocolate landmine, he didn't spill a drop. His elegant glide suddenly took on a swizzy twist, the latest dance craze. Chubby Checker had nothing on him.

I adored going to town with Celia because in my eyes she was the most beautiful woman in the city and certainly the best dressed.

In those days, a well-dressed woman would not be seen without her hat, gloves, matching shoes and handbag. Although Mum was tall, she still wore the highest heels. This was an advantage, as I often came adrift and could always spot her, towering over the general crowd.

Once, in Myer, I had clasped on to her very full circular skirt and was happily following her through the busy Christmas crowd until I looked up at one stage and it wasn't her. I don't know who got the bigger shock. This stranger had lost her little attachment, who must have swapped places with me in the swish and sway of our mothers' voluminous skirts. I let out a wail and burst into tears, clinging on desperately and continuing my hysterical carry-on until Celia appeared with my equally distressed clone. Calm was restored only when we were returned to our rightful seas of embroidered linen and stiffened petticoats.

As a child I, too, was always very well dressed. Because we lived in a poor working-class area, I often came under attack for being so. Not only was I a sissy, but I also looked the part. Suede shoes carried a peculiar stigma during the 1950s and 60s. Just owning a pair – let alone being seen *wearing* them – was almost a confession to being queer. This attitude somehow filtered down to children as well. Of course, my best shoes were suede – imported from Italy, no less – and I always got picked on when I wore them. But it didn't worry me, and I wore them as often as I could. They were olive green with a punched design on them, something like an English brogue.

I can vividly remember the outfit I wore with them. Part of it – a little Norfolk tweed jacket – actually hangs in my stairway, and I pass it every day. I love the label hand-sewn on the inside collar: "Prince Charming". I grew up believing that I was that prince. I had very English mannerisms and spoke with a much more refined diction than most of the other kids at school. Because I spent so much time with Nanna, I inherited her English vocabulary and genteel ways of expression. I will never forget the laughter one day at school when we had to report what we had done over the weekend. I described the gorgeous, black-and-white cows I had seen grazing in a "meadow" in the countryside. Even the teacher laughed.

"Don't you mean 'paddock'?"

"No," I replied. "It was definitely a meadow."

I think that my only regret about being a man is that you can't wear women's shoes. Well, you *can*, and I *have*, but you know what I mean. As a child, I would often put on Celia's shoes and clomp around the house, as I have already described. Later on, when I worked at Le Louvre, Georgina Weir and I became very close. We had the same size feet – well, maybe not exactly but I could squeeze into her shoes – and she gave me the most beautiful pair of black satin YSL evening shoes with ankle straps and tiny diamanté buckles. I adored them and got quite a lot of wear out of them, considering that I wasn't really a great exponent of drag.

I used to fill the columns of my school textbooks with hundreds of designs for women's shoes. Even today, my telephone doodles will often be of the stiletto kind. I recently got a jolt when I visited a blockbuster Andy Warhol exhibition. One of the first things I saw was a sheet bearing drawings of dozens of shoes. From a distance, I was convinced that there had been a mix up somehow – they had got hold of some of my childhood scribbles.

Whenever I alighted from a train at Flinders Street Station, my shoes would shift into automatic and head straight for Myer. I would sometimes try to divert their wilful path. But, no, just like the famous red shoes of the Robert Helpmann film, they had a mind of their own. Some days, when I was supposed to be at art school, I would spend the entire day at Myer. Infatuated with a very handsome man who managed the ladies' shoe department, I would hide behind pillars just to catch a glimpse of him as he went about his daily routine. In the recent past, Myer acquired a slightly tawdry persona. I couldn't imagine spending more time there than absolutely necessary. But the store's fortunes have shifted, and today it is going through a renaissance. The Mural Hall has undergone a magnificent restoration, and once more those ladies of fashion can strut their stuff in all their resplendent glory. Ageless through the Ages!

I can almost taste the six-points-of-salmon sandwich and the chocolate bubbles.

13

A Life-changing Introduction

It never occurred to me, when deciding to embark on a career in fashion, to check whether any jobs were to be had. The popular conception that Melbourne was the country's fashion capital led me to conclude that a thriving industry was indeed out there, just waiting for me to bestow my talent upon it.

I eventually received my diploma of Art and Design with flying colours, I was excited at the prospect of starting my working life. It seemed a forgone conclusion that it would be an easy step to fame and fortune. I had already spent the money. But a sense of bewilderment replaced my enthusiasm after scrolling through the classified pages of *The Age*. Positions offered were few and far between. There *were* jobs for designers, but I lacked the one vital ingredient required – experience!

What to do? Well, my model and muse, Dawn Scott, had become a friend. I had shown her my final-year organdie gown. She had mentioned it to her good friend Rachelle King, who in turn had spoken to *her* good friend Georgina Weir. Georgina was the daughter of Lillian Wightman, the owner of Le Louvre, a salon located at the "Paris end" of Melbourne's

Collins Street. Unbeknown to me, Le Louvre was Australia's premier salon of haute couture.

Rachelle organised an introduction to Georgina – a meeting that would completely change my life. I have always believed in love at first sight ... and this was it. I had never met anyone like her.

Georgina had just returned from Paris and looked extraordinary in a lime-green, see-through chiffon shirt with strategically beaded pockets, burgundy velvet trousers, Maud Frizon backless clogs, and a clutter of bracelets on both wrists. Her eyes were outlined in purple, green and pink, and her talons were painted in a shade called "Bats' Blood". A sharp Vidal Sassoon haircut topped this vision, which I would probably describe today as someone "hit by the fashion bus". She looked as though she had just stepped out of the pages of *Vogue*. She was the very essence of fashion. I was captivated.

I was awestruck! Fortunately, Georgina took over the encounter, rescuing me from my speechlessness and disinterring me from my final-year garment, a mountain of organdie ruffles that I was carrying, and falling into raptures over my frivolous creation. She called her mother, Lillian (known to all as Miss Wightman), who also exulted in its virtues. Taking the gown from Georgina, she clutched it to her waist, pointed her left foot forward, and lifted the skirt high to the side as if she were waltzing out the door wearing it! This manoeuvre was one that I would witness many times in the following years. It was integral to Lillian's performance, part of the act that seldom failed to result in a sale.

Georgina offered me $500 for the dress. Although I didn't see that money for some time, and there was no job on offer as such, she did set me working on a few items for an upcoming charity parade. So, I threw myself into creating the first of the many gorgeous things that I would make for Le Louvre in the following decades.

Soon after this meeting, Georgina and I became inseparable friends, and I was swept up into a world and a lifestyle that I had never imagined.

14

The Haunted Jacket

I enjoyed working for Le Louvre, but a persistent voice in the back of my brain kept nagging me to get a real job! I was constantly scouring the employment pages, forever looking for that evasive job. A couple of positions would always be on offer, but usually at Flinders Lane coat manufacturers or Neat'n Trim uniform suppliers. Hardly inspiring.

One day, while cruising through the situations vacant, I came across a fabulous job. It was working for one of the hot young designer labels of the day, Mr Simon. The position was for their head designer. The word *experience* – that dreaded prerequisite for employment – appeared in big, bold type. After thinking it over, I decided I could get away with a lie over the telephone, so I rang and made an appointment. My design folio looked quite impressive, and I set off, determined to lie my way into the job.

"And where have you worked?" was the first question.

Not as prepared as I thought I was, I confessed the truth. "But if you would only take a look at my folio, I'm sure that ..."

The boss curled his lip and muttered something about wasted time.

His wife was more gracious, and she took my folio as her husband left the office. She seemed most interested, asking about various sketches and chatting with me in general. After asking me many questions – what I had learnt at tech, my skills, likes and dislikes, hopes and aspirations – she excused herself and returned with Mr Grumpy. At her urging, he picked up my folio and shuffled through it. Could I leave it with them? They would get back to me in a few days.

I was over the moon, although everyone told me later that I had been an idiot – they would just steal my designs and that would be that. A few days passed (although they felt like weeks), and I was asked to come back for another interview. Mr Simon – I can't remember his real name – was more affable this time and grilled me for about an hour.

"Can you draft a pattern?"

"Can you grade and size a pattern?"

"Can you cut from a pattern?"

Well, I didn't have to lie. I had learnt how to do all of these at school.

"Yes, emphatically, yes! I can."

It was true that I had all of these skills, but he didn't ask how well I could deploy them. Unfortunately, it wouldn't take him too long to find out.

I started immediately.

I was thrilled. As was my father – he promptly packed up and left home. It wasn't the best period of my life. Suddenly, I was left to care for my mother and little brother, who were both shattered at this turn of events. To say that I had a lot on my mind was no exaggeration. However, I embraced my new job and held the family together with all the energy that I could muster.

My first failure was in punctuality. Every employee had to punch a timecard into a clock at the beginning of each day. It didn't matter if I stayed till midnight; if I couldn't punch the clock before that dreaded red ink started to flow in the morning, my pay would be docked. In my time with Mr Simon, I don't think I ever received my entire salary, not that it was much to start with.

My predecessor, Kevin, stayed on for two weeks, showing me the ropes and rolling his eyes at the sample hand, Jean, when he thought I couldn't see. Mr Simon was quite taken with my folio and didn't seem to want to give it back. He had picked out several designs that he wanted to start producing straight away. A particular favourite of his was the one I call "the haunted jacket", not because of any spooky manifestations associated with it, but because it still haunts me to this day.

The house model was a girl called Annie. Our paths were to cross many times and still do. She was tiny – a size 8, if that. The jacket in question was corduroy and featured many zips and pockets. In fact, there were nine heavy metal zips and six pockets in all. I made the pattern, Jean sewed the sample, and Annie sashayed into the showroom in my first commercial offspring.

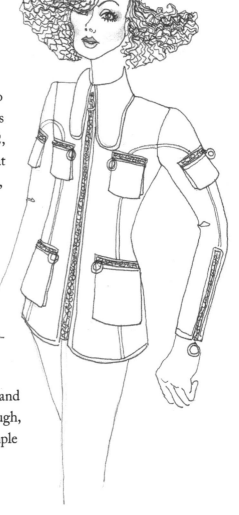

Mr Simon was thrilled. "A winner," he proclaimed, issuing orders to swing into production. He told me to cut hundreds of them in a range of sizes – 6, 8, 10, 12, 14 and even some 16. When I paled at the prospect, he took the jacket and said, "This is a size 12. Grade it two sizes up and three sizes down." When I looked doubtful and confused, he reiterated his instructions.

"And snap to it!"

Although I had started with my size 12 block, by the time we had fitted the jacket to Annie, it was a very tiny size 8. Having learned patternmaking and grading at school, I was competent enough, but I hated it. Anyhow, I took that sample jacket and worked very late over several nights to grade and make all the patterns required. Unfortunately, because the sample jacket was so small, the largest size (16) was actually only a 12 and the smallest size (6) only a 2, a size that didn't actually exist. No one thought to check at any stage of production, and hundreds of these Lilliputian zipperoos were produced. Eventually, when it was too late, the ghastly reality became only too obvious.

When my boss hauled me over the coals, I reminded him of his instructions. He couldn't deny that I had followed those to the letter. But he was right; without experience, I had been ill-prepared for the demands of such a job.

I made more patterns, ordered thousands more yards of corduroy and went into production again. Fortunately, my design proved a big seller. Even the small ones were offloaded (to a children's retailer), and my blunder was never mentioned again. For years, I would see those jackets appear out of nowhere around town. They were corduroy zombies destined to haunt me. I wouldn't be surprised to see one appear on some bright young thing any minute. That retro 1970s look is fashionable again with hipsters the same age I was at the time.

Jean was not only my sample hand – she was also a combination of mother hen, angel, saviour, agony aunt, trouble shooter, negotiator and smokescreen. Despite having worked with Kevin (the designer whose shoes I was supposed to fill) for more than fifteen years, she was sweet to me from the very beginning. She and Kevin had been bolted at the hip, and Jean was upset about him going. But she knew I was way out of my depth and became my lifejacket right away.

Everyone lived in fear of the boss. Hardly anyone talked as they worked, and when they did, it was in whispered undertones. It was all heads down and bums up. I blundered on, balancing precariously between triumph and disaster every day. The modicum of success I experienced when my designs sold well was the only reason I stayed employed.

As the Gown of the Year approached, Mr Simon decided we should enter a variation of a summer jacket design of mine that was selling well.

Made in white linen, this jacket was reminiscent of the 1930s – a bit of Gertrude Lawrence, straight out of *Private Lives*, à la Noël Coward. To go under it, I designed a vampish, backless dress in black bias-cut satin, with original Art Deco diamanté buttons from my own collection. The white linen jacket was to be my next major catastrophe. The design was great, and I thought the sample turned out quite well, but Mr Simon didn't like the linen.

"Vun vare, and it's all crushed!"

He insisted on using bonded linen. In bonded fabric, foam was fused to the back so that it never lost its shape and "vould nevha crush!" Unfortunately, it completely changed the whole look and feel that I was trying to evoke. Nevertheless, the buyers liked it, and the jacket sold well.

The linen had to be ordered from Japan. It took six weeks to arrive, after which it had to be bonded locally. Jean watched me every step of the way. I had the sizing right, and things were running to plan. I did a layout, electing a double cut. (This is when the fabric is folded face to face, allowing you to trace half of the pattern and get two mirror pieces when you cut – for example, a left and right part of the final garment.) I laboured intensely, analysing and checking every stage to ensure the minimum wastage and maximum productivity, I left the mile-long layout on the cutting table for the next day. To my horror, when I arrived (late) the next day, the cutter had laid the fabric and cut the entire order. Unfortunately, he had laid it for a single cut, and instead of 400 full jackets, we had 800 half jackets, with no more linen to be had. Jean swung into action, bundled them all up and hid them in various parts of the factory. Every night, she would smuggle out a little bundle of half jackets and take them home. I don't know what she hoped to achieve by this action, but I was so distressed by what had happened that I thought it was a good plan.

While this was going on, I was making my own entry for the Gown of the Year at home – an Egyptian-inspired gown. Bruck Mills had approached me to design something to promote one of their synthetic new fabrics called "peachface", a dull plastic-like satin. They had also elected the colour: a particularly unpleasant bottle green.

As my twenty-first birthday approached, June and I were busily beading and sewing. Celia rallied for the occasion, deciding to throw me a twenty-first birthday party at home. But the Gown of the Year was almost upon us, and I told her that I couldn't stop sewing; I had to work on the dress. The party went on regardless. Out in my bungalow, I worked away "beaverishly", with June helping me finish the beading. I came into the party at one stage, snarled at everyone, cut the cake and left. Throughout the evening, people would venture into the bungalow, linger until they could not bear the frost a moment longer, then slink off, back to the warmth of the party.

I don't remember who was there. I certainly didn't invite any friends. Auntie Elene and Uncle Brian must have been there, as I recall them giving me a briefcase with my initials embossed in gold. To them, it was just a matter of time before I succumbed to the call of the Commonwealth Bank, and they wanted to make sure that I was kitted out properly for a proper job.

I was quite happy with my finished gown, even though I knew it wouldn't win; the colour precluded any chance of that. Still, it was a dramatic entry and got noticed, particularly by Mr Simon. I had neglected to tell him about my private entry, and for some reason he was absolutely furious. I must admit that it did make our Mr Simon entry pale into insignificance.

Unfortunately, that same day he found out about the 800 half jackets, and he literally threw me out of the building. "You're FIRED!" I hardly had time to pack up my few personal items. He still had my folio, and going to ask for it back was the most difficult thing I had done in my life at that stage. He virtually had steam rising from the top of his head when I brazenly entered his office and asked for my folio back. He was taken aback that I should dare. I think he felt I owed him some compensation for the havoc I had caused in the brief six months of my tenure. Reluctantly he gave back my folio. I tucked it under my arm, said goodbye to Jean in a flurry of tears, and turned my back on my first foray into the big bad world of fashion.

I often wonder whether it is too late to take my unfair dismissal case to the Fair Work Commission, even when the perpetrator is dead. Nowadays, you couldn't give someone the sack the way Mr Simon did.

15

The Hutch

Once again, I found myself browsing the employment sections of the papers, hoping to find another job. With no money or savings, I was obliged to find some source of income. Remembering that Georgina had told me I was welcome back at Le Louvre any time, I put my tail between my legs and once again crossed the holy portal of Melbourne's haughtiest of haute couture salons.

I hadn't seen Georgina for a couple of months, and she had only just returned from a six-week buying trip in Europe. Again looking brilliant – head to toe in the latest mode – she was planning a large charity fashion show in a few weeks and asked me how many stunning gowns I could produce for it.

I was away and running, never to look back.

Georgina was always ahead of her time. The parades she gave for charity were undoubtedly a departure from the discreet, hushed-tone affairs of the day. She would send the poor unsuspecting models out half-naked, dripping in fresh seaweed, or styled as a living branch with six (real) white doves. Nor were her effects purely visual. I remember one parade when she had them come out firing pistols in the air. We very nearly lost one grand old dame from the Western District who was worried that a jewellery heist was underway, threatening her diamonds. There was no such thing as a choreographer or a dress rehearsal; the models would come for a fitting the day before. Then Georgina and I, with her go girls Jane Drummond and Wendy Boland, would somehow pull it all together. The clothes were marvellous – Georgina was like a fashion "ratter", nosing out up-and-coming designers before the rest of the world discovered them. Thanks to her, Melbourne most likely had Chloé, designed by Karl Lagerfeld, before the prestigious stores of New York's Fifth Avenue.

We had such fun in those early years. At one winter-season parade, we showed just about every garment with the knee-high, lace-up boots that were the latest fad from Europe – the only problem being that we only had about four pairs. I would rip them off one girl and furiously try to hook up the laces on the next. How that parade ran without a hiccup, I don't know, but I had a complete collapse afterwards.

Years before the expression "supermodel" came into the vernacular, Georgina's models far outshone the term. My muse, Dawn Scott, was always my number one, but she was only one seraph among the many celestial beings Georgina engaged to show the best clothes the world had to offer. Elizabeth Scarborough could drag a fur coat along the catwalk like no one else. Nerida Piggin was like an enchanted fairy. Rani, a dusky Indian princess, was at least 6 feet tall. They were all divine. Marlo Waters had one wandering eye and hair that was like a sheet of chocolate rain. Julie Wilkinson had lips that could kiss the whole room at once. And I will never forget that Wendy Marshall, a gorgeous creature from Perth, wore the lilac beaded hotpants from my final year collection. The three of us became lifetime friends and Wendy went into business with Georgina, importing clothes for a younger, faster crowd. They called it "little money" (lower cost), as opposed to Le Louvre's big-money business.

Georgina always finished a parade in the French tradition of showing a bride. This became my domain – from my first parade until I left Le Louvre and sometimes even after my departure. Le Louvre was *the* place for a society bride to have her once-in-a-lifetime dress made, and it remains so as I write.

My dressmaking skills were good, but they didn't compare to those of Mrs Ipolli. She sewed all the wedding dresses and unique evening gowns and specific orders for the more demanding customers at Le Louvre. Not "demanding" as in "hard-to-fit" figures – but "demanding" as in, let us say, "fussy"! I have yet to find anyone who could match her skill. Ken, who replaced me at Le Louvre, would come in as a close second to Mrs Ipolli. Tailor Chu, with whom I worked years later in Hong Kong, would come third.

Mrs Ipolli would often make special gowns for the parades. We would beg her not to hand-roll the hems, as inevitably, the gown would be sold to someone not in the same lofty stratosphere as the willowy mannequins. No, she just couldn't bring herself to machine a hem. On so many occasions I would cut off miles and miles of the most exquisitely hand-rolled chiffon just to throw it into the waste bin.

More often than not, I would not only design the wedding dresses but also get the lesser job of making the bridesmaids' dresses, the worst job of all. You would always get such a mixed bag of bridesmaids. Just choose from the following, and you will get an idea: a giant, a Lilliputian, a serious overeater, an anorexic, someone with a fleshy protuberance, someone with huge tits, another with no tits, yet another with only one tit, one with a thyroid problem, one with bad acne, and one so insipid that you would always forget to take her measurements (you would have to call her back another day and say you misplaced her profile card, although we both knew the truth).

It took me years to hit upon a magic formula for bridesmaids. In those early days, it was the most dreaded and challenging task. My first wedding party was the very worst I ever made. It was when I was still trying to please everyone, before I became more assertive. They had decided on lime-green velvet dresses in an Edwardian style.

The dresses featured leg-of-mutton sleeves, a high, ruffled collar, a very fitted cummerbund, gathering under the bust, and ruffles around the hem. I had designed it, I grant you that, but that was before I had seen the six bridesmaids. Imagine my list. One girl was so fat that I couldn't get my arms around her to take her bust measurement. Georgina had to help, while I prayed that I wouldn't need *two* tapes.

As I have said, my dressmaking skills were not as honed back then as they would later become. Having never sewn velvet, I wasn't versed in the many tricks associated with crafting this problematic material. Sewing six of anything was a Herculean task for me, but to tackle six jobs in velvet was an ordeal – although it did teach me an early and valuable lesson. I seriously under-quoted on the job, as it took me three times longer than I had thought to sew each dress. I needed much more velvet than I anticipated and I didn't factor in the unexpected task of completely remaking one dress. When I finally finished them, no one was happy with the result, no one less so than me. I was horrified. The seams were puckered and the hems were crooked. Some sleeves did what they were supposed to do, others did what they wanted to do (sometimes simultaneously on the same dress, but not necessarily).

The gathering under the bust was a particular problem. Because of the nature of the fabric and its grain, the gathering under the left bust looked fuller than the gathering under the right bust. This was particularly noticeable on two girls – the one with no tits and the one with big tits. One girl's high neck was so tight that she was turning red in the face. I think I inadvertently swapped the sleeves of two dresses – one girl had them at bracelet length, and another had them so long you couldn't see her fingers at all. But nothing compared with how bad Miss Goodyear Blimp looked. The velvet wasn't wide enough to put any more gathering in the skirt than I had. Her arms filled out the leg-of-mutton sleeves, even though I had blown out the top of the pattern to the full extent of the velvet's width. Even though the cummerbund had marine-ply backing to keep it stiff, it just disappeared into a roll of fat. And unless someone stood next to her and constantly pulled it down, the back of

her skirt kept getting sucked into her bottom. At one stage, I actually thought that I had forgotten to put her collar on. But, no. It just couldn't fight the battle of the chins.

This was the picture that greeted Miss Wightman when she came into the back of the salon to view the wedding party. Realising that it was far too close to the day of the nuptials to start again, she effused so eloquently about the radiance of the bride that she convinced us that everything else was just a backwash to that portrait of happiness. Even I believed that no one would give a second glance. As we stood mesmerised by her final-quarter pep talk to the lime-green debacle surrounding her, Miss Wightman wasted no time in getting Two-Ton Tessie out of her dress, leaving the poor thing in just her pantyhose and bra. I don't know who got the bigger shock – Tessie, or the rest of us standing there in disbelief. There was nowhere else to look in a room where every wall was a mirror. Not only did we see her from the front, but we also got the back reflected ad infinitum. In Miss Wightman's haste to remove the offending garment from the poor wretch, she had completely ripped out the zip, taking half the garment with it.

Everyone was embarrassed as the members of the fitting disbanded. Still clutching the deflated lime-green zeppelin under her arm, Miss Wightman waved them out the door, wished the bride success and dispensed her usual last words of bridal advice.

"My dear child, remember this," she whispered. "Eyes cast down demurely when you enter the church and as you go down the aisle. Then head back, eyes sparkling, teeth flashing a radiant smile to everyone on the way out."

She didn't have much to say to me as she handed over the velvet marquee. "Just fix it."

She had destroyed the dress. The client had insisted on invisible zips – another complicated operation at any time but one nigh-on impossible in velvet. I had made so many attempts to sew the zip into Tessie's dress the first time around that the fabric had already weakened. Now there was nothing left to sew the zip back into. I had no alternative but to replace the entire back of the dress. When I went to buy more velvet, the saleslady warned me that it was a different dye lot. Of course, when the two were placed together, they did indeed look very different – which meant I had to make a whole new dress. After six dresses, I had learnt a lot about velvet, so my seventh was actually the best made out of the group – although its wearer still looked like the star of that classic B-grade horror movie *The Blob*.

I thought my number was up at Le Louvre, but Georgina and I had become firm friends, and I was given a second chance.

This was in the early 1970s. Everyone was reading *Lord of the Rings*, and I was one of them – I couldn't put it down. On more than one occasion, I would be late or forget fittings because I would be so absorbed by the action in the realm of Mordor. At one stage, when I had to meet an absolute deadline, I asked Celia to hide the book.

Although Le Louvre didn't employ me, I worked exclusively for them.

Unfortunately, I was quite unreliable, unreachable and unpredictable. For Miss Wightman, it was a constant source of irritation that she couldn't get her hands on me when she wanted to. So that I could be close by and reined in when necessary, she came up with a brilliant idea: to give me some rooms not far away in Collins Street that Le Louvre rented for storage. I nicknamed these rooms "The Hutch".

My future stepfather, Duncan, who had just met my mother, worked for a cleaning company, so he helped me clean it up and strip and polish the floors. We compacted Le Louvre's boxes and ephemera into one of the three rooms. In the middle room, we installed a large cutting table and in the other I had a little kitchenette. My first workroom paid dividends all around. I was far more productive and became more important to the day-to-day running of Le Louvre. I could be called on to help in many ways – from changing a light globe to dressing the windows or running up a quick sketch for a prospective bride.

I spent a few happy years in The Hutch and made some great clothes at that time. Georgina almost gave me free rein to do what I liked. Money was never an issue, and I could choose any fabric or trim that I felt like using. I remember making three forties-style dresses for one parade. They were in the finest Racine silk jersey, and I had fox furs dyed to match. One dress was a dusky pinky-beige and had deep fur cuffs. Another was a pale eau de Nil with a huge collar that fell away to show a wholly exposed back. The third was ice blue and had a stole edged in matching fox.

Georgina's friend Rachelle King was (and still is) a brilliant artist whose medium was knitting wool. Working with her was great fun. We would often collaborate on creations for the parades or specific clients.

Miss Hilda King, who was in charge of Le Louvre's workroom, reminded me of the Wicked Witch of the West in *The Wizard of Oz*. Granted, a pale, washed-out, bleached witch, but she did have the hooked nose, the hairy mole on her chin, and breath that could only have resulted from drinking too much witches' brew. There was definitely a hint of "eye of newt" about her. I could never understand why Georgina, who demanded such style and perfection in her surroundings, could have such a harridan in her employ. It was pretty obvious that she couldn't stand the woman, but Miss King had been there for many years, long before Georgina returned from Europe to take over the business. Although Mr Simon got rid of me without so much as a *howdy doodah*, Miss Hilda King was a different matter: she had long-service leave and other entitlements that required a more formal undertaking.

I didn't like Miss King, and she didn't like me. It was clear that I was being groomed as her heir apparent, so she went to no end of trouble to sabotage anything of mine that came through the door. Once, I caught her shifting pins after a fitting I had put aside to take to The Hutch for alteration. She claimed that the pins were falling out, but she was removing them and putting them in completely different spots. Fortunately, the fitting was still fresh in my mind, so I altered it to how I thought it should be, and everything was fine.

At that stage, the workroom was quite substantial – I think there were twenty-six girls there. The made-to-measure business was still huge (before Georgina gradually trained the clientele to accept the idea of stepping into imported ready-to-wear clothes).

The ocelot print was the signature of the house, the raincoat and matching umbrella made in Bianchini-Férier waterproof treated silk a status symbol among the high society ladies of Melbourne, Sydney and Adelaide. A Le Louvre raincoat in ocelot print with a matching umbrella conferred admission to a private club, and they were priced accordingly. In those days, you had to have Miss Wightman's approval to buy one. (Later, Georgina would sell one to anyone who would fork out the money. To me, it was the kiss of death when I made Dame Edna a whole wardrobe in the hitherto-revered ocelot print.)

Mostly the girls in the workroom shared an atmosphere of relative harmony. The only friction was between a couple of Italian women – Esther, a very refined woman from the north, and Rosa, who was from the south and had a touch of peasant about her. ("Anything south of

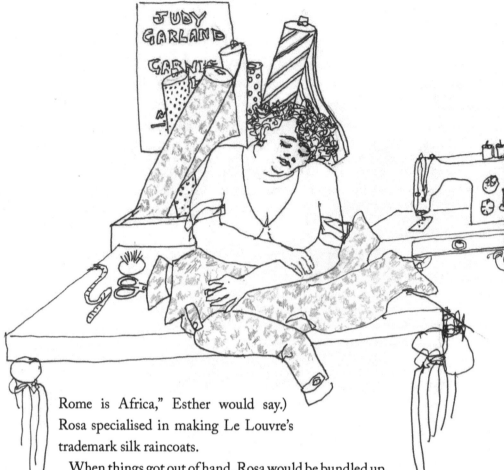

Rome is Africa," Esther would say.)
Rosa specialised in making Le Louvre's
trademark silk raincoats.

When things got out of hand, Rosa would be bundled up
with her needles and thimble and sent to The Hutch with me.
She loved this, as it was a radical departure from her usual work scene.
I had music, radio and lots of comings and goings. She used to fall
asleep most afternoons, and I (unlike the wicked witch) would let
her snooze on. She was well into her sixties and had had a hard life,
so I figured she deserved a bit of a break now and then.

When I thought she had had enough of a rest, I would put on an aria
from *La Bohème*. She would wake with a terrible fright, then burst into
hysterical laughter and run around the room, waving her arms like a
chicken. She always thought opera sounded like a farmyard at dawn.

Over and over, she would tell me the same story about how she lost
her first baby in Italy during the Second World War. The baby was

sickly. Because Rosa couldn't breastfeed it, the doctor prescribed goat's milk. She would walk for hours to the hills to buy this milk from the gypsies, but they cheated her by watering it down, so the baby died of malnutrition. Even after hearing the story several times, I could always shed a tear with her and give her a comforting little hug.

Rosa worshipped Miss Wightman, who had given her a job when no one else would. Whenever Miss Wightman would come looking for me at The Hutch, Rosa would usually burst into tears, smother her hand with kisses, and say, "Oh, Miss Wight, Miss Wight!" Fortunately, this outburst made Miss Wightman think twice about dropping in all that often.

One day, Miss Hilda King handed in her resignation. She had bought a unit somewhere in Sydney and decided to embrace retirement. I was summoned for a drink after work one evening and officially offered the position of head shebang in charge of the workroom. I wasn't that impressed with the salary, but I would have worked for nothing. Georgina was always good with the old routine of dangling the carrot in front of the donkey. "Stick with me, kid, and I'll dress you in diamonds."

How ironic it is that, years later, I would be able to boast the same.

16

Young and Gay

In the vocabulary of Miss Wightman and her generation, the word *gay* still meant happy, jolly, cheerful. The connection with young homosexual men did not register – she referred to us as "sissy boys"! Not that her circle of friends wasn't riddled with sissy boys – it was just never mentioned. Whenever Miss Wightman wanted me to fetch and carry, she would say to me, "You're young and gay. Run up the stairs." It has remained a standing joke between Georgina and me ever since.

I was a breath of fresh air – especially after the rancid breath of old Miss Eye of Newt. Cutting a dash in my fine clothes, I hit it off immediately with Le Louvre's clientele. The fact that half of them fell in love with me was not lost on Georgina or Miss Wightman; indeed we used it to our advantage. Should there be any doubts or sales resistance, a confirmation from me would often clinch a deal. A terrible flirt, I would flatter and tease the clients outrageously. This came naturally to me – an extension of the good manners instilled in me by my mother and grandmother. I would invariably notice a new hairdo, new eyeglasses or a different perfume. I adored them all, but I had my favourites.

Claire Mackinnon was one of my most cherished. She was a former silent movie star, and hers was the most romantic of stories. Her husband-yet-to-be instantly fell in love when he glimpsed her on the silver screen. In the stalls of a dusty, tin picture-house "back o' beyond", he vowed there and then to make her his wife. Within the month, he had set off for Hollywood to seek her hand. He wooed her, married her and brought her home to the cattle station (or wheat farm?), where he continued to worship her till the day he died.

"The wind never touched her" was another of Miss Wightman's famous sayings. Claire was the embodiment of that. She was left a wealthy widow and was sheltered her whole life from the harsh actuality of the real world. Just as pretty as when she shone from the silver screen, she had retained her broad American accent, despite spending sixty or more years in the Australian outback. Claire bought (or was sold) many of the more beautiful evening gowns that floated down the catwalks of Georgina's fabulous parades.

As she was only about 5 feet (150 centimetres) tall, she was responsible for many of those hundreds of yards of hand-rolled chiffon that I would cut off and throw away. Often, I would design a gown or two with her in mind, including that dusky pinky–beige silk jersey dress with dyed fox cuffs.

Another one I made with her as the target was an electric royal-blue gown and an encompassing Spanish-styled shawl with a fringe of handmade rouleau. Each fringe was capped with a sparkling sapphire. The effect was pure Sunset Boulevard, as the stones clattered and sparkled when Claire swept down the stairs like Gloria Swanson, one of her contemporaries and best friends.

We had a little platform in the back salon which made it easier for me to move around when marking the miles of hems to be shortened. It was very hard to get Claire to stand still on this. She always thought of it as a mini-stage and would break into the chorus from *42nd Street* or start doing a little tap dance or soft-shoe shuffle. One way to keep her still was to let her run her fingers through my hair. She loved my shock of hair. It was like a security blanket for her and would keep her quiet until I had finished the job.

"Oh, darlin', you have the most gorgeous silky hair!" I loved this position at her feet because it brought my eyes level with her wrists. She was never seen without three of the most beautiful 1930s Art Deco Cartier bracelets. Number one: rubies and diamonds. Number two: emeralds and diamonds. Number three: sapphires and diamonds. They were better than any matched set I have seen in any auction catalogue or book about Deco jewellery. I was transported back to the Footscray public library, where, as a child, I would spend hours in the grown-ups' magazine section, mesmerised by such gems in the Harry Winston advertisements on the glossy pages of *Réalités* magazine. One day, I noticed she wasn't wearing them and I asked where they were.

"Oh, those lovely boys at Hardy Brothers let me swap them for this gorgeous pearl." (Sissy Boys, for sure.) She delved into her ample bosom and retrieved the ghastliest pearl – the size of a lottery ball – rattling around in a tear-shaped gold wire cage. Furious that Hardy Brothers had tricked Claire out of her magnificent Deco bracelets, I had visions of the three boys later sneaking them out of the safe and mincing around the shop in them during afternoon tea. I was indignant that they should take advantage of such a gullible old woman. But who was I to cast the first stone? Here I was, removing another hundred yards of hand-rolled chiffon from the hem of a gown for a faded movie star who had nowhere to wear it and probably never would. I often wondered if she had any room left in her closets to hang them. She did seem to get a lot of pleasure, though, from that Lotto pearl and the many dresses she bought from Le Louvre, so who was I to question the ethics involved?

One of my favourite old chooks would always have some sort of alteration on the go. No matter what, she would devise an excuse to come into Le Louvre for a fitting. It was on account of her that the expression "squashed beaver" was introduced into the terminology of Le Louvre–speak. This client would remove all her clothes before I could stop her, no matter what the alteration. It could be a tight cuff on a blouse, some loose buttons, a faulty zip or the hem on a jacket. I would have to summon up a look of complete composure and slight captivation when I entered the fitting room to find her sprinting around, wearing nothing but pantyhose.

"Oh, Gregory, you naughty boy," she would say, blushing. "You caught me."

It didn't matter if I waited half an hour; it was always the same game. Miss Wightman refused to believe me, but she never risked entering the fitting room before I had a chance to get this client at least half-dressed. As for someone not wearing an undergarment, I was considered scandalous for inventing such an outrageous story.

Old Mrs Smithe, who resided in a suite of rooms on top of the old Windsor Hotel, was another client who was enamoured of me. I was the only person in all the years she had shopped at Le Louvre who understood immediately what she meant by the word *Petersham*. It is a milliners' ribbon, often used in waistbands on skirts and trousers. She would buy a suit and just say this one word, "Petersham". She was very old and not really batty, but she didn't waste words. I understood what she wanted and obliged – putting in an extra piece of "Petersham" so that, after a large lunch, she could let her waist out and not lose her skirt as she left the restaurant.

Mrs Smithe's life story, as told to me by Miss Wightman, was fascinating. She had lived at the Windsor since the 1930s. As a young bride, she had just built an enormous mansion in Toorak when she and her husband embarked on a grand tour of Europe. I think it may have been their delayed honeymoon. They went on a shopping spree to furnish their new home, purchasing some treasure in every city they visited. Parisian antiques, Italian mirrors, carpets, grand pianos, chandeliers, silver, crystal, linen, cutlery, crockery, along with modern European gadgets and electrical appliances – everything needed, from the basement to the attic, in the dream home in Melbourne waiting for their return. However, on their first night back, a burglar broke into their bedroom. Mrs Smithe got such a fright that they moved to the Windsor Hotel and she stayed there after her husband passed away until the day she died. When everything arrived home from Europe, it was put into storage and forgotten. The undiscovered treasure was not unearthed until her affairs were being sorted out after she died. Imagine unpacking all those mystery boxes. I wonder how the Steinway sounded.

Miss Wightman would share other anecdotes about Mrs Smithe. How she would hide all her diamonds in the sugar bowl, only for it to be removed by room service maids, sparking a search through every sugar bowl in the hotel. How she kept every newspaper since the day she moved into the hotel and how they were stacked to the ceiling in every corridor, making the passages almost impossible to navigate. She and Miss Wightman were great mates. Their long lunches at the Café Florentino were made even more enjoyable after I appraised Miss Wightman of the role of Petersham.

Old Mrs Smithe was the mother of another of my favourite clients: Le Louvre's very best customer, José. She, too, lived in the clouds. Having bought the city's first penthouse, in Spring Street, José seldom left her eyrie except to go to the dentist or the doctor, both in the building next door. She hardly ever came into Le Louvre; we went to her – and like

a travelling circus at that. I'm sure the Collins Street crowd must have thought we were either gypsies hawking their wares or a Chinese dragon a few streets out of whack.

The clothing racks always had wobbly wheels, like those rogue shopping trolleys, and we would zigzag our way up to Spring Street, trying to steer thousands of dollars' worth of haute couture. José was always first to see the collection. We would show our selection try them on her, and then prepare for the various games that followed.

Her first pick would be left overnight for her to play with. The next day a rack with the "definite No-Nos" would be collected and returned to the salon. These would be the sleeveless, backless or very outrageous. She always wanted at least to *see* the outré, as they were the playthings, icing on the fantasy. We would go back for a second session to narrow down her selection to the "Maybes", and another lot would come back. Then I would return the next day, usually with a couple of the rejects that she would have had a sleepless night thinking about. Had she made a mistake? She would then try the whole lot on again for my approval and comments. I would analyse her choices and figure out solutions to any doubts about fittings and alterations. Then I would help her narrow her options and decide between several outfits she pretended she wasn't quite sure of.

José and I had a special bond – we both suffered from psoriasis. Hers was a severe case, mine just developing. We would discuss our conditions at length, and she would give me various creams and lotions to try. She kept me in one very expensive scalp lotion for years – she carried stock.

Money was no object to José, but she still enjoyed complaining about the exorbitant cost of the clothes and how she was being ripped off. It was just one of her games. There was always some drama with at least one outfit. A belt would go missing, only to be found later, wrapped around a tree trunk halfway down Collins street. The print in a blouse looked to be a different colour from the skirt. Or the lining of a suit would go all-electric when she went down in the lift. Her games were all designed to string out the time we spent with her.

I remember a huge drama involving a Fendi fur jacket. It was in the days before Fendi became what it is today. In her usual trendsetting discoveries, Georgina had brought home the latest thing – an unlined, unstructured, throwaway possum jacket. They were fabulous, a total departure from any previous notion of a fur jacket. We got an urgent message from Spring Street one Monday morning. José hadn't slept all weekend because her Fendi jacket was full of holes. Having held it up to the light, she had seen the sun stream through it like a colander, and she was having a conniption. I was dispatched pronto to assess the situation.

These jackets were actually made from all the bits that the furrier would normally discard – scraps and offcuts. Because José's jacket had been made from possum bellies, each little patch had at least two nipple holes. We had to convince José that the possum belly was the most valuable piece of the poor animal's pelt, that such fine pieces as those in her jacket were hard to come by. When she was still not convinced, we had to call in an outside opinion – a furrier from one of Melbourne's oldest fur salons. José was still dubious. The furrier had been slipped

$100 to extol the virtues of the rarity and quality of the possum coat while not even hinting at what he really thought of the "It" jacket of the year. (He said later that he had never seen such a piece of rubbish in all the years he had been in the industry – not since his apprenticeship at the age of fourteen. He would have expired had he known how much the toggled-together scraps from the furrier's floor had been sold for.)

That season, Georgina had two jackets, and the second one also caused problems. The other customer came out in a rash from the unlined fur touching her skin. I had to line it with silk chiffon so that there would still be a suggestion of the unlined effect. Worse, it had accidentally been sold with a Paris Metro ticket in the pocket – Georgina had worn it for a month while buying the collection.

Although we always officially presented the collection first to José, there was another client who always managed to get in before her. Mavis Powell had the uncanny knack of knowing when the clothes would arrive. We would be unpacking them when she would suddenly appear in a misty shadow at the door, pick out several of the very best to be put aside for her, then vaporise. I think she must have known someone at the Customs Office.

Le Louvre's clientele were great ladies. I don't remember who was what or from where, but many of them had humble beginnings. One was the daughter of the boom gates operator at Box Hill railway station. One started off on a velvet swing at the Tivoli Theatre. And another was the daughter of greengrocers – behind her back, people would make a little gesture like swinging a bag of nectarines. Yet, they were all very grand and ladylike. Some were difficult, but most of them were a delight. Even a few of the difficult customers became favourites, as they were so quirky. I never knew what to expect next.

One such client, I nicknamed Mrs Condom. There were a couple of reasons for this, the main one being that she looked like she had been squeezed into one. She was a rather large woman, and her clothes were always very, very tight. That was how she liked them. The first time I was called to a fitting, my heart skipped a beat. After squeezing into an Agnona coat, she was in danger of exploding – the buttons were straining, and the belt just met. Agnona was known for its exquisite garments all fashioned from double-faced wool. With double-fell seams, they looked exactly the same inside as out – as a result, they didn't require a lining and had no seams to let out. I was explaining the reason I couldn't let it out and suggesting a bigger size when she interrupted me.

"Oh no! I want it taken in!"

I was flabbergasted, but Miss Wightman gave me the nod to play along. Try as I may, I could not grasp hold of any fabric to pin – it was so taught. I finally got some pins in, but the moment she took a breath, they all popped out. Making some excuse about faulty pins, I told her that I knew how much to take out. "Please leave it to me. Come back next week."

I soon got to know Miss Wightman's various nods and winks. I would often spend up to half an hour pinning a fitting, only to have her immediately remove all the pins when the client had gone. She thought there was nothing wrong with it. This was often the case. Most faults were in the minds of customers. They would come back the next week to a garment that hadn't been touched, yet express delight.

"See! Isn't that so much better?"

"Oh, yes, I can move my arms now."

"Yes, it's much better with that panel removed."

And my reply? "You were absolutely right!"

I had done nothing, of course, but we had to carry on through the charade and charge for the alteration so as not to be caught out.

Sometimes, I had to go behind Miss Wightman's back. When I thought the alterations were necessary, I would try to remember where the pins had been before she removed them, especially in cases where sleeves covered hands. Miss Wightman would just push up the sleeves in the way she wore all her clothes, but not everyone wanted an evening gown that made you look as if you were about to start washing the dishes.

When Mrs Condom came back the next week, complaining that the

Agnona coat was still a little loose under the arms, I pointed out that she was wearing a sleeveless dress and to think of winter when she would be wearing a jumper.

Some clients had that uncanny eye that could pick a fraction of an inch difference in the level of a hem at fifty paces. So I devised a trick that could get the hem of a floor-length gown perfect. Instead of trying to pin the hem, I would calculate the dress length by measuring the distance from the floor (perhaps 17 inches above). This worked perfectly, except for one time when a new girl didn't know my method. Eager to please, she stayed back one night, cut the skirt off at 17 inches, and then shortened it by another 2 inches. I don't know how I did it, but I convinced the client that I thought a short dress was better than floor-length. My neck was saved by oozing charm. Not that I was ever swamped with gifts, but often clients would give little tokens of appreciation.

I always refused any gifts of gratitude that I thought inappropriate. A toyboy, I was not. (Although I did finish up in bed with one client, her name will go with me to the grave.) When a former lady mayoress gave me a ticket to meet her in Hawaii, I returned it with my regrets. I told her that I couldn't go at such short notice and faces were saved all around. My most treasured memento of those years is a letter that the daughter of one of my most favourite clients found when she was sorting out her mother's affairs. It was a letter from me thanking her for some little gift she had sent me. In it, I also thanked her for having the best set of legs that had ever stepped through the doors at Le Louvre. Of the thousands of letters she had received during her life, that was the only one she had kept.

Those legs had been what helped me convince her that she was better off in the short dress than in the long.

17

Has Anyone Seen Miss Wightman?

On the subject of legs, Miss Wightman had a very shapely set of pegs to hold up her very shapely form. Le Louvre was famous for ocelot print, and that's what she wore. She wore the salon's signature ocelot print raincoat even in summer.

But that ocelot raincoat and matching umbrella were not the only pieces the salon was famous for. There were dresses in several different weights of silk, cashmere knitwear, and diaphanous chiffon evening gowns. The most famous dress can still be obtained today. It's known as "The Pleated Model".

Quite often, a client who had recently returned from overseas would pop in for a cup of tea wearing something she had purchased abroad. Miss Wightman hatched a conspiracy with me to make the most of such opportunities. If she liked a piece, she would somehow manage to get it off the unsuspecting soul, and I would whip it upstairs to take a pattern. When one woman was reluctant to comply, Miss Wightman spilt the

cup of tea on her so that I could take it upstairs to "fix" it.

Another client brought in a dress she had purchased from Le Louvre in the mid-1930s. It was by Edward Molyneux, an Englishman working in Paris and one of the top couturiers of his day. We got the Molyneaux upstairs, I took the pattern and later modified it, and "The Pleated Model" has been a best seller ever since.

Passing through the doors of the immaculately polished copper façade, one was seduced into a world of refined elegance. Voluminous clouds of ombré-toned silk tulle screened the windows fronting the street. You could see the world passing by, but no one could see into the inner sanctum. (A madwoman liked to sit in the window, and Miss Wightman was quite happy to let her. She wasn't a client, just an eccentric off the street.) Inside were some fine ormolu desks (which were French) and an armoire showcasing jewellery, handbags, handmade roses and ostrich feather boas ("the add-on sales", in retail lingo). Antique gold mirrors reflected the light from alabaster lamps. But no dress was on display.

You only got to see what was thought to be suitable for you. Heaven help you if you attempted to open the mirrored doors behind which the collection was sequestered. Miss Wightman reigned from a high carved sofa scattered with ocelot skins that took pride of place, so she blended in. Once she was going to some winter charity gala, and I made her a long, cashmere-wool ocelot skirt to wear. Of course, when she wore it while seated on the sofa, you couldn't see those shapely legs. In fact, she completed disappeared.

"Has anyone seen Miss Wightman?"

18

Dressed to Kill

Of all the carrots that Georgina dangled, the one that appealed to me the most was the added bonus that she would dress me for work. Consequently, during my years at Le Louvre, I was the picture of sartorial elegance. Graham Fell, although not then the dear friend he later became, declared me to be one of the best-dressed men in Melbourne. I had not worn such beautiful, imported clothes since Celia had dressed me in nothing but the best when I was growing up. In the intervening years, I hadn't been able to afford anything beyond hippie chic. At art school, I dressed entirely in Indian shirts and kaftans. Even during my high-school years, my clothes came from The House of Merivale and Mr John, which was something of a knockoff of Biba of London.

I acquired quite a few outfits from that modish, snazzy, jazzy, flashy Collins Street store with Celia's indulgence. It was such a thrill being ripped off by the barracudas who worked there. I was "in love" with one in particular. Phillip was gorgeous and could see me coming a mile off. Like his colleagues, he had absolutely no scruples. I know that everything I ever bought there was stock that wouldn't move, but I wanted to believe

Phillip when he told me that I looked fantastic. He was very good at bringing you another pair of trousers just before you had the other pair on (or off).

My dear friend Keith worked for them some years later and would tell me horror stories that rang far too true. He said the staff would run bets as to who could sell the most shocking pile of overpriced crap to poor love-struck adolescents (like moi). My favourite story concerns a prospective groom. He was after a black suit, but Keith had only a pin-striped one.

"Just try this for size, and I'll get you a black one down from Sydney," he promised.

That night, Keith took the pin-striped version home and coloured in the chalk stripes with a black Texta. Anything for a sale!

As for ties, I had nearly enough to wear a different one each day for a month. My very favourite, I remember well. The design motif was of an elegant woman in the Art Deco style walking a Borzoi hound. I wore it with a silver brooch from the 1930s, featuring almost the same design. Pins and brooches were a little bit "out there" for a man to wear, but that didn't stop Georgina from buying them or me from wearing them. I had this great jumper with a landscape of trees and mountains across the front. To accessorise it, I built up a collection of flying cranes in grey mother-of-pearl. They crossed my chest and flew right off my left shoulder, always attracting a comment or two at the bank.

My very best piece was a birthday gift one year from Georgina and Wendy Marshall. I still treasure it. From the 30s again, it was a jazz trumpeter cut from ivory set in a gold mount.

⦁⦁⦁⦁⦁⦁⦁⦁⦁⦁⦁⦁

I don't know how she did it, but Georgina would always arrive home from Europe with suitcases of clothes for her partner, Kent. Now, twice a year, she had to add my wardrobe, and I suspect she put some of mine on his tab. As I watched her unpack the booty, she would catch a glint in my eye when I spotted something of Kent's that I really liked, and I would often find it in my pile later on.

She always bought me two unstructured cotton suits for summer, one navy and one beige, a look that lasted only one season. A linen suit or jacket, and beautiful Zanobetti shirts from Florence, were usually included. Years later, on the first trip I made to Florence after leaving Le Louvre, I thought I would just drop in and buy myself a couple of Zanobettis. I nearly fainted at the prices – nothing less than $100 and this is going back more than forty years!

For winter, Georgina was at her best. I love winter. You can get really dressed up – just keep adding. Grey flannel, tweed, corduroy and velvet were all part of my look. One year, she brought me back a bottle-green velvet suit, which I adored. (I think the silk tie with the lady walking the Borzoi had a touch of the same green.) I used to have huge fights with Miss Wightman about this suit. Being very superstitious, she accused me of killing off all of her friends. Unfortunately, it may have been true – every time I wore the bottle-green suit, some old chook would fall off the perch. The day after I had worn it, we would hear the news that Lady So-and-So had been found dead in the bath, clutching her last gin and tonic. One day, three died within hours of each other, and my suit was banned forever. I didn't like to point out that they were all in their late eighties and that natural attrition was most likely to blame for eroding her dwindling circle of drinking buddies.

After observing the ban for a year, I thought I would risk an outing. Sure enough, one of our best clients from Adelaide, who had only been into the store the week before to replace her ocelot raincoat, curled up her toes within hours of me slipping into the suit and stepping through the copper doors. I have never seen an order for an ocelot coat finished and dispatched with such alacrity.

One of the most beautiful collections that Georgina stocked consistently was an Italian range of women's suits and coats made from the finest Australian merino wool. The house of Agnona was famous for its superb tailoring, great classic style, and that double-faced wool construction that ensured lightness as well as warmth. They also made men's clothes and, one year, Georgina said I could order a coat as part of my winter clobber. With my knack for choosing only the best – a talent I have retained since childhood – my coat turned out to be the most expensive coat Agnona ever produced. Unfortunately, for some reason, they believed that it was an urgent order, and it arrived, at great expense, in its own hanging wardrobe within a fortnight of my ordering it. It would have been cheaper to send me to Italy to pick it up! One of the few times that I witnessed Georgina blanch was when she saw that invoice.

Still, it *was* a divine coat. Unfortunately, one night when we were all squeezed into a car coming home from a party, a member of our inner circle, Frances Dumeresque, burnt a hole in the shoulder with a cigarette. I cleverly re-cut the raglan sleeves into a double shoulder line and replaced the burn with what used to be the belt – and it became even better.

I wore Giorgio Armani when he was Walter Albini. Other favourites were Valentino, YSL and anyone stylish in between. Georgina didn't buy me shoes, but I certainly did. Anything left after my antique purchases I spent on footwear.

In the years that have passed since then, my image of impeccable sartorial elegance deteriorated quickly. Now that my lifestyle has changed and I don't need to be on display, I usually buy just one or two "good things" when in Europe. I also have an extensive wardrobe of clothes from the days when I designed for Shanghai Tang. I really like them and just might develop into an eccentric who keeps wearing them into old age.

"Mummy, there's that funny old man in the shredded Chinese jacket."

"Don't point, darling. Mummy will call the police."

For years, I wore exclusively Japanese designers. I remember standing in the Yohji Yamamoto shop in Paris, trying on yet another black suit not dissimilar to the three I already owned at $3,000 a pop. For the first time, the voice of reason asked, "Gregory, do you need another black suit?" With the shop employing tactics similar to the heavy sell at Le Louvre, I knew it would be a battle to get out without buying that suit. Four adoring salespeople, like a noose around my neck, were telling me how fabulous I looked.

Suddenly, I knew how to escape. I was wearing a wooden Buddhist prayer bracelet that Mark had recently brought me back from a buying trip in Taiwan. When I pulled at it, the cheap elastic snapped, and a hundred beads scattered to every corner of the store. The four salespeople dropped to their knees, trying to collect them. While they were distracted, I was out of that suit in a flash and at the far end of Rue Cambon before they knew what had happened. That was it for Yohji.

I still wear one of those suits, and it's still stylish after more than thirty years, but I love buying things from Target and Kmart these days. I can't understand how they manage to produce clothes of such high quality so cheaply. Oh, come on, Head in the Sand! It's slave labour, don't you know? Their big men's section has boomed in the last few years. Of course, clothing with a 32 inch waist (such as I wore in my Le Louvre days) have long since gone. I remember those fancy clothes all going at once.

When I lived in Avoca Street, South Yarra, we had a plague of moths. I thought they were so pretty as they fluttered throughout the house. I didn't heed people's warnings and left them alone. As a result, they ate my Agnona coat, my velvet suit and all of my cashmere sweaters. My greatest regret was a favourite jacket, the best that Georgina ever bought me. It was in the softest cashmere you can imagine, with a very subtle herringbone pattern in the palest beige and taupe. It sounds hideous, but it was very beautiful. I wore the trumpeter on its lapel and always felt like a million dollars.

"Clothes maketh a man."

Well, maybe not. I feel just as happy today in my Target T-shirts as I ever have in the finest clothes. But I will never forget how good that jacket felt, how it hung on my shoulders, and how it turned heads and garnered admiring glances as I walked down the Paris end of Collins Street.

Maybe it was the diamanté clip in my hair.

19

Come Fly With Me

I wish there had been such a thing as a frequent flyer program during my years at Le Louvre. I would have clocked up many miles and made it to Europe long before I ever did. I had never flown on an aircraft until Georgina took me on the travelling Le Louvre roadshow to Sydney.

I was in my mid-twenties and still working from The Hutch. Sitting in a window seat on my very first flight, I felt like a little boy getting a reward for being good. I was so excited as we flew through a brewing storm. Mighty flashes of lightning lit up two vast banks of clouds. It was so dramatic. I kept trying in vain to get Georgina's attention. When placed in any moving mechanical object – be it a plane, a car or a St Kilda–bound tram – she would immediately fall asleep.

Meanwhile, now feeling like Mickey Mouse in *Fantasia*, I had to stop myself from conducting along to God's sideshow. Since this entrée to the clouds, I have flown through some violent storms but never one to compare with the breathtaking grandeur of that electrical extravaganza. I could barely contain myself, thanking the stewardess enthusiastically as if she had arranged the whole thing for my benefit.

Georgina turned on me like a viper. "Don't ever thank them. Don't ever look at them. And never smile," she said.

I couldn't understand her antipathy towards cabin crew (as we call them today). From then on, of course, I went out of my way to thank, look and smile, just to annoy Georgina. Maybe it was because they were pretty, which seemed to be a requirement in those days.

There was another thing I used to do that would drive Georgina nuts. When returning from anywhere into Melbourne – knowing that she would always have some kind of fruit on her – I would reach into her bag, confiscate it and dump it in the quarantine bin provided. I took great delight in doing this, and she would become furious. I hate to think of the fruit flies she has transported over the border since I haven't been around.

At least four times a year, the circus travelled to Sydney and Adelaide, where Le Louvre's patronage was almost as strong as in Melbourne. I thought it was fabulous when I first went along. We took the premier suite at the Wentworth Hotel, Sydney's top five-star hotel at the time. It was a suite of rooms that could be endlessly added onto. I was allocated a fold-up bed, a "Purse", as we called them. Although camped in among the racks of chiffon and silk, I didn't think twice about the arrangement. It was years before I graduated to a proper bed. After a long day setting up the circus, my favourite thing was to order room service and watch the telly in the big salon. Everyone else went out to dinner, while I always ordered a filet mignon, followed by ice cream with hot chocolate sauce.

Setting up the circus was such fun. Miss Wightman would strip the room of all paintings, shoving them behind sofas or in wardrobes – she couldn't stand paintings. Eventually, hotel management put a stop to this by screwing them to the walls, but in the early years they were the first things to go. Then the furniture would be pushed up against the walls. Any pieces she found especially offensive would be expatriated to God-only-knows where. Then I would start draping and swathing miles of silk and chiffon. Using furs and ostrich feather boas, I would create eye-catching, ostentatious displays, transforming what only hours before had been simple sofas or side-table lamps. Once, I caught a length of chiffon smouldering on such a lamp. But what did we care about safety issues? Decor was all that interested us.

Adelaide was a tougher assignment to redo, as the hotel was not as grand as the Wentworth. Although we had a similar arrangement, with a series of rooms that opened up to one another, it lacked a grand salon and any other focal points such as we had in Sydney. The suite was furnished with dark furniture that could only be described as Spanish Hacienda Ugly. The abundant carving was all plastic moulding.

We did our best, however. Miss Wightman performed her usual trick, cajoling the management into taking most things away – until they eventually put their foot down. The first year I was there, I was in the suite with Miss Wightman before everyone else had arrived. Impatient to get things moving, she convinced me that I could move the heavy, Moorish-style dining table out of the room and up the corridor. This being my first visit to Adelaide, I assumed that was what always happened. It took me half an hour of pushing and shoving to manoeuvre that massive brute of a thing through the doors and out into the hallway. Since it was almost as wide as the passage, I couldn't see where I could put it that wouldn't block someone's access.

"No, no," she insisted. "Push it up to the end, where the maids' cupboard is. They're like magicians' rabbits. They can squeeze in anywhere."

About halfway up, I heard an almighty crack. The table had snapped in half. This certainly made it easier to move, but how was I going to explain what had happened? Gingerly, I rested the two halves together at the end of the hall, leaving just enough room for the rabbits to get to their warren of sheets and towels. Then I hightailed it back to the suite. I don't know what transpired, as the subject was never mentioned. The following season, we encountered the same suite of furniture but were banned from removing it. Maybe the table healed itself. You couldn't see any evidence of the wound.

Sydney and Adelaide were not just miles apart geographically; they were different in so many ways. Adelaide women exhibited the style and deference of landed gentry, in contrast to the Sydney clientele's flashiness of the nouveau riche. Both cities had their charms, but Sydney won hands down for a boy who had never been further than Mildura.

My first visit there with the Le Louvre circus was undoubtedly an eye-opener. The policeman's son was shocked at the general attitude of "We're paying for it, so it's ours." The first day, at lunch downstairs on the terrace, I was sitting next to Miss Wightman when she eyed the salt and pepper shakers. "Oh, they're nice," she said before slipping them into her bag. Because we would entertain clients throughout the day, there was a constant stream of room service with tea and coffee, point sandwiches, biscuits and nibbles. Georgina would always order more linen napkins than were necessary, with most going into her suitcase. I still have some of a particular damask design that I fancied. I couldn't actually purloin them myself, so every time they would appear, I would hint at how much I liked them, and Georgina would pilfer them on my behalf.

It was an incredible, every-man-for-himself feeding frenzy whenever we packed up to leave the Wentworth in Sydney. Miss Wightman particularly liked the little silver teapots and cutlery. I hate to think what might have happened had she faced today's airport security with what are currently considered potential weapons in her possession! Although she was always loaded down with loot, she managed her copious handbag as if it held nothing heavier than a hairbrush, a bottle of Shalimar and a chiffon scarf.

I was shocked, as well, by the behaviour of Georgina's secretary, Janet. The most Protestant and upright member of the troupe, she only ever seemed to have her clothes dry-cleaned in Sydney – she would arrive with a suitcase full of dirty clothes and send them off at the hotel for cleaning. It all went on the bill. How the Wentworth could keep track of what went missing, I wouldn't know, but I suspect all the napkins, teapots, towels and robes went on the bill too.

Georgina hasn't changed one bit over the years. Recently, when checking out of her Milan hotel, she was presented with a hefty bill for misappropriation of hotel linen. Those very smart linen napkins that we had been dabbing on our lips for years were actually bidet towels intended for dabbing more unseemly orifices!

I had my favourite clients in both cities. Elsa Jacoby was a highlight of any visit to Sydney. She had a theatrical background and was a million laughs with a few whiskeys under her belt. (To this day, I pour a very heavy Scotch. Miss Wightman taught me how: "Darling, just pour till the ice floats.") Elsa was a big woman with a big personality, and I would have to make special clothes with her in mind. She would come into the hotel, smugly thinking that nothing in the ready-to-wear collection would fit, and she would be safe. After a few whiskeys, however, she would be surprised to find herself decked out, head to foot, in a whole new wardrobe for morning to night.

Each season, I would calculate how much weight she might gain, and I was always on the mark – until one year when she went on some special diet. Down to a stunning size 14, she shocked us all when she spun in and around the room. Our first thought was: "What are we going to do with her custom-made size-20 outfits?" However, Elsa was so pleased with being able to fit into ready-to-wear that she bought more than she ever had before. As usual with fad diets, she later put it all back on, and some. So, we resurrected those dresses that we thought we would never sell. Once again, she was out the door, outfitted and outwitted.

Elsa never arrived before the cocktail hour, and she would end up singing, dancing and wearing my feather-and-fur decorations out to dinner. Quite often, she would get carried away and wear them home, only to find charges for them on her bill. Huge silk flowers were all the go one year. She had them pinned to her in every imaginable spot as she left the hotel looking like a giant rose bush in high heels.

A woman known fittingly as "Matron" was possibly Le Louvre's best Sydney client. As happened with a few of our eccentric clients, we never actually saw her wear any of the clothes she bought. The first time I met her, everyone else was out to lunch and I almost shooed her away. When she appeared wearing a white polyester Neat'n Trim uniform, my

first thoughts were to get her out of there ASAP. "Go. Go. The dirty towels are behind the bathroom door. Quick. And, while you're at it, empty those ashtrays."

Fortunately, something about her attitude and the way she was smoking her cigarette sent me a warning before I did so. Clearly, she felt quite at home standing there. Matron owned several large nursing homes and was RICH. She would buy outfit after outfit without ever asking the price. I never, ever saw her wear one of the hundreds of things she purchased over the years. When I would return to check the fittings and alterations, she would always be wearing the same white polyester Neat'n Trim uniform, holding a lit cigarette in her hand, and radiating that attitude that sparked my intuition not to judge a book by its cover.

One of Adelaide's most senior matriarchs, Mrs P.B. Angas Parsons, became my client exclusively after she took quite a shine to me and I had her around my little finger. She must have been in her late seventies and still drove an original FJ Holden when making her forays to the centre of Adelaide to shop with Le Louvre. A very soft mint-green, that car was in immaculate condition – not a scratch or dent – which I found amazing after I saw her drive it once. She took off like she was racing in the Adelaide Grand Prix. Without looking in any direction, she lurched into the stream of city traffic, then slowed to a crawl.

Mrs P.B. Angas Parsons had a distinct, harsh Australian drawl that was as dry as the thousands of miles of dusty cattle country she owned. She also had a bad case of osteoporosis and was very hunched over. When I showed her clothes, I virtually had to put them on the floor for her to see them properly. Getting things to fit her was difficult. I think that's why she liked me, as I only showed her things that I knew were soft on the body and easy to alter. Her skirts fell at least 6 inches longer at the front. Once, she came in with a skirt on back to front – it fell to her ankles at the front and showed her stockings and suspenders at the back. So that this wouldn't happen again, I always marked the front waistband with four big Xs embroidered in red thread. Money was never mentioned. To at least eight or nine outfits at a time, she would snap either "I loik it. I'll 'ave it" or "I don't loik it. I won't 'ave it."

Out of all the clients I dealt with in Adelaide, there was only one that I dreaded. She was an Adelaide matron and a tragic case. She was usually charming and sweet, but I soon learnt that you had to be very quick and keep her animated; the moment she became pensive, she would break down with self-pity and grief. Years before, she'd had both breasts removed in a radical mastectomy. No one warned me before my first encounter with her, but they all cleared out, knowing what to expect. If she had to spend a long time in front of a mirror for a fitting, she would start crying, then beat her chest, rip open her blouse, and scream, "Look at what that butcher did to me." It was one of the worst experiences of all my years at Le Louvre. It happened every time, but nothing could prepare you for witnessing such grief and I didn't know how to console her. After a few times, I just had to pretend it wasn't happening., After the fitting, she would compose herself, have a cup of tea, and go on her way as if indeed nothing *had* happened. Breast cancer research and the charities associated with it have become very dear to my heart, and I am sure that my exposure to this sad woman first formed my strong connection to that cause.

I would have to return to both cities to check on the alterations and deliver and fit the clothes ordered from Racine in France – clients would buy from models, and their orders would arrive six or seven weeks later. Usually, I would go on these one- or two-day trips alone, but sometimes Georgina would come with me, especially if she had friends to see or a party to attend. On one such visit to Sydney, some special event was happening at the Wentworth, so we couldn't get our usual suite and finished up in a very unsatisfactory room of inferior quality. It had two single beds and not enough room to swing the proverbial cat, let alone comfortably fit all of our boxes of clothes.

We were expecting someone I shall call Mrs Mac. A surgeon's wife from the eastern suburbs, she was very particular, always wearing hat, gloves, shoes, bag and jewels to match. She was tedious beyond belief. Although we tried to make the room as presentable as possible, she didn't seem to notice. All she did was embark on an incredibly long and tedious story about her husband buying her a large diamond ring and hiding it in the bottom of their bed. She was decked out to death in a winter white outfit from one of our Sydney competitors, Nellie Vida.

Halfway through the session, Georgina popped off to the bathroom to eat some of the large, tossed salad that she had made in the bathtub. While she was there, she used the toilet but she didn't flush it because you could just about hear everything in such a small room. When it came time for Mrs Mac to change into her fitting, she slipped into the bathroom. Later, when she needed to change into her next outfit, I suggested I leave the room and I popped into the bathroom (with my mind on some avocado and tomato in the bathtub salad). To my horror, I saw, halfway down the toilet, Mrs Mac's multi-stitched, fully-fashioned white wool twill belt. I pulled it out. Half of it was now bright yellow.

"Georgina," I called. "Could I see you for a moment?"

When she saw the belt, we both broke into uncontrollable, hysterical laughter – except that it was controlled uncontrollable, hysterical laughter because we couldn't afford to make a sound. I was writhing on the bathroom floor, and Georgina fell into the bath with the tossed salad.

"Is everything all right?" Mrs Mac trilled from the room.

We had been gone for some considerable time, trying to compose ourselves.

"Be with you in a minute."

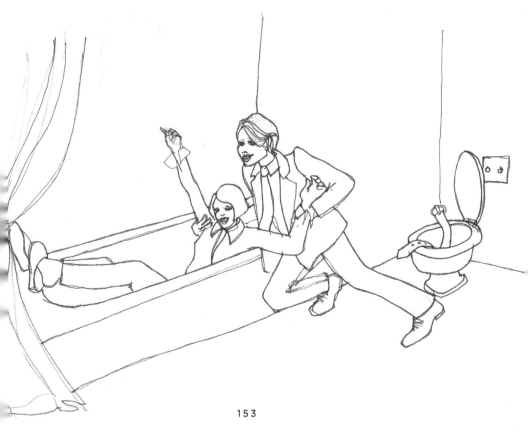

Our plan was to keep her occupied while I would try to wash the belt. So, I suggested getting her going on the ring story again.

"And how many carats did you say it was?" I heard Georgina ask as she returned to Mrs Mac, closing the bathroom door behind her. I washed the belt with the only soap to hand. This being pink Cashmere Bouquet, it turned it into an apricot colour, much to my horror. After much rinsing, I managed to remove all traces of urine but was left with a very damp belt. I used every bit of toilet paper and tissue we had, wrapped it up and jumped up and down on it, trying to exert maximum pressure on the paper so that it would soak up as much moisture as possible. When I had exhausted every method that I could remember from Martha Gardener's household hints, the belt looked pristine, although slightly perfumed with notes of roses, lilac and violet. At least it was nearly dry.

After deliberately spilling a little water on the floor near the door, I emerged from the bathroom, clutching the damp belt and hoping my face had returned to its normal colour.

"Your belt touched the floor and got a little damp, Mrs Mac, but I think it will be fine."

A look of horror engulfed her benign countenance.

"It didn't fall in the toilet, did it?" she snapped.

Obviously, this had happened to her more than once.

"No, I can assure you," I lied through my teeth. "Just a little water on the floor."

We managed to hold our composure throughout the tedious mechanics of assembling all her "winter white" accessories, which took ages. We bade her adieu, begging her to bring in the new diamond ring for us to admire on her next appointment. I hoped she wouldn't lift the toilet seat before going, as it was full to the brim with masses of yellow and pink paper.

For weeks afterwards, we spasmodically fell about laughing. However, for all my expertise, try as I may, I couldn't get that tomato stain from the bum of Georgina's good YSL pants.

20

The Apple Isle

Although we had quite a few clients from the Apple Isle, numbers didn't warrant a visit from the Le Louvre travelling roadshow. Or so management believed, their reluctance and neglect reflecting the mainland's attitude towards Tasmania generally. As a defence, our elite Tasmanian clients displayed a certain aloofness and snobbery, even delusions of aristocracy. In fact, we still refer to one of them as the "Tasmanian Princess". I am sure there was a lot of clucking about Mary Donaldson when she hooked Frederick and became an actual royal princess.

"It should have been me!"

Our two favourite Tasmanian clients lived in Launceston and came to Melbourne at least twice a year to "fit out". Sisters who owned the only good pub in their town were both fabulous and vivacious women, especially considering the environment in which they were reared. They were quite big spenders, and their Melbourne shopping forays were a delight to all. In a moment of distraction – or maybe as the clincher for a difficult sale – Georgina promised them that she would bring a collection to Launceston and put on a fashion parade as a charity fundraiser.

You would have thought we were Hollywood movie stars, judging by the treatment we received on arrival. The local media were there with cameras whirring and flashing. They made us wait until the plane was empty, so they could capture us disembarking. I half expected to see a red velvet cushion in front of a square of wet cement so that locals could take imprints of our celebrity hands and feet and place them later on in the "Mall of Fame" next to those of Merle Oberon and Tommy Hanlon Jr. Accompanying us was little Annie, she of the "Haunted Jacket" fame. As our star mannequin, she got most of the attention, of course, because she could pose for hours on end à la *Vogue* magazine, with hands on hips, head thrown back, lips pouting and face scowling.

It was winter, and I was wearing a symphony of winter beige tweeds and cashmere, featuring my ivory Art Deco brooch on the lapel of the jacket. My hair hung in a heavy sheet over my right eye, and I was attempting to grow my first beard. Having settled in our rooms, Georgina and I thought we would take in the sights of the town. After throwing on another couple of layers, we swept through the revolving doors of the hotel, arm in arm. We looked to the left, and we looked to the right. Before the doors had a chance to slow down, we swept back in. The bar had a roaring fire, and a drink before dinner held much more appeal than the bleak streetscape we had glimpsed. We never saw more than that fleeting moment, as we didn't leave the hotel for the next four days.

Georgina and I bunked in together as we often did while I gave little Annie the room booked in my name. The hotel had old-fashioned ways, including bringing guests an early morning "cuppa", whether they wanted it or not. Let me set the scene.

I had taken a fancy to wearing long, Victorian broderie Anglaise nightgowns, which I discovered when rummaging around country antique shops. I had included one from my collection on this trip to

Tasmania. It had a ruffle down the front, and big gathered sleeves that finished in ruffles covering the hands. Unfortunately, having lost all its buttons, it fell open right down to below the navel. At 6.30 the first morning, there was a sharp rap on the door. Having been sound asleep, I awoke in that dazed state of not knowing where or who you are when staying in strange places, so I leapt out of bed without thinking, bound for the door.

Outside was a startled housemaid in a black-and-white uniform. And there I was, greeting her in my be-ruffled Victorian nightgown that stuck out like a circus tent over a very stiff "good morning" erection.

She started to say, "Good Morning, Miss Weir. Your morning ..." But, seeing the tent pole, the unbuttoned ruffles and the beard, she scuttled the tray and fled. I can imagine the maids fighting the following day over who would bring the good morning cuppa so they could cop a look at "Miss Weir". We had become the talk of the town!

Launceston society ladies were lining up to perform as mannequins at the gala charity parade, which was to be held on Thursday evening. Georgina targeted those "models" who had the potential to buy – she focused a lot of fittings with an eventual sale in mind. This ploy was successful, as the husbands got quite intoxicated on the evening itself, and several tightly knotted purse strings were loosened with a bit of alcoholic lubrication.

One of the most beautiful gowns I ever made was a wedding dress. (I would make several versions of it in the years to follow.) Traditionally, every parade finishes with a bride, and Georgina chose a plain-looking girl to wear this gown of mine in the finale. The poor girl had no chin to mention due to an unfortunate rear-ender with a horse. At the time, I pleaded with Georgina not to choose her, as I thought she would become the town laughing stock. Looking back now, though, I realise that choosing that girl gave her a happy memory that she would cherish forever.

I didn't see much of the evening as I was backstage choreographing the whole thing. The models I was dressing and undressing were far more interested in how they looked rather than how smoothly the show was running. I would have to rip them away from the congestion around the only mirror, reassure them that their heifer-like ankles didn't look puffy in that length of skirt, then boot them down the catwalk. Getting them back was another challenge. Several of them got stage-struck, finding all the applause and whistles so captivating that they would do an extra lap – and throwing my running order completely out of synch.

Georgina's partner, Kent, and a buddy of his had flown over for a long weekend. They had started drinking on the plane and hadn't let up since arriving, so they were having a whale of a time. For some reason – moral or otherwise – the idea of Georgina sharing a room with Kent was frowned upon, so I stayed where I was ("the other Miss Weir"), and Kent and his mate were allocated a room above the revolving doors. One or the other of them blotted his reputation (or enhanced it) by peeing out the window later that evening, narrowly missing a departing reveller. The parade must have been a great success because I know we had a busy selling day, the wives taking advantage of those loosened strings before their spouses sobered up.

On Friday evening we were guests of honour at a dinner held by a leader of Launceston society at one of Tasmania's most historic homes. The house had walls 10 feet thick, and the hostess proudly showed us the scars of the spears in the heavy cedar shutters that had repelled a marauding Aboriginal assault. Later, I found myself wishing that they had been successful in their attack.

The hostess gave us an extensive tour of the house before dinner. We finished up in the children's wing, creeping into a room that was more like a crypt than a nursery. In this cold, cold place, two tiny snap-frozen tots were asleep in their beds, the only indication of life being the sparkling frost on their pillows where their breath had formed icy crystals. As we left the room, I covered one up, the poor mite having dislodged the bedding as little kids do. I prayed it would survive till the morning.

Then we entered a baronial dining room with at least thirty people seated along a massive oak table. As guests of honour, we were placed with the roaring log fire directly behind us. I don't think I have ever been so cold and so hot within such a short period of time. I removed as much clothing as I could, but I had an Antarctic-worthy, long-sleeved thermal garment (known as a spencer) under my polo-neck cashmere jumper. This particular spencer, borrowed from my mother, featured tiny, embroidered roses and a scoop neckline decorated with rather delicate lace. So I knew when to stop removing layers!

As I sat there sweltering, I glanced down to the end of the table and saw clouds of frosty breath – the heat that was so roasting my rump hadn't made one iota of difference to the farther reaches of the cavernous room. I wish the saddle of beef had been as well cooked as I was, because something I ate that night gave me the most horrendous food poisoning. The roast was carved from a big silver salver on wheels, of the kind usually only found in hotels like Raffles in Singapore or the Savoy in London. The salver crept towards me like a giant shiny slug. As I was about the last to be served, my beef was not just cold; it could only be described as "blue". Or maybe it was the peas that did it, because by the time they arrived, they had refrozen – the packet always warns of the dangers of such a practice.

That evening we moved from the hotel to the ancestral home of our

"Tasmanian Princess", yet another magnificent heritage-listed home. I started to feel unwell as I was shown to my room, one of the less significant rooms on the second floor. My first question was about the location of the closest bathroom, the necessity of visiting becoming more urgent as the minutes passed. I spent the most gruesome night, with numerous dashes to the bathroom. Unfortunately, it was so far away that I had to anticipate involuntary motions well in advance. My Victorian nightgown, having been worn all week, was already slightly sad, but by the next morning it was in an appalling condition (both coming and going).

No one realised I was sick, so no one was perturbed when I didn't turn up for breakfast; everyone thought I was just having a long-needed sleep. It was only when the mother of our princess saw me hiding behind a Doric column on a mercy dash to the loo that my sorry state of health was discovered. Georgina has never been able to cope with illness or death – I was close to the latter, but she didn't want to know. The mistress of the house, on the other hand, was marvellous. She managed to extract me from the Victorian nightie, gave me a good sponge down, and popped me into a pair of her husband's flannelette pyjamas. She must have taken the nightgown away and burnt it, because I never saw it again.

There was a full-scale house party on that weekend, and it wouldn't have surprised me if there had been a race to hounds. I spent Saturday and Sunday delirious. All that I remember is the sound of Champagne corks popping, glasses clinking, people laughing and voices scrambling. Florence Nightingale would occasionally test my temperature, apply a cool cloth to my brow and disappear. Early Monday morning, I awoke to see Georgina staring at me. When I blinked, she was gone – back to the mainland. I was too sick to travel, so she just abandoned me, my fate in the hands of the powers that be.

The powers that be nurtured me back with bowls of chicken soup, coddled eggs and dry toast. By Wednesday, I felt alive again. It came Friday, and my nurse was very reluctant to let me go. For one spooky moment, I saw my life ahead as the mysterious howler in the forbidden west tower. A life of clunking keys. Trays left by terrified servants outside my door. A life without human contact. A life without sunshine in a prison where my burgeoning beard would eventually sweep the floor. A life that was forgotten, overshadowed by the misty memory of marvellous merriment so long ago.

"Remember that weekend party?"

"Gregory *Who*?"

21

Fashion Clouds

One of our best clients at le Louvre was married to the chairman of TAA. She thought highly of me and suggested that I submit designs for the forthcoming revamp of the air hostess uniform. Given plenty of notice, I was very excited and worked diligently for months on the project.

I researched fabrics to find the most practical, serviceable and economical. I designed a whole wardrobe that went easily through the seasons and the washing machine. It was a "this goes with that" wardrobe of co-ordinates in the chic and stylish colours of navy, grey and white. My knitwear interwove the TAA insignia, as did the matching carry-on luggage that I am sure Fendi copied years later. The collection was drip-dry and non-iron. It breathed. It was cool in summer and warm in winter. The sleeves of the overcoat even inflated to become another emergency slide in the case of a crash. There wasn't a single angle that I hadn't given thought to. What's more, it was kind-of modern and stylish.

On the day of the presentation to the board of directors, I was confident that we would get the contract. Although not precisely fitting into Le Louvre's realm, it would be a very lucrative deal that we could easily manage to contract out. I was done up to the nines in a new Italian unstructured suit by Giorgio Armani (before he was Giorgio Armani) and feeling on top of the world.

Just as I was about to step into the taxi, Miss Wightman – who had not shown any interest in my project – suddenly announced that she would come with me, then took off down the street to Frederic Muller's to have her hair combed up. I had to wait for her to change into a fresh ocelot ensemble and for the girls in the workroom to press the 20 metres of chiffon she always threw around her impressive chassis.

Incidentally, this was the most dreaded task of any in the workroom, calling for devotion above the call of duty. These copious chiffon scarves were always drenched in the best and most expensive French perfumes, mainly Shalimar, but there was always a little bit of lunch somewhere hidden in the many folds. Often, the unlucky girl called upon to press these voluminous chiffon banners would need an oxygen mask or at least 10 minutes on the back stairs to recover from the task.

Anyway, when Georgina had finally powdered her mother's nose and put on a touch of lippy, we were already 40 minutes late. When we finally entered the vast boardroom – after taking a wrong turn and getting lost in the corridors of power at head office, we were over an hour late. Miss Wightman drew herself up to her full stature and, with a swish of chiffon, strode the length of the boardroom table, spinning a fantastic tale of courage and bravery in the face of death. She spun the most audacious lie I had ever heard.

"My dears, I am so sorry we are so late. We were in the most terrible accident on the way here in the taxi."

They all expressed concern and surprise, as we certainly didn't look as though we had been in an accident. Neither of us had a hair out of place, nor a scratch, bruise or even a crease. They all looked amazed, but she couldn't leave it at that.

"We rolled over three times."

That's when I looked like I had actually died in the crash. The colour drained from my face. They all turned to me for confirmation, as did Miss Wightman. I went from grey to ruby in a flash and meekly pronounced, "We were very lucky."

With the board members unsettled and impatient to get on with the meeting, I was invited to pitch my proposal. I passed around the storyboards, explaining the advantages of modern advancements in textile technology and how I had blended the latest fashion trends with a classic style that would give the uniforms a life of many years without needing to be constantly updated. I could see a few appreciative nods ... that is, until the drawings reached Miss Wightman. She took a cursory glance at my magnum opus and exclaimed, "Rubbish. This is all rubbish. That's not what you need!"

She then proceeded to tell the board exactly what they did need: pure silk crêpe-de-chine little blouses with a pussycat bow at the neck; and a little imported Racine suit from Paris, in red wool jersey with gold buttons. None of this synthetic, drip-dry nonsense. "Rubbish, rubbish, rubbish."

I was mortified. While Miss Wightman gave the board a minor dissertation on feminine deportment and the importance of hostesses lowering their eyes when serving the tea, I gathered up my months of hard work, knowing in my heart that any chances of our contract dictating style in the fashion clouds were doomed.

On the way back in the taxi, Miss Wightman chirped, "Well, that seemed to go rather well," and I almost wished we *would* do a triple roll to put me out of my misery.

22

Never Button Up a Balmain

Lillian Wightman was famous for her quips. "Never start a meal on a lake" was one of them. In this piece of gastronomic advice, she was referring to soup, an unnecessary course in her opinion. For her, it took away from the delight of a pre-dinner whiskey. Another little gem – "What's born in the bone shows in the ankle" – was trotted out frequently, often in a desperate attempt to dredge up something positive to bestow upon an important client's daughter or a plain bride. It hinted at good breeding and refinement when a stock report would have been more relevant to the heifer in question.

As mentioned already, Miss Wightman had very good pegs with nicely shaped ankles. She also displayed a curvaceous figure with an ample bosom and generous hips. Georgina, on the other hand, had no hips or derriere. But she *did* have legs that went on forever. At the height of YSL dressing, she could be mistaken from the back for a man – and often was. Luckily, she had great tits! Sometimes, at the end of a big day, Georgina would snuggle up next to her mother on the ocelot couch in the large salon. Lillian would run her hands down her daughter's legs.

A wistful look would pass over her face as she lingered at the ankles. A curse on that George Weir and his Irish genes!

"A large box with no ribbons" was a saying she used when referring to a coffin, especially when reminding a reluctant customer that "you can't take money with you".

"Nothing in your size" was her first greeting to any poor Japanese tourist who would accidentally wander through the door. Before they could replace the lens cover on their Nikon SLR, she would spin on her heels, beat a hasty retreat to the upstairs office, flop in a chair and try to regain her composure. ("They tortured our boys, you know.")

But one of her favourite sayings was not of her own making at all, despite the claims she made to it. "Never button up a Balmain" was an excuse for any garment that didn't fit. And *I* was the one who invented it!

In the early days of Georgina's buying trips to Paris, she had entrée to two of the old *Maisons de Couture*: the houses of Balmain and Molyneux – two of the great names of the golden era of Paris fashion. (Molyneux is pronounced with a hard x, as in the hard t of Moët et Chandon.) When buying, she virtually fulfilled the wish lists of Le Louvre's best customers. She knew their sizes, their preferences, the colours that flattered them, their pet hates and phobias. One Sydney client, for example, adored Balmain while loathing Molyneux. Quirkily enough, another Sydney client loved Molyneux yet detested Balmain. These women were of similar age, stature, social standing and affluence. They also shared a total dislike for each other. It was always a disaster should they shop at the same time.

Georgina had a deal with these *Maisons de Couture* to buy the samples at the end of each season. Samples were the garments paraded before the clientele in order for them to make their selections, after which orders would be made to the client's exact specifications. The only problem with these garments was that they were extremely small. The armholes, in particular, were cut very high and tight because they looked better on the models, who didn't have to worry about lifting their arms or raising a hand to their mouths to eat (and by the size of them, they never did).

This particular season – it was winter – Georgina returned with two woollen suits, one plain (Molyneux) and one in a speckled birds-eye tweed (Balmain). As luck would have it, both of the above-mentioned women turned up to the first Sydney showing, overlapping within the same hour, both lured by the promise of their favoured designers. It wasn't precisely pandemonium, but it was busy. Everyone was demanding full attention. I shall call the women by the names of their favourite designers.

Mrs Molyneux spotted the Balmain jacket and adored it, so Miss Wightman ordered me to quickly switch the label to Molyneux because she wouldn't buy it if she saw that it was a Balmain. After I had switched the labels, Mrs Molyneux tried on the Balmain (which now had a Molyneux label). She loved it. But, because it was costly, she said she would think about it.

Meanwhile, Mrs Balmain arrived. She spotted the Balmain (which now sported a Molyneux label) and said, "Oh, yes, I can pick a Balmain at a hundred yards." Out came the Molyneux label, and back in went the Balmain. But she wouldn't commit either.

Later in the afternoon, Mrs Molyneux turned up after a lengthy lunch, wanting to try on that suit again. So, the labels were swapped once more. Yes, Mrs Molyneux would buy the Balmain (which was now a Molyneux again).

(At this point, I should explain that the suits were sporting different labels in the skirt and jacket.)

Then Mrs Balmain rang, saying she was still interested in the Balmain. "We are so sorry, but it has been sold."

A hand was held over the telephone, and a hushed conference ensued. Had she seen the Molyneux (which was now a Balmain)? No one thought so – because she had spotted the Balmain/Molyneux at the precise time that Mrs Molyneux was trying on the other switched label.

You think *you're* confused! It was a case of magic mirrors and revolving doors the whole time this was going on. We didn't want the two women to meet.

"We do have another Balmain." (Actually, the Molyneux.) "You must come back in and try it on."

She dutifully arrived and was shown the new Balmain, which was the Molyneux. But she didn't like it quite as much as the real Balmain, which had been the Molyneux. She couldn't quite put her finger on it.

Unfortunately, she was putting up some sales resistance – mainly because it was somewhat smaller than the real Balmain. In fact, there was a 4 inch gap where the buttons didn't meet. An awkward moment followed. It was pretty evident to everyone that this jacket didn't fit her!

Suddenly, from nowhere, something popped out of my mouth.

"But you never button up a Balmain."

"Oh, yes!" everyone chorused. "Never."

She didn't bother changing. She wore it home!

23

Rollers

I was a natural when it came to hair. From a very early age, I was always trying to do something to my own. Getting rollers into short hair was a challenge to be reckoned with – I became an expert, and it didn't take me long to figure out how to avoid the ridge made by the elastic grip. From my early training with rollers, I later developed the skill of cutting my own hair. I have had psoriasis since I was about fifteen. One of its worst and most irritating symptoms affects the scalp. To avoid embarrassment at the hairdressers, I taught myself to cut my own. People would say, "Who cuts your hair?" and more often than not I would end up cutting theirs. Once, after I had cut Janet's hair, a hairdresser complimented her. Because she had not long been back from London, she said she could pick a Sassoon cut a mile off.

It all became a bit too much after a while. At Le Louvre, not only would I design and make the bridal gown, I would have to dress the bride and do her hair and make-up as well. Miss Wightman would deliver a throwaway line and I would cringe. "Don't bother with a hairdresser, darling. Gregory's marvellous." Come the day of the wedding, I would find myself with the bride, five bridesmaids, the mother of the bride, her mother and the odd interstate guest needing a comb-up. I eventually put a stop to this value-added service. Mind you, in all the years I did it, I was never offered a gratuity or as much as a bottle of Champagne.

I stopped it because of a disastrous incident involving the wedding of the governor's daughter. It was just after the marriage of Princess Anne and Captain Mark Phillips, and the gown Anne wore inspired our dress. Needless to say, it had medieval sleeves. The family tiara was retrieved from a dusty attic, or at least it looked as though it had been. It was an unremarkable, dull arrangement of diamonds and sapphires, which they thought rivalled the very jewels of the Majesty they represented. This, and the veil, were to be the crowning glory of a magnificent ensemble. This girl was much like Princess Anne – undeniably horsy – although more attractive than the princess. She would often come for a fitting for her dress while still hot and sweaty from the saddle.

The day of the wedding was one of the funniest of many during my time at Le Louvre. My mode of transport in those days was my mother's Morris Minor, affectionately known as Bluebird. She was a slightly beaten-up little bomb, and what duco she had was royal blue. Georgina and I loved her and would tootle around everywhere in her, and I would often drive her to afternoon liaisons with a very handsome French ambassador who was married at the time to a famous international beauty. Anyway, Bluebird took me to "Gov. House" to dress the bride and, as usual, do the hair. I had never been there before and, driving a somewhat incongruous vehicle, I needed to do a lot of explaining to get through the various security checks. Being somewhat overawed as I approached, I drove straight over the red carpet. As I parked Bluebird, I glanced in the rear vision mirror and saw two liveried footmen furiously (and not too successfully) vacuuming the tyre marks with an ancient Electrolux. I had just driven through a big puddle and left a muddy impression right under the porte cochère.

The effervescent bride greeted me with the news that she hadn't washed her hair because she thought it would be "easier to manage".

I'm sure she thought she was doing the right thing but I couldn't get a bobby pin to stay in for more than a couple of minutes – they just slid right out. My major dilemma was how to anchor the veil and tiara without actually resorting to drilling a hole in her head. In desperation, I requested a hair roller instead of a hammer and nail. Eventually, a tatty selection was delivered from the depths of the servants' quarters. My idea was to wind a hank of hair around a roller and somehow lodge the tiara and veil into it. I chose the least offensive offering, a pale blue roller that had set many a bouffant over the years. It seemed to do the trick. Although the veil was the length of a football field, the hundreds of yards all came from one tiny point, so there was nothing to hide the mechanisms that would serve my purpose. As a test run, the bride jigged around and shook her head, and everything seemed to be firmly in place, so we both felt confident it would work. At this stage, we were running late, so my next predicament was how to get to St Paul's Cathedral before she did because I would have to arrange everything and send her off down the aisle in perfect style.

I flew out, into Bluebird, back over the red carpet and off down St Kilda Road. This tree-lined boulevard runs directly from Government House into the city, finishing up at the cathedral. The police had cordoned off all intersections to ensure the bridal entourage had an uninterrupted passage. I could see the Rolls-Royce catching up behind me, so I put my foot flat to the floor and ignored the police, who frantically tried to flag me down. If it had happened these days, I would have been shot by a SWAT team.

As I approached the intersection outside the cathedral, the Rolls overtook me and drew up outside the heavy bronze doors, which are opened only on state occasions such as this. To the amazement of the attendant crowd, I slammed on the brakes near a startled policeman and leapt from Bluebird, leaving her little heart still pumping wildly. I instructed him to take good care of her and ran to untangle the bride as she attempted to extract herself from the mess she had created with the veil. I smoothed it out, fluffed it up, turned the bouquet the right way

up and sent her on her way. Everyone in the packed cathedral turned to watch her procession to the altar. She did look spectacular. A blue ray of light from a stained-glass window caught a few diamonds and sapphires, and the tiara lit up, sparkling as she made her first steps on the arm of her proud and distinguished father.

My sense of relief then turned to disbelief as I watched her continue down the aisle. Halfway along, in perfect timing with Mendelssohn's

Wedding March, the elastic gave out, and a pale blue roller started bobbing and swaying at the end of a limp ribbon of hair. The bride never complained to me, nor did any of the guests who rang to congratulate me on my triumph. I can only presume that the tiara and the hair harmonised while the curler fell off and rolled away under a pew.

After this incident, I refused to attend to another bride's hair, although it didn't necessarily curtail my hairdressing career.

24

Mendelssohn March

Here comes the bride
All dressed in white,
Sweetly serene in the soft glowing light.

The first wedding dress I ever made was, of course, for Teddy. As already mentioned, certain items in my mother's jewel box served as the basic foundations for many of my designs. The item I called upon most was a wide, elastic-threaded cuff of diamantés set in frosted glass. This piece was so versatile that it was in constant demand. It was a perfect cummerbund, a 1920s-inspired head wrap, a Queen Mary–style choker or a bustier. And it provided the springboard for my first wedding dress: the bodice of a Givenchy / Audrey Hepburn style of gown. I would wear it myself when I wasn't using this elasticised cuff in one of Teddy's gowns.

One day it just gave up, the elastic worn out from being forced over my head too many times. Hundreds of little frosted glass settings shot off in every direction. I gathered up as many as I could, but they kept turning up for years in the most peculiar places. Mum would look at them with a bewildered expression. Having never seen her wear the diamanté cuff, I didn't expect that she would recognise this sparkling little beacon found wedged under the skirting boards as having anything to do with the adornment she had treasured as a young woman and worn to many a wartime-services dance. I kept the salvaged pieces. Many years later, I used them on a Judy Garland–inspired jacket I made for my friend, Stephen.

My first real wedding dress was the ruffled extravaganza that I carried over my arm when I first waltzed in through the portals of Le Louvre. That began the tradition of my making the wedding dress for the finale of the Le Louvre parade.

I was always allowed to make it as a surprise, so Georgina and Miss Wightman never saw it until it closed the parade. Often, my creations were unconventional, to say the least. Miss Wightman would get furious, saying they would never sell, but they always did. Several stand in fond memory. One was a nude-pink, silk-jersey gown that slithered over the body. Its medieval-inspired sleeves laced up the arms and formed long points that touched the floor, echoing the languid train. Another was an explosion of silk net over shaded silk that had bunches of violets caught up in the multilayers of the skirt and an outrageous ruffle over somewhat exposed shoulders.

The most scandalous of all was a white silk-jersey dress that dripped off a bodice of silk tulle with strategically placed leaves and flowers barely covering the nubile young model's essentials. Miss Wightman and a few of her cronies got the vapours. We finished up-selling and copying that dress several times.

Thank goodness, the lime-green velvet fiasco that I described earlier turned out to be a singular aberration; the society weddings of that era stand out in my memory as beautifully staged dioramas. In my mind's eye, I can still see one setting on a privately owned cliff at Portsea.

Six bridesmaids fluttered in the breeze like seagulls, giant organdie bows on their shoulders reminiscent of ruffled wings waiting to take flight.

Nothing with any wedding ever went precisely to plan, but we usually averted any major catastrophes. I remember one mercy dash against oncoming peak-hour traffic because we had left the bride's shoes behind. She had to commandeer her mother's slingbacks, which were two sizes too big. The dress was in exquisite gold lace. Instead of a veil, I had made a cage around her head of heavy honeycomb gold netting. Although she had promised her intended to give up smoking, this last-minute disaster tipped her over the edge. She so desperately craved a cigarette that I had to poke one through a hole in the net while trying to avoid setting her alight.

After a couple of near head-on collisions, the shoes arrived. But too late, as the bride had left for the church. She, too, was fashionably late. Fortuitously, the few minutes' delay meant that the sun set at the precise moment when the doors of St John's in Toorak opened and the bride entered. She looked so fabulous. Like a golden angel coming to life from the magnificent stained-glass windows above the door, she proceeded to the altar, *Here Comes the Bride* being accompanied by a percussion clip-clop of the borrowed slingbacks. The golden cage around her head (although not in flames) glowed like a luminous halo. Somehow, we managed to smuggle the shoes back to the bride in the front pew, but there must have been something wrong with those too. After signing the vows, she clip-clopped back up the aisle, but she looked so magnificent that I don't think anyone picked up on it.

One bride nearly didn't make it down the aisle at all. It must have been 1974, the year of *The Great Gatsby*, starring Robert Redford and Mia Farrow. The 1930s strongly influenced fashion that year and provided the theme for this wedding. I dyed metres and metres of silk chiffon in Lapsang Oolong tea to get the perfect shade. Cut on the bias and dripping with floating panels and inset godets, it was, in fact, like a 1930s tea gown. Fastening the tiny, tiny buttons down the back required a good half hour of manual dexterity. It was set off by a giant picture hat that dipped over one eye – gossamer antique roses under the brim framing the face, the blooms with just a hint of blush.

Often, I didn't attend early negotiations, only meeting the future bride when I discussed the design and submitted drawings for approval. I had been introduced to her merely as Paula. It was an Easter wedding. Come the big day, I found myself with the dress but no information as to the bride's full name or where she lived. I had assumed that Janet would put the information with the dress, and she had just assumed that I already knew. Janet had gone hiking in the bush, Georgina was away on a secret tryst, and I couldn't find Jane or Wendy or anyone else who might know. I had no idea what to do. Sitting on the end of my bed, staring at the bag containing the orphaned dress, I wracked my brain and tried to dredge up any clue as to the lost bride.

My head filled with passages from F. Scott Fitzgerald. I was confusing emeralds, like beacons at the end of the dock, with diamonds as big as the Ritz when "Mathoura Road" suddenly came into my mind. It was something more concrete than Daisy Buchanan and West Egg, Long Island, so off I headed.

All done up in a new, unstructured Italian suit, I clutched a giant hatbox and Le Louvre dress bag over one arm as I searched on foot. Mathoura Road is rather long, so I had no choice but to start at one end and work my way along with determination and hope in my heart. I gave myself plenty of time, but I was beginning to lose faith after an hour had passed. Then, halfway along, my door knocking on the opposite side of the road alerted the bride. She opened her door and waved me across. With a radiant smile and a sound of relief in her voice, she exclaimed, "I was beginning to worry."

I was only a bit late, but I wasted no time in getting her into the dress, aware of those hundred or so buttons to do up. The cars arrived. She slipped into the perfectly matched satin ankle-strap shoes, took the cascade of shaggy roses that dripped to the ground, and departed for Rippon Lea, where the wedding and reception would take place. The guests were all gathered by the edge of the large lake, which was filled with waterlilies the same colour as the dress. As the bride walked towards a little oriental bridge from the other side, you could catch glimpses of her through the trees and reflected in the water. On a small island, still within earshot of the assembled friends, she met the groom. It was so romantic.

I took to the Champagne, feeling such great relief as my stress vanished. I felt as if I were at a fabulous Jazz Age party with Scott and Zelda, Jay and Daisy. All thoughts of what might have been dissolving, not unlike Fitzgerald's hopes of the American dream.

The ballroom at Rippon Lea, a 1930s addition, was the perfect setting for that wedding. It was also where a near disaster happened in the years after I left Le Louvre. Everything had run like clockwork with this wedding. Not a hiccup had disturbed the making of the dress or the fittings. Everything had been finished and delivered in plenty of time. And, once again, I had been invited to the reception. (I was often asked to the wedding receptions.)

The fabric was a jacquard – a quite inexpensive rayon that I had found in the dungeons of the Job Warehouse (see Postscript). The dress was 1940s-inspired – and the fabric could have been hidden away since that time, just waiting for me to find it. The dress had big shoulders and a crossover draped bodice and hips. The skirt fell in a huge circular train, which could be brought around to the front for the photos (such as in the wedding portraits of friends and relatives that filled one of my mother's biscuit tins, which I had unearthed – a great source of inspiration).

It must have been the heat from the bride's body. When she alighted from the Rolls-Royce under the porte cochère at Rippon Lea, a crushed wreck emerged. During the whole construction, the dress hadn't had as much as a single crease and I had hardly touched it with an iron. The dress looked fine from the front because the bodice and hips were all draped, but the train was now a wrinkled mess. I nearly died.

In a panic, I ran off to the kitchen to see if I could track down a housekeeper. My thinking was that they would have to iron tablecloths, so there must be an iron somewhere in the establishment. I begged and pleaded with the manager. He was reluctant to help – until I eventually dragged him to see my predicament down by the lake, where the bride was having her photos taken. His mean, little mouth puckered up even more than I thought possible and he gave in.

Like a spider waiting for its prey, I set up the iron in a little antechamber just by the main door to the ballroom.

"Ladies and gentlemen, please be upstanding for the new Mr and Mrs Evans."

Everyone turned to the door, holding their Champagne glasses high in the air.

Nothing! The band started again. "Ladies and Gentlemen …" Nothing!

I had hijacked the new Mrs Evans as she went past and shoved an ironing board up her bum. It was full steam ahead as I endeavoured to iron the crumpled, rutted, crinkly train.

All silly and mushy, the bride and groom didn't hear the third introduction and didn't seem to care. Then the best man came looking, found my lair and dragged the couple off for the fourth attempt. I could hear enthusiastic applause as the newlyweds made their grand entrance onto the dance floor for the bridal waltz, the refreshed train following obligingly – still hot and steaming, but as smooth and calm as its colour (clotted cream).

<hr />

Often, Miss Wightman would get to a bride before Georgina and I had had a chance to do so and said bride would finish up with "dress number one". Miss Wightman loved point d'esprit, a fine net with tiny hail spots all over it. Dress number one had a strapless satin foundation underneath a bodice with a very high neck, very full sleeves, and a very full skirt cinched at the waist with a very wide sash that had a very big bow at the back. It was a classic, beautiful gown – an easy formula, a fait accompli. But I felt that Georgina and I had much more to offer. Sometimes, feeling thwarted, I would drop a name or two, mentioning girls who had had dress number one. Melbourne society was quite tightknit in those days, so the prospective bride would usually know the family, and I would win the day with an alternative original design.

I remember a shocking incident with dress number one. I was at the parents' home to dress the bride, tizz the hair and so on. The home was in the leafy depths of Toorak, and the garden was beautiful, occupying at least an acre, if not more. (The house has gone now, and three mock-Georgian monsters stand in its place.)

They had decided to take some photos in this garden. Being unable to resist art directing every detail, I had made big satin bows for the family Labradors and went out to check the scene. It was a stinking hot day, and the lawn was covered in thousands of tiny flies. I belted back to the house and told them the situation. However, the photographer insisted he knew best and, no matter how much I pleaded, he refused to budge. You can imagine what happened next. The dress filled up with thousands of tiny flies whirling around in the layers of net. The hundreds of hail spots had corresponding black spots – except that the latter were in a trapped frenzy. Thinking that I was attacking the favourite daughter, the Labs got overexcited and lost their bows as I swatted away furiously. I tried everything to get those flies out. A vacuum cleaner helped a bit, but their little wings got stuck in the holes, and I just couldn't shift them. They flew around furiously for hours.

"What's that humming?"

In the finished album, the photographer fogged out the flies, so the photographs didn't look so bad. But the swarm took the enchantment

out of that wedding. Rimsky-Korsakov's *Flight of the Bumble Bee* might have been a more suitable wedding march.

〰〰〰〰〰〰

Here comes the bride …

Lovely to see
Marching to thee
Sweet love united for eternity.

Eternity? Somehow, I don't think so. I can only think of a handful of my brides who are still with their grooms. I did a few of my first brides' second weddings and at least two of their third.

What is it about a wedding? Is it a fragile faith in true love? The yearning that Jay felt for Daisy in *The Great Gatsby*? The one particular person who can fix what's missing? The illusion of a perfect match and happy-ever-after?

Or is it just another opportunity to dress up in a new frock?

Postscript: Job Warehouse

Job Warehouse was an excellent source of fabrics. Having started in business before the Second World War, it has been closed for the past twenty years or so now. The windows didn't change for forty years, so you could see things that I remembered from my student days. Since vacated, this rabbit warren of a shop with storerooms occupied some of the most valuable real estate in the Melbourne CBD; I was always risking life and limb to find fabrics and other things for my various projects. Actually, I must have known about it before art school, as that's where I bought the hanks of black raffia that I used to make Cleopatra wigs for my fourteenth-birthday "stage spectacular".

Rumour had it that a prominent Jewish family in the schmutter business kept it going to give a mad old uncle who had survived the Holocaust something to do. And mad he was! He was always ranting and raving and throwing people out onto the street – but only if you didn't know how to handle him. There were rooms and rooms of treasures. Rolls of fabric, some of them pre-war, reached right up to the ceiling, but you couldn't get past the old tyrant to reach them.

The very worst thing you could say to him was that you were "just looking".

"Looking, looking. I am not for looking. I'm for buying. Get out!"

One of my approaches was to give him something specific. I would say, "I want to buy six yards of emerald-green satin with little red ladybugs embroidered on the border." Happy as a sand boy, he would go off hunting for it, leaving me plenty of time to scramble around in rooms that were out of bounds I would find marvellous things. Sometimes, he would come back with the emerald-green satin with embroidered ladybugs, and you would have to buy it. Still, it was always worth the risk for the true treasures your archaeological excavation had unearthed. When there were several of us, the other ploy was to get the prettiest girl to flirt with him. He always fell for this one. The girl would have to give him a kiss on the cheek. If we took longer than expected, he would also get to pinch her on the bottom.

For years, I continued to buy marvellous material using my diversionary tactics. For $2 a metre, I sometimes bought wonderful things that looked like they cost hundreds – probably the only occasions when I made a profit. I only got caught once. When I was at a formal party and had a little too much to drink, a client waltzed up to me in the beautiful gown of rainbow tulle that I had made her and announced to her circle of admirers that I had bought the fabric in Paris just for her.

"No. No," I blurted out. "I didn't [slurring]. I got it at Job Warhousshhhe."

I had a lot of explaining to do the next day. Fortunately, Job Warehouse was a little-known secret, and I convinced her that I meant "Avenue Jacob Housseur", just off the Avenue Foch.

I hadn't been to Job Warehouse for years, and the last time I did go, there was no sign of the old uncle. Someone who could be a mad nephew seemed to be in charge. As I left, I heard him berating an obvious fashion student in search of a treasure.

"Looking, looking. I am not for looking. I'm for buying."

25

Going Solo

I loved working for Le Louvre. I had a great interaction with the clients and managed the workroom quite efficiently. I worked with beautiful clothes and still was able to express my creativity. My private life was entwined with Georgina and her circle of friends, and we had enormous fun working and living in each other's pockets.

In a few short years, my relationship with her had reached a very intense stage. As well as being quite confused with my prospects and the path my life was taking, Georgina had become so reliant on me that I had to ring her to wake her up first thing each morning. The routine became ridiculous. She wouldn't get dressed until I had chosen her wardrobe, and I would sit on the edge of her bath and supervise the hair and make-up.

We had a very dear mutual friend called Doozi. Georgina had gone to art school with him. Even though he didn't like me at first – because I had grown so close to Bubby, as we called her – I eventually became friends with him too.

Telling me that my situation was going nowhere, Doozi badgered me to leave Le Louvre and go out on my own. So, that's what I did – in most harrowing circumstances. Georgina and I had a drink in the office after work one night, and the cord was cut. She sat there at her desk, fiddling with an unsigned check. I don't know if she was going to offer me an incentive to stay, and I often wonder what I would have done if she had. Soon afterwards, I left for my first overseas trip, not having any plan as to what I would do on my return.

Back in Melbourne, Doozi was very helpful, drumming up business for me. There wasn't a friend of his who he didn't coerce into having a new party frock or something made by me. Gradually, through word of mouth, my name became well known, especially among well-dressed Jewish women. They set me on the path of creating some of my most beautiful weddings, as well as dresses for many of the glamourous bar mitzvahs that Melbourne hosted. That said, my clientele came from every creed and stratosphere. I became close friends with a few and retained treasured memories of all of them – the Good, the Bad and the Ugly.

Georgina didn't speak to me for years as she was heartbroken by my "betrayal". She accused me of stealing clients from Le Louvre, which I didn't. On the contrary, I turned down clients I had become very fond of there over the years.

Although painful, the break was as necessary for her as it was for me.

Incidentally, I later found out that Doozi was duplicating my ridiculous morning wakeup calls to Georgina, as was Kent when he came on the scene!

26

Twelve Sleeves

I was rudely awakened by a call early one Monday morning. Some chap asked me how busy my schedule was and if I could do a wedding in two weeks. Somebody had already made dresses for his bride to be and her bridesmaids but he didn't like them. He had heard, in his words, "You are the best" and wanted to start again. Being early Monday morning and having had only a few hours' sleep (Sunday night was a big night on the disco circuit), I was hardly sensible and replied, "Yes, I could". With no time to waste, he suggested a meeting at 10 am. Having no idea what time it was (8 am, in fact), I suggested 1 pm.

Driving up to the large Toorak mansion that he nominated, I recalled that it had once been the childhood home of a friend of mine, but a designer of the moment had recently given it a total makeover. I was ushered into a small, dark study/library. It was all ebony and chocolate, with suede sofas, smoky-glass coffee tables, antique leather-bound books and a big vase of intoxicating lilies. I sunk deep into the suede and took in the various "vinaigrettes" (as I like to call them) that the designer had arranged for just such an opportunity as a 1pm appointment.

On the largest coffee table lay an open book about Rembrandt. Next to it – on a small, gilt artist's easel, lit by a single spotlight – was a little framed drawing. Sure enough, on cross-referencing, the book and frame displayed the same drawing.

"Hmmm!" said a thought bubble. "Put your price up and don't *um* and *ah*."

I was then summoned into a larger study/office, which was as white and bright as the other was brown and dark. The future groom was sitting in a giant swivel chair behind an enormous, white marble-and-chrome desk. Hanging on the back of the chair was an exquisite gamine-like creature. She reminded me of the French actress Jean Seberg. (Seberg was an American actress, but I think of her as French because she was a bigger star in France.) This was the future bride, and she may as well not have been in the room at all. After being introduced, she played no part in the interview; she didn't utter a word. Meanwhile, the groom moved from one end of the desk to the other, dragging her back and forth as he did so.

He explained that he wanted something sexier than the boring dress she had chosen. More explicitly, he wanted her to look like she was wearing almost nothing. Being quite unambiguous, he wanted to be able to get at her pussy without too much messing about. "Easy access," he intimated. "Before, during and after the service." She giggled and tousled his remaining hair.

"Do I have the dress for you!" I exclaimed, trying not to look shocked. "I'll be back in the morning with sketches."

The wedding dress that I had in mind had caused a minor scandal at one Le Louvre parade. I had made several modified versions since then, but here was my chance to pull out all stops. I thought a silk taffeta dress with my (current) signature sleeve would be just right for the bridesmaids. I was back in the morning with the drawings. The bride to be wasn't there, but the groom was thrilled with the slit (slut) skirt and backless, frontless, barely covered bodice. I had to get a move on, so I asked when I could take the girls' measurements. He had already arranged that for 6 o'clock that evening.

He didn't ask the price at that appointment, and she didn't ask about the dress.

"Don't you want to know what it's like?" I prompted her.

"Oh, okay."

I showed her the drawings. She liked them – just as the bridesmaids liked the dresses in white Valentino taffeta that I had designed for them. One girl was quite relieved, as the previous dress had been a shade between cobalt blue and ultramarine, with a beaded belt. I didn't have the usual sizing problems as they were all almost perfect size 10s – I could have cut identical dresses, and they would have all fitted, even if mixed up. But the girls were all divine and would have looked stunning in anything. Miss Seberg was fabulous, with a figure like a boy – quite narrow through the hips – but with a perfectly exquisite bosom. I made an appointment with her for Thursday and the bridesmaids on Saturday.

With so little time to complete the job, I must have been totally loopy to take it on. I had to get some help, so I rang my ex art-school teacher, five-carat Margaret. Luckily for me, she was going through a dry spell and promised to come in the next day. She drank! I didn't waste any time and stopped to buy the fabric at La Modiste on the way home. There was just enough taffeta for the six bridesmaids' dresses. Because I could cut that design with my eyes closed, I set to work for the rest of the day. I wanted them cut and ready for Margaret the next day.

"There are twelve sleeves here," she exclaimed incredulously when she turned up. I hadn't told her the whole truth – nothing about the number in the wedding party, nor the date (which was only eleven days away). She had a minor conniption and had to sit down to take it all in. I told her not to worry – *I* wasn't.

"I know I can do it. *We* can do it!"

She got down to it, separating the sections and grouping sleeves, bodices and skirts. I was a bit fazed, I must admit, when I saw six white taffeta mounds taking up the entire cutting table. Anyway, I started on the wedding dress. It was extremely fragile based on a bodice of silk net and had to be handled with the utmost care. One mistake, and you would have to start again. Because the bride was an almost perfect size 10, I was confident that I could fit the dress to my dummy; it would need few if any adjustments, so I charged on regardless.

For the first fitting, the dress consisted of a long-line bodice of a single silk net with a very narrow under-skirt of the finest Racine silk jersey. This narrow cylinder of an under-skirt fell from just above the area of the groom's specific erogenous concerns. At the back, it flared to a train. At the front, it split in two, almost from the point where it began.

Of all the naked women I saw over the many years I made frocks, this bride was one of the most perfect. With flawless skin that softly embraced a lithe, fit and sensuous frame and not one ounce of fat, she was like a live commercial for Cashmere Bouquet soap, Nivea cream, Dove moisturiser and Oil of Olay all rolled into one. Her sensuality balanced Essence-of-Whore with an ambiguous, boyish and raffish innocence – the two blending into elegant femininity. There was no hint of the anorexic, baton-like body that so many young women aspire to nowadays. Although I had finally realised my sexuality, even *I* had stirrings.

Once an aspiring model, she had been badly disfigured in a motorcycle accident. Whoever was her plastic surgeon must have been a genius. On close scrutiny, you could find a few scars, but they only added to her allure. Scraps of gossip about her previous membership in a notorious motorcycle gang fuelled my imagination. I envisioned her as a contemporary Helen of Troy, battles being fought over her in amphetamine-strewn carparks in Sunshine or Broadmeadows – speed-freaked rival gangs striving for supremacy, with her as the prize.

The fitting went perfectly. I explained to the bride that what she was trying on was only the shell of her dress, and there would be several more layers. Yet, she still expressed the opinion that it was too rude – even for her. The bridesmaids' dresses came together like a dream, with few alterations needed. I didn't have all six dresses for the fittings – I just used the one dress several times, taking out each previous set of pins before the next girl.

With only five days to go, Margaret started to panic. She couldn't see how we could possibly get the job finished without moving into top gear, so she decided to move in to my apartment at Avoca Street. We made up the Biedermeier sleigh bed for her in the main salon, and we worked all day and into the night as the deadline approached.

As per Murphy's Law, something that could go wrong did go wrong. As I was appliquéing a delicate swirl to one sleeve, everything went down into the guts of the mechanism in the sewing machine, where it got chewed up and covered with oil, requiring a whole new sleeve at the twelfth hour. Fortunately, it was done in time for the final fittings on the day before the wedding.

Everything was perfect. The bride's dress looked like it was melting on her body and would drip off any second, leaving a puddle of giddies and swirls. With oversized ruffled sleeves like outstretched wings, the bridesmaids reminded me of a flock of white doves – fussing, preening, billing and cooing – all more interested in how *they* looked rather than the bride, the fitting object of attention.

Paying no heed to superstitions about seeing the dress before the big day, the groom was delirious about the final presentation. In a trial run of his anticipated moves at the nuptials, he groped at various parts of the blushing bride and was more than satisfied at the easy access provided by the design. He handed me a large wad of cash, which I counted on his insistence. I couldn't wait to get home and count it again. Before I left, though, I had a sneak preview of the décor, as the wedding was taking place at the house.

Kevin O'Neil, Melbourne's number one florist, had pulled out all stops. In the garden, the swimming pool was full of white waterlilies, and urns spilled out trails of orchids. Throughout the house, tall crystal vases held towers of oriental lilies and roses, bouvardia and tumbling showers of stephanotis and jasmine. Gardenias filled shallow bowls. The mixture of perfumes was heady and intoxicating.

The next day, I was there early (well, on time anyway) to put the finishing touches together. As I placed a single layer of silk veil over the bride's simple haircut, I was thrilled with the effect. It was one of the most sensational wedding parties I had ever made.

Stories and gossip abounded for days after. Apparently, the groom allowed his bride's former motorcycle gang to pay their respects. On Harley Davidsons, they roared through leafy Toorak and into the garden, wished her well, toasted her with Veuve Clicquot, and roared off after half an hour.

Maybe the groom should have paid attention to superstitions about seeing the dress – or perhaps the dress itself was to blame – but rumour has it that the groom expired "on the job" (as the saying goes) during the first week of the honeymoon! Months of speculation about foul play and wills followed. Apparently, there was a prenup. She had to be married for a period of at least five years before becoming a beneficiary. After an indecently short period of mourning, the grieving widow married her deceased husband's business partner.

I wasn't called upon for another gown, and I was disappointed to never see her again. I thought I had a client for life! But my hopes were dashed with the demise of my patron, the deceased. I did see her again years later, a trail of chequered misadventures in her wake. The most scandalous being when she dumped drug lord number two and ran off with a notorious queen. They fled to the country and established a horse stable, breeding polo ponies. She had filled out a bit and was almost matronly wearing a Chanel suit!

27

Money No Object

As an opening gambit, one couldn't hope for a better prospect. As far as Melbourne Wasp weddings go, this was a significant date to be circled on the calendar in the hope one would be included in the guest list.

While not old money, the groom's family were prominent in the town; some, though, thought the girl to be a bit of a scrubber. Her step into Melbourne society was aided by the indisputable fact that she was a ravishing beauty and had a vivacious personality. Obviously, she was being groomed to fit smoothly into the family's hospitality empire; an upfront asset like this girl could be seen as a valuable investment. The first interview was with the future mother-in-law, so I don't know if the bride assumed that's who would be paying the bill, but when the question of the budget was brought up, the future mother-in-law's response was, "Money is no object". My eyes lit up and my imagination ran wild. I designed a fabulous gown influenced by Auntie Lorna's entry in the Gown of the Year all those years before. It was knee length at the front and swept into a train at the back.

The fabric was again from Valentino, a pure silk taffeta overlaid with the matching organdie. The colour was somewhere between clotted cream and the palest banana. The dress was strapless with a tiny jacket that carried through the skirt's design: an explosion of pleated organdie fans. I think I should have received an engineering degree for the complexity of construction required by the execution of the design. The underskirt had a boned and hooped undercarriage worthy of one of the grand dresses of the court of Louis XIV. I spent hours underneath it, flat on my back, during the fittings, like a motor mechanic reconstructing the transmission on a souped-up roadster. It was weighted and balanced so that it sat perfectly, and didn't gather momentum and sway to and fro when the bride swept down the aisle. It stood up when it was off the dummy. The hundred or so fans that made up the skirt were circles and half-circles of crisp organdie and were all hemmed by hand before being sent off to the pleaters. They were then sewn onto the taffeta underskirt, again by hand, as you couldn't get anywhere near the machine with my engineered fabrication. It reminded me of the Sydney Harbour Bridge from underneath; all that was missing were the rivets. Once it got going, it had a life of its own: it crossed the room by itself once when I knocked it off the cutting table. Hours and hours went into creating this beautiful gown.

But I was only interested in the look and didn't fully think out the consequences. I was also making the outfits for the bridesmaids, the matron of honour, the flower girls, the page boys and the future mother-in-law. Everything in the entourage was a variation of the Valentino taffeta and organdie. The outlay for the fabrics alone ran into the thousands of dollars. I never dreamt of asking for a deposit, thinking there would not be a problem.

Although everything ran fairly to plan, I had to put my head down and bottom up. The fittings went well, and everyone seemed delighted, except the future mother-in-law – who, when her dress was finished, decided she didn't like it and wanted changes. Her dress was in two pieces, with a sunray pleated skirt and what essentially was a short-sleeved T-shirt. The fabric was navy chiffon that was stripped and shot with multicoloured

lurex. The T-shirt was solidly beaded in all the colours. It was very simple and over the top at the same time. I loved it and thought that, for once, this woman, who had a reputation for tending to "gild the lily", looked elegant and chic but with an added luxe touch. Three days before the wedding, she decided she wanted a ruffle around the sleeve and the simple T neckline made into a deep plunge, also with a ruffle. I couldn't believe what she was demanding, and we had a huge fight, she making all kinds of threats. I refused to ruffle up in compliance, and words flew around like daggers. Eventually I threw her out. My last words to her as she yelled, "Where am I going to find a dress, with three days to the wedding?" were "I don't care."

She went straight to Le Louvre and found a dress with the ruffles she was after. Alarmingly it had see-through lace panels that revealed her panties. It was cream crêpe de chine and designed by Karl Lagerfeld for Chloé – a stunning dress, but a little "mutton dressed as lamb" on her. Come the day of the wedding and, although the dresses were complete, some hand finishing still needed to be done. I was running late and by the time I tore into the tree-lined avenue of the bride's parents' suburban home with all the dresses, there was a palpable air of panic.

The bride was standing in the middle of the road in her dressing gown. With a head full of hair rollers and a face mask, she stood one arm raised, shielding her eyes like a midshipman on the lookout for land; luckily, I just missed her. The one complication that I hadn't foreseen was that she couldn't sit down in the dress. She could sit, but when she did, the skirt sprang out in one direction or another, often up over her face exposing more than anyone but the groom should expect. The problem was the seating arrangements at the bridal table, and I suggested they get a stool that could slip under the dress.

Unfortunately, down the chain of command, a bar stool instead of a small stool was delivered, and it was the most unusual sight as she towered above the rest of the bridal party. The consensus was the wedding was a triumph, and I had lots of feedback from clients who were at the wedding. The panties got tongues wagging and, as no one knew about the fight with the mother-in-law, I spent some time explaining and denying responsibility. I could finally sit back and take a break, clean up the chaos resulting from the previous weeks of toil, and prepare to start on the next undertaking. I sent off the invoice to the bride's parents and, as a special treat, took myself to a matinee. I think it was the latest James Bond movie.

The explosions and mayhem on screen were no comparison with the to-do that resulted from the presentation of my bill. The parents obviously presumed that the mother-in-law would foot the bill for the wedding, as she had orchestrated every aspect of the spectacle: the dresses, the flowers, the cars, the reception. I had never met the mother of the bride until the last fitting. They offered me $500 for the wedding dress, saying that's what they thought my dresses cost, while the base cost of the dress exceeded $1,000 in just the fabric and the pleating. The mother-in-law, who by now absolutely hated me (and who could blame her?), refused to be drawn into the matter and denied any knowledge of the "Money No Object" scenario. My friend John Potter offered one suggestion to their claims that they couldn't afford to pay my account, which was for them to sell their house. We all got a laugh out of that one! I can't remember the final arrangement that we came to, but I lost money on the deal, learned a valuable lesson and never let any presumptions on anyone's behalf hold sway. I had an act of final revenge when I sold the navy beaded dress to one of the mother -in-law's social rivals, who wore it to much acclaim during the next round of Toorak parties – much to the chagrin of the old dame, who didn't dare show her panties again.

28

Brides

I often wonder what happened to a certain bride with no groom. I had an appointment with a very brusque-sounding young woman for an early-evening appointment. She was short and swarthy, with thick curly black hair and two eyebrows on a collision course to become one. Her name was Greek, and she looked the part. She wanted an engagement party dress and a wedding gown. When quizzed about dates, she was evasive – six weeks would be fine for the engagement dress, and there was no hurry for the wedding gown. There would be a suitable period after the engagement, she joked. But it wouldn't be a shotgun affair.

Some information, however, she gave up without prompting. She was a solicitor, had her own business and had just paid more than $1.5 million for a large house up the street (top dollar in those days). Yet, when asked specific questions, she didn't answer, was very vague or threw a question back at me as a diversion. About the bridesmaids, she said that she hadn't decided on the final party. She also said that I was expensive (although I only charged $500 for bridesmaids), but not out of the question.

I didn't foresee any problems in coming up with a suitable design. She had a good little figure. Although diminutive, she was in proportion and had no heaving bosoms or tummy rolls to disguise. For the engagement, she decided on a one-shouldered, long, navy-blue taffeta dress, a variation on a black evening gown that I had trotted out a few times. The high ruffle on one shoulder always gave the body some extended length, as did the long slit in the skirt. For the wedding dress, she wanted taffeta again, this time with a draped, crossover bodice, quite a plunging neckline, dropped waist, full skirt to the back and somewhat inflated sleeves. Ivory, rather than white, was a flattering tone for her complexion.

The fittings went well. The navy dress was very becoming and the wedding dress most elegant. As often happened, she relaxed and, after subtle hints, she decided to have the eyebrows shaped and her hair layered in a tousled style off the face for the big day. A bouquet of gardenias was suggested, with a few placed in her chignon to finish the picture.

When both dresses were finished, she seemed in no hurry to collect them. Although *she* was in no hurry, I *was*. I lived a fairly precarious hand-to-mouth existence at the time, and the rent was due. She paid in cash when she did finally pick up the dresses, so I opened a bottle of Champagne and made a toast to her and her fiancé. She choked and spluttered. After recovering, she giggled nervously and confessed that she didn't have a fiancé. But she was a woman on a mission and had everything planned – even schools for the children she was going to have with the man she hadn't met yet. Jokingly, I asked about the honeymoon. In all seriousness, she said she had chosen the exact villa at the Hotel Bora Bora in Tahiti. She just had to fill in the dates.

Not knowing what to say, I wished her luck and hoped everything would fall into place. Not long afterwards, the economy experienced a bit of a slump. When driving past her house, I noticed that it was up for auction. I rang her office number to enquire and found it was no longer connected. I never heard from her again. I can only hope that her plans and dreams were fulfilled. How awful if her ivory dress turned yellow waiting for an outing from its calico bag!

Some brides-to-be have been dreaming about their big day since they were little girls. There is nothing more devastating than to have those dreams shattered. I am afraid I have been guilty of undoing dreams a couple of times. All the same, I have no regrets – the results exceeded what anyone (including the perpetrator) ever imagined.

One starry-eyed bride came to me clutching a scrap of guipure lace that she had carried around since her teens. Although it was rather grey and grubby, it was to become the dress of her dreams. The nature of the lace dictated the style – constructed, fitted waist, full skirt. Yes, I could find it! If not the exact one, then one almost the same. Delirious with delight, she floated out of Avoca Street, her dreams about to be realised.

My gut feelings are usually correct, and they were telling me that this material was not right for this girl. I had a length of beautiful pale-gold lamé that I had bought in Paris a few years earlier. It looked like the covering on a heavy ottoman, but it fell like liquid metal when draped on the bias. When she came the next week to see the designs, I had draped a length of almost identical lace from La Modiste on the Biedermeier sleigh bed. She flipped when she saw it; it was exactly what she wanted. I excused myself – I would be back in a minute. On return, I unfurled the length of gold like Priscilla, Queen of the Desert.

"This is what you should have."

To say she was taken aback was a mild understatement. While she stood in front of the mirror, I draped the fabric over her and showed her my design, the antithesis of everything she had ever dreamed about since age fifteen. It was an empire-style, bias-cut dress with a deeply scooped neckline and long, tight sleeves. A drape fell from under the bodice, which was solidly beaded in pearls and gold.

Unfortunately, it was well over her budget. I apologised for shocking her, explaining that I hadn't been able to sleep, so dismayed I had been at the idea of her in the guipure. I thought she was going to burst into tears, and I was right. When she regained composure, she exclaimed, "I love it." We both burst into tears and the journey towards the aisle from that day on was a dream. The dress turned out brilliantly. She was thrilled, and I like to think that I uncovered a different side of that starry-eyed girl who came in clutching the grubby piece of guipure.

One of my favourite wedding gowns was made for a good, down-to-earth Aussie girl whose parents owned cherry orchards. My design was a Grace Kelly–inspired gown, like the one she wore to get married in the film *High Society*. It was white organdie with multiple layers of circular skirts. I hand-painted bunches of white-on-white cherries on it. Everything went smoothly, and the dress was divine. For the mother of the bride, I found a Valentino crêpe de chine festooned with cherries and emerald-green ribbons.

Come the day for the final try-on, and mum and daughter arrived with bright-red hands. (It was the beginning of the cherry-picking season.) Mum was okay because her dress had sleeves, and she could just buy some short gloves over the counter. But the bride was cherry-stained to the elbows, and her dress was strapless. Elbow gloves being impossible to find, I spent the next two days hand-sewing some. After the wedding, the only way she could get her ring off was to cut off one finger of the glove. All that work was wasted!

Inspiration is a tricky thing. Sometimes, it comes in a flash. Other times, it never comes. Some brides just don't inspire.

Once I had a bride who sent me numb at first sight. I have no idea how she got my number, as most referrals came word of mouth. At the given time, she arrived with an entourage. It was the closest I have ever come to a panic attack.

Let me set the scene. My Avoca Street salon was at the top of a large Victorian house with all the trimmings. Before you got to the front door, you had to negotiate iron-lace verandas and an elaborate iron-lace stairway at the entrance. Then one and a half flights of stairs to my main room, which I called the "Frock Shop".

This girl arrived with her mother, grandmother, sisters, best friends with babies in arms, another baby in a pram, plus a neighbour. There must have been at least eight people in all. They decided to bring the pram all the way to the top, even though I suggested leaving it on the landing. Getting the grandmother in was more challenging than the pram. My first thought was, "What if she carks it?" I finally got them settled in different spots around the room. Everywhere you looked, there was someone: on the Biedermeier sleigh bed, the Madame Récamier, the sofas, the armchairs, the dining chairs. They surrounded me. I felt like the ringmaster at a circus. Looking around, I couldn't pick which one was the bride – there was not one young, fresh and innocent face to be seen. Meanwhile, they all looked at me, waiting for my act to begin.

"Bring on the tigers!"

They were not the type of clientele I usually catered for. There were two tracksuits and at least one pair of Ugg boots! Where on earth had they come from? Broadmeadows, Frankston, Rowville? Ah, Essendon! Yes, there was quite a bit of money in Essendon. Had they come through my friend, Maree O'Brien?

I didn't know what to do! How could I get out of it?

When I established who the mother was, I thought I would start with the budget. She wasn't fazed by my price. Bugger!

The date of the nuptials? In twelve months!

I seized on this and said I was sorry, but I was going to Europe in two months and would be away for three months, so there was not enough time to do it before I left and not enough when I got back as I had a booking then already. I said that I wished they had told me before they had made the appointment and not wasted their precious time. "I am sorry. Thank you very much."

Well, they didn't react. They just sat there. Were they waiting for the clowns?

"Well, thank you again," I said. "I hope you find someone who can help you. Good luck."

Still, they sat. The baby in the pram woke up, screaming. They all looked at one another, not grasping the situation. Then they all looked at me expectantly, as if I'd been joking.

"Let me help you up," I said, pulling on the old woman, who was sinking slowly into the Biedermeier sleigh bed. I had to get them moving. Unfortunately, it took about half an hour of awkward silence to get them out.

When I returned to rearrange the seating plan in the big top, I took a peep over the balcony. They were still milling around the front gate with bemused looks. I think it was during one of those periods when Georgina and I weren't talking. For a moment of spitefulness, I thought of sending them to Le Louvre. But I knew she didn't have enough zebra sofas to seat them all, and even I couldn't be that mean to Georgina (or *them*, for that matter).

No bride has left me without a tale to tell. I can't pick my favourite over the years. The Mantello girls? The English girl who flew from the Middle East for fittings? The Jewish bride that I made look like something from *One Thousand and One Nights or Arabian Nights*, causing such a stir within the Jewish community? Or my dear friend, Chrissie, who thought it would be wonderful to have her own wedding dress remodelled for her daughter's upcoming nuptials? (Her ex-husband nearly died when he got the bill because remodelling was much more complicated than making a new dress and much more expensive! I often wondered if Chrissy had planned that manoeuvre to get back at him.)

There were happy brides, sad brides, even tragic brides. There were tears, and there was laughter. One bride punched her mother, knocking her for six. One bride nearly killed me with stress. There was one who lost so much weight after the dress was finished that it wouldn't stay up. Another one put on so much weight that the zip burst at the altar.

Not too long ago, I had a call from a girl who cried when I told her I had not made a wedding dress for many years. I had made her mother's dress, and she had been waiting all of her life for me to make hers. That was a hard one. I considered coming out of retirement, but the timeframe didn't work for me.

Who knows? Maybe I haven't lost my touch.

29

Elva

One of my favourite women friends first appeared – as happened so often during my career – as a client at my front door. She had got my name from someone I knew from the disco dance circuit, Richard, who worked at Raymond Castles, a fancy shoe store where she was a huge spender. She wanted an evening gown, something that wasn't so easy to buy off the rack in those days. Richard had warned her of my quirky personality.

"If he doesn't like you, he won't work for you."

Mindful of his words, she had set off with my number and a determination to make me like her. Rather foolishly, she booked an appointment for 9 o'clock on a Saturday morning. Friday night being a big night out on the dance circuit, this had not been such a good idea.

I had fallen into bed at about 5 am. When the doorbell rang at 8, I awoke in a panic. But my watch reassured me that it couldn't be this new client. Feeling relaxed, I threw on a kimono and answered the door. Well, there she was – Elva. Clutching a bunch of yellow tulips, she rattled off an apology.

"I hope I'm not too early."

A bit nervous, she confessed that she was basically a bit of a tart. Then, registering the state of my attire, she realised that she was indeed a bit too early and rattled on a bit more. As I wasn't fully awake, her repeated apologies washed over me, just like the water in the quick shower I took following her admittance to the "Salon". I think she must have been gripping the tulips a little too hard – they refused any sort of guidance, insisting on arranging them*selves* in my vase. But I can't imagine anyone on this earth not liking Elva instantly. She was what is often described as "an original" or "a breath of fresh air".

We talked and swapped a little history, she filling me in on her status as "the other woman" in a marriage. She was going to a ball where she wanted to make a big impression on this man in her life. She wanted elegance and class – two things that she didn't always get quite right in her enthusiasm for life. We made another appointment at a more realistic time.

When she came back, she loved my drawing. It was an elegant black dress in heavy moiré taffeta. An oversized ruffle (like a swelling tide) discreetly followed a high split in the skirt, continued up over her bare shoulders, stood up like a lizard's warning behind her head, and then went on down the back to start again. It was one of my most outstanding gowns – a great success that saw active service for many years and was later borrowed by a whole new generation of her family.

It was the first of many gowns I would make for Elva over the years. She would put up with any discomfort to look good. Often the gowns I made for her were complicated to get into and out of. Some almost required a map and instructions. One solidly beaded dress had a big slit up the side. When the beads slashed her tights to ribbons, she just took them off on the dance floor and continued on. In some of them, she could never go to the toilet without getting completely undressed. And breathe? Who needs to breathe? She had a saying – "If you want to be comfortable, wear a tracksuit!"

Elva lived for the races and was constantly being photographed for the papers and magazines. I made all her outfits for Ascot, and the clothes

I made for her were unlike anything I made for others. Ever prepared to go that one step further, she had the temerity to carry off the many eye-catching outfits we created together.

What I loved most about Elva was her laughter and the funny stories she told about her complicated love affair. She would often accompany her man, Trevor, on his overseas trips and holidays. More often than not, the wife would be up the front in first class with Trevor, while Elva was strapped to the wings.

One such trip to Acapulco was my favourite story. They were all booked to stay at one of those exclusive resorts. When the hotel transport arrived at the airport, she was dismayed to find that only three guests were heading for the resort and there was only one limousine. Thinking a threesome would not be a good idea, Elva held back, determined to make her own way when the coast was clear. Once Trevor and his wife had left, she discovered that not much else was available. So, she flagged down a local bus and somehow made it clear where she wanted to go. The San Malenous bus was only too delighted to help.

Now picture this: a beaten-up, dilapidated, rusty wreck on wonky wheels ... peasants spilling out of every window ... chickens in crates tied to the roof ... a pig ... suitcases groaning at the seams ... boxes with "hot" stereos, fans and microwave ovens from across the border ... a huge bale of hay ... and Elva with matching hot-pink luggage.

Locals and peasants are supposed to stick to back roads, staying out of sight of fancy resorts. The opportunity to see "Los Trios Muchos Grandiosos" resort up close was too good an opportunity to let slip away, so the whole bus whooped with enthusiasm at the prospect of delivering "la Señorita" to her door. They took her to their hearts completely when she enthusiastically joined a rowdy peasant ditty. With an explosion, a cloud of dust, exhaust fumes and a rousing chorus from the squawking chickens, the bus arrived at the resort at precisely the same time as Trevor and his wife. Despite having left the airport area much later, the back roads meant the bus had a shorter journey.

Elva spilled out of the bus, followed by her matching set of luggage.

Trevor pretended not to notice her. But the staff, who had lined up to greet the incoming guests, were captivated by this fantastic apparition. Thus did their love affair with the "Señorita Australi" begin. No matter how low-key she tried to play it, the mariachi band would strike up whenever she entered the dining room. Everyone from the front desk to the gardener would scream out an enthusiastic greeting whenever she appeared. Of course, the star treatment made it extremely difficult for Trevor to pay little visits to Elva's villa mid-afternoon or midnight.

"Who is that outrageous woman?" Trevor's wife enquired.

Back on home turf, the wife eventually found out.

Elva had a falling out with her best friend. This "friend" sent a cryptic note to the wife urging her to "follow the jogger". Trevor had a habit of going for an early morning "jog", during which he would place a brick in a specific place if it were "on" for an early morning "jig". Elva would drive past and, depending on the placement of the brick, either scoop him up or drive on. As it transpired, this betrayal was the best thing the ex-best friend ever did.

A few years later, after the divorce, Elva and Trevor married. They enjoyed a wonderful marriage for many years, sharing true love and joy together, the brick now solidly in situ. I made the wedding dress, of course, and I will never forget the fittings.

In Elva's contentment, she had filled out a little. So, we decided that a girdle was called for on the happy day. The dress was ice-pink silk devoré velvet with a cherry blossom motif. It featured a draped cowl neckline and a narrow skirt with a softly draped swathe on the hip. Trying to get Elva into the girdle was so funny. We bounced around the salon like two mating kangaroos, trying to stuff bits that didn't want to be stuffed into this antiquated figure-firming cincher. We both finished up on the floor in hysterics.

On the day, I made her bouquet and a whisp for her hair, then sent her off looking the absolute picture of blissful elegance.

Elva always described her life as like riding in a lift. She had been to the basement a couple of times and said there is only one way to go from there – she would be happy to take the ride to the penthouse, making all stops on the way. Well, she hit bottom in a very hard way when Trevor passed away. She discovered that he had gambled all the money, and their house had a reverse mortgage with a negative balance.

Luckily, a wonderful well-heeled niece came to the rescue, installing her in a comfortable retirement village. There she struck up with one of the few available gentlemen. They enjoyed several years of delighting in each other's comforts before he passed away and she suffered a series of health setbacks. Because the village would only accommodate residents in perfect health, she had to leave.

Once again, Trina, the niece, came to the rescue, this time installing Elva in a nursing home that was on a par with a five-star resort. Although her health had deteriorated, her personality seemed to shine more brightly. Such was her contribution to the ambience of the home that the management joked about putting her on the payroll. Every day, as if for the first time, she would chat to all the ladies who had dementia, brightening their day. She organised parties and activities.

She complained so much about the food that it improved dramatically.

I was roped in on several occasions. One of the most fun was a pre–Melbourne Cup make-your-own-hat party. I supplied all the materials – flowers, feathers and so on – and several glue guns. It was a riot of a day. I worked harder than I ever had, running from one to the other. I think I actually assembled all the headpieces that day and I was exhausted. They made a film, which the marketing department used in promotions.

Every Christmas, Elva played the Christmas fairy. One year, she rang me to tell me that she would be the Christmas fairy one more time, even if it killed her. I made her the most beautiful fairy dress in red-and-green tulle, embellished with holly and tinsel and a matching magic wand. The party was a great success, so they threw two more for the residents' families and one for all the residents with Alzheimer's.

Another of my best clients also lived in this home, so I introduced them. Their paths would not have otherwise crossed (except maybe in a marquee at the races). Indeed, this other client, who I also regarded as a friend, would have previously looked down her nose at Elva. But in their final social sphere they became the closest of friends. Elva and I dropped in to see her this particular Christmas. She hadn't responded to any stimulation or eaten for days but her face lit up when she saw Elva wearing the fairy dress. She called Elva to her bedside and whispered, "Don't go."

Sadly, not long afterwards, Elva did go. She had a fall, broke her hip and never recovered. But remembering the sparkling smile of this truly remarkable woman will always brighten my day.

30

The Red Dress

In all my years of dressmaking, my instincts were my best guide. I only made mistakes when I allowed others to influence my decisions. Women would come to me clutching photos of dresses, swatches of fabric and sketches of dreams – all dismissed with a flick of the fringe. They would want a blue suit and finish up with a silver evening gown. They were always thrilled with the end product, even if they had taken a somewhat circuitous route to reach it.

When I let several of my good clients have their way a couple of times, the results were disastrous. After a while, the client would come to regard herself as the designer. Against my instincts, I would give way to her ideas and make that elusive dress or blue suit, only for it to be a catastrophe. One such incident involved a bar mitzvah of significant importance. Of course, even the most modest bar mitzvah is important, but this one was a whopper.

Georgina's partner, Kent, used to tell a joke about rivalry within the Jewish community. With everyone trying to outdo each other in extravagance, one man manages to throw the ultimate bar mitzvah –

on the moon! It's a great success and the main topic of conversation. "So Maurey, what did you think about the bar mitzvah on the moon?" someone asks. But all of the fuss has put Maurey's nose out of joint. "It was okay. Not much atmosphere."

Well, this female client had invited hundreds of guests to her bar mitzvah, and she was out to impress. As I had a reputation for churning out a good frock, she had come to me. When she returned to see the sketches of the "black dress" she had requested, she chose a one-shouldered design composed of hundreds of hand-cut petals that diminished in size until they finished at the shoulder. It was made from an embroidered spotted net, each petal sewn on with a diamanté. It was my favourite design, and I was pleased she had chosen it. Measurements were taken, and an appointment for a toile fitting was made for the next week. Then she dropped the bombshell: she wanted it made in red!

A colossal argument started brewing. I tried to explain that the design would not translate to red. It would not suit her in red. It was a black dress only. A foreboding tinkle of the chandelier above warned me that a jamboree of storm clouds was gathering above. Her best friend was with her and supported this transformation to red. (I eventually banned all friends.)

"No!" I stood firm. "It's a black dress, not a red dress!"

The storm broke. Floods of tears and wailing – yes, wailing – beset the salon. She begged, she pleaded; she offered to pay more (a first). She was determined to have red. She had told everyone she was wearing red, the whole theme of the event centred on her in red. The catering, the flowers, the invitations all rotated around RED.

I counter-begged. I pleaded to let me design another dress in red. I had a fabulous idea for her that would knock everyone's eyes out. She wouldn't budge. I didn't want to budge either, but the prospect of this woman standing in tears till midnight saw me capitulate. She had been there for hours and didn't seem to want to leave. I just wanted to get rid of her, so I capitulated.

Later in the week, she returned for the fitting of the toile – a calico version of the dress to be. (This was before I learnt to stretch the process out so that they thought they were getting value for money!) The toile needed only minor adjustments. I even levelled the hem.

I could produce a perfect dress from a toile. I made the dress in red, and it looked stunning, but I just knew it would be terrible on her. When she came for her next fitting, it was finished. I swung open the doors of the frock shop and proudly revealed it. She let out a gasp. It was beautiful. When she put it on, however, my instincts were proven correct. She looked absolutely appalling in it. She got a dreadful shock and stood there in stunned silence for what seemed like hours. I looked up. The chandelier was tinkling. Then she burst into tears. The tears built up into sobs and convulsions. She was inconsolable. I had no idea what to do. In the end, I just put my arms around her and held her until I thought she had calmed down. When I let her go, she copped another look at herself in the mirror and started all over again. I closed the doors to the armoire and suggested that she get out of the dress.

I had noticed that this woman wore a lot of perfume, but as I fitted her for the toile, I observed – or *detected*, I should say – a strong body odour beneath that mask. Because of her anxiety, she had sweated more profusely than usual. Not only was the dress soaked all down the front from tears; it was also sodden under the arms and around the waist from perspiration.

I hid it away. After she calmed down, I said gently, "I told you it was a black dress." Wailing started again. Although it did cross my mind to slap her to her senses, like a scene in a Spencer Tracy / Katharine Hepburn movie from the 1930s, I desisted.

The bar mitzvah was only a week away. What could she do? I said I could make her the red dress I had proposed before, and she reluctantly agreed. I would need a fitting for another toile as this red dress was strapless and slightly more complicated. She agreed to return in a day or two. I immediately ran around to La Modiste, a shop where I bought all my couture fabrics, and bought 6 metres of red heavy silk crêpe. That night I stayed up into the early hours making the toile.

The next day Georgina called to tell me all about what had happened there the day before. My client had visited Le Louvre looking for a red dress and had put one aside. In a hysterical fervour, she had run me down to anyone who would listen, claiming that she would ruin my business and never darken my door again. Later that day, I heard from several other sources that she had been all over town, cornering the market on red dresses. She had two on approval and two put aside.

In any case, I continued to work on the toile, building a bodice that I could use to construct my design. In the afternoon, Elva happened to be passing by and paid me an unexpected visit. She spotted the red petal concoction hanging in the dress shop and wanted to try it on. I tried to dissuade her, but she was insistent. She didn't notice that it stank to high heaven. It fitted her perfectly and looked fabulous on her – the dress needed an Elva to carry it off. She twirled around the room, fluttering the petals the way I had done all those years before with my crêpe paper sparrow's wings. She wanted it; she loved it; she had to have it.

"What's that funny smell?"

I got her out of it quickly. As she sniffed under her arms, she admitted to a busy day. But she was puzzled – she was sure that she had put on her antiperspirant.

When I had completed my toile, I rang my bar mitzvah client and let her know that I had heard what she had been up to. Having no idea that Georgina was my closest friend and that the network of poofs and fag-hags that worked the fashion network had filled me in over the hotline, she vehemently denied that she had been running around town looking for a red dress. Yes, she would come in the morning for a fitting.

I was pleased with the fitting. It was just a calico under-structure. It didn't look like anything, but I was satisfied that it served my goal of giving her support and figure control. She didn't look impressed, remaining silent throughout the process. At least she didn't break down. However, she brightened when I showed her the fabric. It was beautiful, with weight and fluidity, and it looked costly (which it was).

I started the dress. It was all draped from one side, with the folds and pleats from the skirt and the bodice meeting on the hip and caught on the left-hand side in a diamanté bow. It was a masterpiece of construction, each pleat and fold caught by hand on the calico structure underneath. The base, which was boned and stiffened, smoothed out any lumps or bumps that would be accentuated by fabric so unforgiving as the crêpe. When the client tried it on, she was as stunned as before ... but this time with disbelief at how good she looked. I was thrilled; she was thrilled; the whole town was thrilled. The moon had nothing on it.

I had gone out all guns on this dress. I was exhausted, but it was worth it. My reputation was intact. In fact, it had gone up a notch or two, and I had made an unexpected sale with Elva wanting the red petal dress.

I went to the armoire and was bowled over by the pong when I opened the door. I resolved to send the dress off to the cleaners the next day. In the meantime, I hung it out of the back window to get some air.

I proceeded to clean up the devastation I always left in my wake. I hadn't been shopping for weeks, and there was no food in the house, so I decided to treat myself to dinner out after a visit to the supermarket. I was out till late, and on returning home I forgot about the red petal frock hanging out the window.

That night there was an incredible storm with gale-force winds and lashings of torrential rain. It rained all the next day, too, and still I didn't remember Elva's dress. The following day, the sun shone, and about midday there was a ring on the door. It was Elva with some sandwiches and Champagne. She couldn't wait any longer for the dress; with Trevor having had a big win at the races, she had cash.

With a sinking realisation that the dress she was so looking forward to must be in shreds by now, I could only hope that she hadn't come from the car park at the back of the house and seen what was left of it. Keeping her busy setting up lunch, I leaned out the back window and was surprised to find the dress still there. Not only was it still there; it was as fresh as a daisy. In fact, it seemed to have more life. The petals were perky and fluffy, the red was redder than any red I had ever seen, and it smelled like sunshine!

Once again, Elva dazzled whenever she wore it. She never learned the story of that dress, although I'm sure she would have enjoyed it if she had.

31

Mark

The most important man in my life and the determining factor in its path is Mark. It has been so for nearly forty years, and I am writing this chapter on the anniversary of the day we met.

I will never forget the first time I saw his face. I thought I would die on the spot as my heart skipped a double beat. He was the most handsome man I had ever seen. I still feel that today. I think he becomes more handsome as the years go by.

I had been away on holiday in Noumea with my hairdresser friend Peter Fell and his wife, Susan; and friends Peter and Nolly Kordel. We had a ball. I returned on a Sunday feeling totally rejuvenated. I was thirty-two and, having just wasted two valuable years feeling sorry for myself over a broken heart, I thought it was time to start living again. I was slim and had a good tan (I could never get darker than gold), and I was desperate to see my friends. I rang everyone, but no one was home. It was before mobile phones and being available 24/7. I couldn't think where they could be, but I figured I would find them at Pokey's later that night, as that was where you went on Sundays.

Pokey's was part of the Prince of Wales Hotel, a rather rough watering hole in St Kilda in the days before it became gentrified. Sunday night was big. There was a $6 buffet tea, a spectacular drag show, and dancing till the early hours of Monday morning. How we ever got up and went to work, I will never know. Doug Lucas was the MC and the comedy drag relief. With the most enormous glittery lips that never seemed to wear off, he used to do an old Vikki Carr number, *It Must Be Him*, with a telephone where he would whirl the receiver around and tangle himself up in miles of coiled flex. I always found him hilarious.

Wanting to expose my golden tan, I ripped the sleeves and neck from a new black windcheater and off I went, little knowing that the night ahead would change my life forever. Pokey's was packed to the gills with the regulars in their regular spots at their regular tables after they had filed past the bain-marie and plated a roast lamb dinner, chicken in pyjamas or a lasagne. I could never quite bring myself to partake in the offerings, although it did seem good value at $6. My best friend, Graham, and I would usually finish up in Carlton at two o'clock in the morning with a toasted mortadella sandwich and a double chocolate milkshake. Tonight, however, I couldn't find a single person I knew, let alone any of my regular dancing partners. I watched the show from behind a pillar to keep an eye on the door if Graham et al. should arrive late.

After the curtain call, the mirror ball started to spin, the music blasted out at a million decibels, and the party began. I did the circuit and the other room with the piano, where old queens from another era would crowd around the beaten-up old Steinway and sing *Shine on Harvest Moon*. I think I fought my way to the bar and bought a double Cointreau on the rocks – I loved the colour it went in the ultraviolet light – and then cruised around trying to look relaxed. I was ill at ease in situations like this where I wasn't part of a tag team. Trying not to look desperate, which at this stage I certainly was, I circulated and then found a position near the dance floor. I often would dance by myself, but I wasn't quite ready with only one Cointreau under my belt.

If not on the dance floor, I was certainly close enough to feel part of the general swing of things. I was enjoying watching people when I spotted this stunning, slim, dark creature approaching me. He came right up to me and said, "Do you want to dance?" I was so shocked that I turned around, thinking he must be talking to someone behind me. There not being anyone behind me, but still not believing this absolute gobsmacking beauty would want to dance with little old me, I replied, "Who, me?"

"Yes, you!"

I think I swallowed the Cointreau glass and all in an effort to rid myself of it, and we proceeded onto the dance floor to find a spot. I like to think I have a degree of prowess and natural skill on the dance floor. Well, this first hop with Mark was a disaster. I couldn't concentrate, I couldn't hear the music, I couldn't get the beat. I was in a panic that he would clear out at the first chance he saw of escape.

Come a break, he asked me if I would like a drink. Going against the etiquette of such occasions, when you never drink anything more expensive than a beer, I said I would have a Scotch and soda. He was still undeterred. We made our way back to the action, and I started to feel more relaxed and able to dance with him. I still couldn't believe this was happening to me, when my next big concern started to cloud over me. What sort of watch was he wearing?

Now you may begin to be of the opinion that I must be a nut case to even think of such a thing. The most handsome man in the world is interested in me, and I am worried about what kind of watch he is sporting. I have fortunately managed to discard the many phobias and apprehensions that have impeded my perception of the world and the people therein over the years, but I could barely talk to someone if I didn't like their watch. So, there we were, crowded like gyrating sardines, and I am trying to manoeuvre Mark into a position where I can set eyes upon his timepiece. Anyone else would be trying to check out other parts of the anatomy, but no, I am trying to see his wrist.

A very rousing song, a big hit of the day, which funnily enough became "our song", came on and up shot his arms above his head. Thanks to Melissa Manchester and *You Should Hear How [He] Talks About You*, my fears were allayed, and the most elegant of gold watches was exposed on a most elegant wrist. Thin as a gold coin, with no numerals and a fine mesh band. I knew then and there that this man was special. I have kept this watch in a box by the bed ever since. I often think, "What if it had been a Casio digital or something waterproof to a thousand fathoms? How would have things turned out?"

Feeling very reassured as to the calibre of this dreamboat, I was delirious, and we enjoyed dancing and flirting and making eyes and smiles at each other. All of a sudden, I realised the time and said to him, "I have to go." He was absolutely flabbergasted, as I am sure this had never happened to him in his entire life. I said goodbye and started to leave. He grabbed my arm and asked me why. I was reluctant to tell him, and I must have been an absolute fool even to consider the choice I was making.

"They are broadcasting Princess Grace's funeral at 11.30. I can't miss it!"

He held me tighter and whispered in my ear, "I have a television!"

Well, I never did get to see Princess Grace being popped in the ground, and the rest is history.

They have been the happiest years of my life, and I think I love him more each passing year. It is not hard to love him as he is the most beautiful, kind, wise, thoughtful, generous, loving, caring, patient, tolerant and forgiving person, and I am thankful every day for his existence in my life. We have been a good combination and found qualities that have complemented and promoted each other's talents. We have successfully woven a life together that has enriched us emotionally, physically and financially. I think if we hadn't met I would still be running up a frock in a back room overlooking a car park in South Yarra or Prahran.

Nothing Mark ever does upsets me, although it is quite clear many things that I do bother him. I asked him about this once, and he told me that "every day" he lets something that I do go. It's forgotten, forgiven, swept out with the rubbish. The only things that upset me about Mark are things that I imagine. I will sulk and brood over these things until he finally clicks and undoes my knots.

Early in our affair I thought he was seeing someone else. A man would ring and say, "Can I speak to Mark?" If Mark wasn't there the man would just hang up. I was too cut up to ask who it was. This went on for at least a year. It turned out to be his brother who was too shy to speak to me!

I can't pretend that there hasn't been the odd glitch and hiccup over the years, but we have never really fought. There were a few rocky moments early on, and once I remember driving off with him screaming at me as he desperately tried to hang on to my windscreen wipers, "If you go, then never come back!" I did, of course – the very next day.

I think it has lasted so long because I never expected it to last the week, the month, the year, the decade; I am still surprised that I am here. We enjoy each other's company and are happiest when we are by ourselves – not that we don't enjoy our wonderful friends and the world we share. We were never apart for more than a few days until I went to work for Shanghai Tang in Hong Kong; what was meant to be a fly-in-fly-out consultancy turned into a full-time job. The pace and pressure of work and living there started to overwhelm me, and I suddenly realised that time was rushing by, and the one thing that was most important to me was threatened. My life with Mark was more important than the prestige, challenge and excitement thrown my way, so I decided to come home. I didn't want to lose the most important man in my life, the man that I hope to grow old with (Who am I kidding? I *am* old) and love to the day I die. (OMG, that could be any day now.)

My Mark, my true love.

32

Hair

I have never thought of myself as a "sight", a description often used by my mother to describe one whose unusual appearance sets them apart from the crowd: someone odd. She would generally emphasise the degree of the sight with other such sayings, a favourite being "The things you see when you don't have a gun." She made this observation once, not realising that the "sight" in question was, in fact, her beloved son.

My stepfather was working and living in Bahrain, where my mother had joined him, and they were returning home to Melbourne for a visit. I went to pick them up from the airport. Looking back, although bitterly hurt at the time, I can see how my mother could have made such a judgement.

I had not long returned from my first trip to London, where I had fallen victim to one of the trendiest hairdressers of the day. He was Japanese and very creative in styling and pricing. After streaking my long hair, he had proceeded to perm it. This had taken hours, as he'd used hundreds of tiny rollers, and I had an abundance of hair. Looking like Louis XIV revisited, I had risen to take my royal leave, only to be ordered to another

throne, where he had come at me like Edward Scissorhands. All that I had left after he had finished was a bit of colour close to the roots, and the overall effect, although still tightly curled, was of spots. I looked like I was wearing a leopard beanie. Although I had left the salon considerably poorer and in a state of shock, I had grown used to this hairdo by the time I returned to Melbourne, and I liked my new look.

My haircut, however, does not give the complete picture of the "sight" that ran with outstretched arms towards the gobsmacked woman who was wishing she had a shotgun. I was also wearing a full-length fur coat. "So what!?" you may say. Although not politically correct these days, back then, it was quite a fashion statement for a man to be seen in a skin other than his own. Apart from the fact that I was wearing it on a fairly hot day, this particular coat could be described as a "sight" in its own right.

It was raccoon, also spotted, and made me look like a fugitive from a Hollywood college football movie from the early 1940s. Although too long for Mickey Rooney, it could have belonged to him. It now belonged to my friend Doozi. I loved it and would borrow it on any pretext because "I looked so fabulous in it." This return of my long-absent mother seemed the perfect occasion for my newly matching coat and hair to enjoy another outing. As with every other thing I have done to shock my mother in my life, she soon got used to it.

I have done so many things to my hair over the years that it's a wonder that I have any left at all. I have been every colour, length, kink and curl imaginable. Not all of the many different looks were successful. For a few years, I shared my Avoca Street flat with John Potter, who was at the peak of his hairdressing career at the time. I don't know if it was me, or the women, who drove him to early retirement. He was always trying out something new on me, an only-too-willing guinea pig.

John decided my hair needed a few days' rest after one attempt to go platinum blond had gone seriously wrong. The resulting shade could only be described as "chromium yellow". I couldn't be seen in public, as I looked like an escaped, genetically engineered, mutant canary. We worked out a roster system for friends to drop food parcels and other staples such as magazines and gossip. My friend Graham had agreed to do the next drop, and I devised a very amusing mask made from a large supermarket paper bag to wear when I greeted him at the door – he had only *heard* about my hair.

Unfortunately, I had forgotten entirely about making an appointment with a prospective client. It didn't matter to me how rich or important someone was; if I didn't like the look of them, I wouldn't, couldn't, didn't take them on as a client. After this woman had changed her appointment several times, I had lost interest in her and had completely forgotten she was coming. She was very nervous about seeing me in the first place, as she was aware of my reputation for being slightly eccentric. When the bell rang, I put on the bag-mask and opened the door with a grand flourish – "Ta-Da!" – thinking it was Graham. The woman was somewhat taken aback, to say the least, and was not at all reassured that I was perfectly normal when I removed the Safeway bag; she got shock number two with the resonant canary plumage.

After a somewhat awkward interview, she departed, saying she would think about it. I was more than pleased that she did ... and didn't.

The next attempt at platinum was moderately more successful in that the result was interesting. The hair around my neck and ears, being harder to dye, remained dark, and the rest was pure Jean Harlow. The effect was similar to having plopped an English badger on your head.

That evening, I was having dinner at one of the newest, fanciest restaurants in town, Café La, on the top of Melbourne's recently opened Regent Hotel. My darling Margaret would never take any money for all the help she gave me, so I would often take her out for fancy treats. I was aware that a group of serious businessmen at a nearby table had taken an avid interest in me. I overheard one of them say, as I passed their table on the way to the bathroom, "See, I told you it was a wig. You can see his real hair sticking out from underneath".

Peter Fell was one of Melbourne society's golden boys of hairdressing – a friseur extraordinaire. We nicknamed his easily recognised signature style as "Toorak Windy". It was bleached, teased, stood 2 foot tall, and was lacquered to resist a typhoon. Most of Melbourne's society matrons were or had been clients of his at one time or another. He even did house calls. One fabled beauty had her hair done in her bed. There was nothing wrong with her – she just didn't much care to leave it. Peter was Graham's brother, and we often all went out together. At the time, when my hair was very long, we would be out to dinner and he would suddenly get the urge to do something to it, much to the horror of fellow diners. All of a sudden, my hair would be corn-rolled or, all the better, whipped into a French roll if I happened to have a few diamanté pins on me (which was often the case). We would then head off to a club and dance for hours on end. Never would a hair be out of place, no hair spray! – he was very good.

Peter would bring one of his best clients' wigs home to style. His mad Jack Russell terrier would go berserk, swoop them off the table, and take off. He felt particularly amorous towards one wig with blond tips and loved to give it a shag. He would shake the wig furiously while racing around the house, barking and growling until he decided that he had yet another kill under his belt. Then we would find it abandoned by the back door. One went missing for weeks until he went and dug it up from under the azaleas. A dry shampoo and some hot rollers, and the client was none the wiser.

When I worked at Le Louvre, my hair was very smartly styled at Ndumsky, two doors down. (This beautiful copper-fronted salon was pulled down in the small hours of the morning by an unscrupulous developer who knew he would never have been granted a permit to do so. Only the façade of the original Le Louvre building at number 74 remains of the beautiful streetscape that is still called "the Paris end" of Collins Street.) My hair was cut in a very heavy, blunt fringe that hung down over my eyes. I would pin it back off my face as I was working so that I could see what I was doing. Again, the pin was often a diamanté or a silk rosebud on a clip, which I would forget about and then wander off to lunch or the bank and be puzzled by the funny looks I would attract.

I think the only way for a woman of a certain age to wear her hair is long. Drawn up and off the face in a classic knot or French twist is the most flattering and elegant of styles. Miss Wightman's hair was down past her waist and looked fabulous in an Edwardian knot on top of her head. She always amused me when describing going to the hairdresser's as "a visit to the laundry".

I will be eternally indebted to one other head of hair: the flaming red mane of the Duchess of York – "Fergie". It is due to her that Mark and I established our business. I met the lady herself once and she asked me to tell her the whole story, which she had heard about from David Tang. She was highly amused and said she should be paid a commission. I laughed, but somehow I got the feeling that she wasn't joking.

It was at the time when she had just become engaged to Prince Andrew, and the whole country had gone Fergie-crazy. Mark was speaking to a Sydney friend who asked him where her cousin could find Fergie Bows in Melbourne – she was coming down the next day to buy for her fashion accessory company. Mark said that we had them and to come and see us before anyone else. We didn't have any, of course, so I sat down that night at the kitchen table and made ten bows out of old scraps of dresses and anything else I had lying around. When the cousin arrived in the morning, she said they were just what she was looking for and placed an order worth a few hundred dollars. Later that week, Mark said he was going to make an appointment with one of our largest department stores to show them our new venture.

Back then, Mark was working for his cousin's music business – which bored him. So, every now and then, we would dabble in some "little money"–making scheme. Lately, we had been making windcheaters. One night before we were living together, I had been running late to meet him and noticed a few spots down the front of my white windcheater just before stepping out the door. Not having anything else that was as clean, I had taken it off and splashed some coloured inks across the front to hide the stains. Everyone had loved the look, so Mark saw an opportunity and I had started making them. We sold quite a few.

All the same, back to the bows, I, being a total pessimist, told him not to be so stupid.

"Who would be interested in these terrible bows?"

He, being the supreme optimist, ignored me and off he went. He came back with an order for $125,000 worth. We didn't have a clue where to start. It was a considerable number of bows, the most expensive being $5. We conned everyone we knew into action, even finding some outworkers by taking a stab at Vietnamese names in the phone book. One of those girls ended up working for us for over twenty years – Mai became a member of the family and would acquire two houses and a new chin!

Somehow, we got the bows made and delivered. They all sold, and we had a new business. We bought our first house from the profits and have never looked back.

I think the funniest thing that ever happened to my hair was during a trip through the Middle East. Once again, it was rather long. Becoming sick of it in the heat of the desert, I decided that it must all come off. We were in Amman, the capital of Jordan, and staying in the best hotel in town as a reward for having had to stay in several less salubrious establishments on the way. Having made the decision, I set off to find a hairdresser. I didn't have to go very far, as there in the lobby was a fine-looking salon, befitting its setting in a very stylish hotel. A man was fussing around, tidying and sweeping up. Not speaking the language, I made my intentions clear with a series of Marcel Marceau gestures as I sat down in the burgundy leather barber's chair. But he had obviously finished for the day and mimed likewise. "No" may be universal, but it was an answer I wasn't prepared to accept, so I kept on and on, with a few begging gestures thrown in for good measure. With a final shrug and a look of exasperation, he put down his broom and threw a cotton wrap around my shoulders.

What took place next was a fantastic display of dexterity and showmanship. Not since London and the Japanese of a thousand rollers had my hair undergone such attention. He would lunge at it with a tail comb, catch a section and flip it into the air and, before it fell back into place, attack it with the scissors, sometimes taking a snippet and sometimes a chunk. I was most impressed and was enjoying the whole procedure until a man came rushing into the salon. He was squealing like a stuck pig and started beating and cursing this artiste at his work. The poor man cowered and tried to stave off the blows. Finally, he grabbed the broom and fled the scene.

The assailant was horrified and immediately babbled away in German (people always think I am a German). I was so relieved that he hadn't started beating me as well that I started talking, trying to calm him down. He soon picked up and changed to English. He couldn't begin to apologise enough for the regrettable situation, and the man would be sacked immediately. My artiste was, in fact, the hotel cleaner. Such are my powers of persuasion that the poor man had caved in and was just trying to oblige. The real hairdresser did his best to save what was left of my hair. The result was not the most stylish or flattering of haircuts, but it was undoubtedly one of the most memorable.

The one lesson I have learnt over all these years about my hair is the old truism: It always grows back.

33

A Hat Story

For a few years my mother had a job at the Rothmans cigarette factory in Maidstone. It was a security role – her job was to check bags, bras and panties for cigarettes that had "fallen off" the conveyor belt. She worked at some ungodly hour after midnight, checking the female night-shift workers as they signed off. As no one in our family smoked, the job offered no perks except for the marvellous cardboard cylinders that the tobacco arrived in. She would bring them home and turn them into hatboxes. They were made out of heavy cardboard – and I mean bulletproof-heavy – and were the perfect size for hats.

When Celia redecorated her bedroom, she used leftover wallpaper to create her first pair of these hatboxes. The wallpaper design focused on an ivy-like creeper, which didn't cling to a garden wall so much as waft and float around an impressionistic interpretation of bricks. Covered in this artistic triumph by the roll, in shades of grey and lilac, the two boxes that she made doubled as bedside tables, being just the right height. She drilled holes in the lids and inserted mauve silk cord for the handles. This made it somewhat easier to remove the lids, but they were still extremely difficult to dislodge because, in the time that passed after a hat was put to bed, an incredible vacuum would build up. I think scientists might have found answers to the origins of the universe had they studied what went on among those hats between outings.

Because it was so difficult to get at them (removing Excalibur from its rock would have been easier), they didn't play an essential part in my dressing up. However, every now and then, I would make the effort – if only to admire them, as I thought that hats didn't do much for me.

In the 1950s and 60s, a woman wouldn't be seen dead going to town without a hat. Celia had some beautiful ones. My favourite was made of fine straw, with a very shallow crown. Its brim was wide at the front and even wider at the side. In defiance of any sense or reason, it then cut away sharply to almost nothing at the back. This hat also featured a bow (of black velvet ribbon) and a fantastic hatpin (a giant pearl with two bands of diamonds at its base).

At least, I thought they were diamonds. I would sometimes steal this pin for several days at a time, hoping that Celia wouldn't be going out in that hat. It was a great help when securing a veil or an explosion of tulle to Teddy's head. It was also a majestic addition to a crown when Teddy was Elizabeth I. Unfortunately for Teddy, the pin would have to be thrust right into the top of his head, through his neck and down into the body to achieve the desired effect – well worth any discomfort.

Among Celia's winter hats, I awarded the prize to a donkey-coloured felt hat with a wide floppy brim that came right down over one eye. There were also several berets. One was white felt, with a long silk tassel which hung down almost past the ear. It swung from a jewelled dome, reminding me of the Taj Mahal. Another was the softest shade of lilac, with a bunch of velvet violets pinned on the side. Both looked great on Teddy.

Other pieces came with veiling. A collection of flowers or a single silk rose would perch cheekily on the forehead and hold the veiling as it skimmed over the face. It is a look that I have always liked, and for several years I included such pieces when showing our millinery collections. Although slow to capture the imagination of buyers, these precursors to the "fascinator" did eventually sell. In fact, they have made Mark and me a lot of money over the years and are still the rage. Things just go around and around. (Sometimes, I want to give these buyers who know nothing about fashion a good whack. They think they have just invented something. One buyer recently thought she had created the butterfly!)

Celia made many of her hatboxes for friends. She would even sell them at the church fete to raise money for the ladies' auxiliary. As I struggled with those lids, I never imagined hats would play an essential role in my career later in life. I hold no pretensions to being a milliner but I do know that the success of our hat business has sparked envy and disdain among the clique that professes to be so. As with the way our company was conceived thanks to the Fergie Bows, Mark saw an opportunity and took it.

When handmade woven raffia hats were all the rage, he took one to the Philippines and had it copied for a fraction of the cost that they were selling for in Australia at the time. Once again, we cashed in. When buyers showed interest in seeing our better and more formal hats, we turned on that same old sixpence: a few weeks later, there they were. I was relieved that Mark never crossed paths with the whitegoods buyer. Knowing his tenacity, we would have a range of refrigerators, washing machines and dryers before you could say "Energy rated".

No business ever can escape the curse of Murphy's Law. Every year, something goes terribly awry. In the early raffia days, one container arrived full of unblocked and shapeless hats – we had to block them ourselves to get the order delivered on time. One race season, we had exhausted our entire supply of black hats, so we had to call on a local manufacturer to make supplies, only to find that they turned bright red after a day in the sun. During another race season, I spotted a young lass wearing a style that I had bought from the same supplier – it looked like it had melted. Incredibly, she had enjoyed so much Champagne that she didn't even realise why she was crashing into everyone, and everything – her drooping hat had moulded itself over her entire physiognomy!

No matter how much care and time are spent ensuring that the flower matches the feather matches the ribbon matches the straw, all of these components will invariably arrive in different tones. If you are lucky, tonal is fine. It's when they clash that you are really in trouble. I have to admit, though, that some of our best sellers have been accidents.

The Melbourne Cup carnival is a marvellous time and, of course, was a mainstay of our business. It provides women with an opportunity to dress up and wear hats, something rare in today's everyday life. Previously people took more care in their appearance; style and grooming were important. Today we only dress up for special occasions. Thank goodness there are still big public events like the races; otherwise, there would be nowhere to indulge in such pleasure.

Not that I think a matching combination of hat, shoes, bag and Woolworths trolley will ever catch on, but I do despair at the lack of pride that I see everywhere around me. In all the years that I sewed couture, I only made beautiful evening gowns, party frocks and wedding dresses. I often wonder what I would be making today if still in that line.

Has that world gone forever? I don't see it anywhere. Not at the theatre, opera or ballet. When I went to the premiere of a new musical, I sat next to a tracksuit! If you make an effort to dress up, you feel entirely out of place when surrounded by cardigans and sports clothes. "This is the end," I thought.

Will the hat be a thing of the past? Will sunhats only be worn in the desert and on the beach? If the ozone layer is repairing itself (as I read somewhere), will the sun-smart, roll-up beach hat that has been our bread-and-butter line for years become obsolete as well?

Perhaps I should send Mark looking for that whitegoods buyer. I have a marvellous idea: a thought-activated oven that chooses the menu, cooks the dinner, then washes up!

34

Shanghai Tang

What is the right time in a man's life for a midlife crisis? Halfway? If so, where does that happen today? Life expectancy keeps being prolonged as the decades roll on. In the eighteenth century, a fifty-year-old would have been a venerated old man. Nowadays, he is driving around in a Porsche with a trophy blonde wife.

What is a midlife crisis, anyway? When I was about to turn fifty, I wasn't aware that I was going through one. I felt jaded with our business – sick of hats, trims, all and sundry. Our business had evolved into a golden goose. I recognised the benefits that collecting its never-ending eggs had given us. Somehow, though, I had grown tired of it all.

What symptoms was I displaying? Was I crabby, snappy, critical, short-tempered? Did my eyes roll back into my skull at the slightest analysis of my mood?

I don't know why, but much to Mark's horror I went by myself to a "white party". Exclaiming that there was "nothing for me here", I stormed off to find that there was nothing there for me either! I shudder at the thought now – I wore white satin shorts and an ostrich-feather boa, and all I can recall of this party was the cash register in my eyes totting up the number of white feather boas we had sold to that stadium. Soon after arriving, I left – or *tried* to leave, I should say. It was ludicrous. A long queue of spaced-out queens waited for very infrequent cabs. It made me furious that most were heading to the same destination but each taking a single taxi. I thought I would never get home. When the next cab came, I galvanised into action and arranged for the next bunch to share the fare. Unfortunately, I was so clever that I filled this cab and it left without me. Mark decided to do something to rescue me from myself.

The prestigious Hong Kong brand Shanghai Tang had its flagship store in a splendid Art Deco building in central HK, which boasted an equally magnificent and stylish interior. Shanghai Tang was the creation of David Tang, a Chinese entrepreneur who was more English in pretensions, mannerisms and aspirations than any of Monty Python's eccentric characters. His fashion brand was a meeting of two cultural elements – Oriental with a Western slant. At least, that was the concept. David's list of friends was a Who's Who of Anybody Who's Anybody. A trendsetter and a jetsetter, he was one of the world's most stylish men.

Unfortunately, however, his business had fallen into a state of damage control. Although he had been brilliant in conceiving it, I am not sure that he had been wise in his choices of people delegated to run it. A flamboyant but disastrous opening of a New York store didn't help. There was also talk of embezzlement along the way.

A major French conglomerate was in the process of acquiring the company. Our dear friend John Axcel had been appointed CEO and his task was to restructure the company. Somehow, he and Mark decided I would make an excellent design consultant. A plan was put into effect that would see me spending up to a month at a time in Hong Kong, overseeing a design team and planning the strategic focus for its fashion direction. A month or so there (then home for six weeks) sounded great on paper. And the next thing I knew, I was heading to that ex jewel in the crown for English colonialism in the Far East, Hong Kong.

Although David had lost control of the company, he remained as creative director, with the power of veto on all aspects of design. I should have heeded my first instincts: it wasn't going to work. Our design sensibilities were too far apart. Given five objects to arrange on a table, I would most likely devise a group of two and three, whereas he would place all five in a row. Symmetry versus asymmetry.

David took an instant dislike to me. No matter how hard I tried, nothing I did pleased him. From the very beginning, the consultancy plan went flying out the window. Instead, I was hands-on, doing everything – designing the women's and men's clothing ranges, the children's wear, the homewares and gift collections. I had two design assistants and, although they worked diligently and showed great dedication and enthusiasm, the situation was overwhelming.

Meanwhile, David would go on shopping sprees at Etro, Dior and Takashimaya. After an hour's whirl through some elite boutique in New York, London or Paris, he would decide on a whim that we would have to change the collection that we were midway through working on. After discovering a rare thirteenth-century bowl, he would decide that our next tea set would be based on its complex, intricate decoration. It would take us hours and hours to modify the design to fit on a teacup, especially given that the techniques and secrets used on the bowl had gone to the grave with the emperor. He would be outraged at our ineptitude and storm off.

"Cancel the whole idea."

So much time was wasted on futile design exercises. He would bring clothes that cost many thousands of dollars and be furious when our version – which would have to sell for a couple of hundred dollars – didn't look and feel the same. On a rainy day, he would fly through and demand new designs for our umbrellas because he didn't like the ones in the store. Over the next few days, I would then have to drop what I had been working on and design umbrellas instead. No wonder I was always behind schedule! I would have to jump from one thing to another. (The umbrellas were marvellous, by the way. One favourite design was purple with a lime-green lining printed with a forest of bamboo.)

The only blessing was David's constant jet-setting – which meant that he didn't see everything that got through to the stores. And all the things I managed to sneak past him were a success. For a winter collection, I designed beautiful shearling coats in olive, chocolate and steel grey for men and the softest pastels for women. They had raw seams and an unconstructed air about them. They were also very heavy and extremely expensive to produce. In a fit of pique, David flung one to the floor, screaming that they would never sell. They sold out within a week and couldn't be repeated because of the timeframe. He would never admit he was wrong.

On a trip I took to India with Mark, I designed a collection of solid-beaded cheongsams, the traditional Chinese garment. They were unbelievably beautiful and cost next to nothing. A particular favourite of mine was white with a blue willow-plate pattern. A matching little cashmere cardigan was beaded with the same design. Haute couture for a cost price less than US$100! Back in Hong Kong, the team was so excited as we were unpacking the collection of ten that one of the office girls, Lisa, hurriedly modelled them in front of David, still wearing her winter boots.

When he had seen all ten gowns, he turned to me and said coldly, "I don't like the boots."

The collection was squashed. However, when the new London store opened later that year, they were looking for anything to add some glamour, so the ten gowns I had made were resurrected and dispatched there. They sold in the first week for more than $5,000 apiece.

I hand-painted some white organdie jackets with designs like the sacred mountains on Chinese scrolls. Teamed with black satin trousers, these jackets also had black-and-white ostrich feather cuffs. David hated those too, but I snuck them into the store, and someone famous (I think Bianca Jagger) bought one on the first day.

For a winter collection, I teamed gold-flecked fabrics, tweeds and denim with intricately cut leather-and-suede jackets printed with delicate oriental designs in gold. All very subtle and so different from anything Shanghai Tang had shown. Weeks of work had gone into design, fabrication and sampling. David swept into my studio, took one look and told me it was all "Crap, Crap, Crap". We had to start again from scratch, with only weeks to go before the production deadline. Unless he had seen something in a fancy shop, he couldn't accept that it was any good. He had no imagination, and absolutely no faith in me. Perhaps I might have been a bit early, but gold appeared on the catwalks of Paris and Milan two seasons later.

My consultancy turned into a full-time residency, with the trips back home fewer and further apart. After working six full days a week, I would stop for breath on Sundays. There was no time for much of a social life and I missed Mark. It was stressful and not the solution to my problems (even though I hadn't recognised that I had some).

After I left, Shanghai Tang franchises popped up in all the major cities worldwide, and the investors put a lot of money into PR. Flip open any English or Italian *Vogue* at that time and you would see glorious full-page advertisements promoting its image to the world. During my time, though, there was no budget for such things. My right-hand girl, Judith, and I decided that the spring collection was too good to let go unrecorded. Fabulous, lush and extravagant, the collection – including much of the knitwear – featured beading and embroidery.

I had found these terribly kitsch, foam-backed synthetic blankets in the market on an excursion to source fabrics. My favourite had cute lion cubs in a huddle. Others had big fat pandas eating bamboo, horses galloping on a beach or tigers stalking in long grass. The colours were garish – skies in electric midnight blues, moon and stars in fluorescent yellow, greenery like emeralds on crack, and tree bark that glistened like caramelised golden syrup. Imitating the look of velvet pile, these blankets looked as if a fairy had waved a magic wand over them so they could catch the light every which way. This particular fairy being captivated with them, turned them into the most beautiful appliqué padded evening jackets. Using heavy, dulled satin in tonal variations, I coordinated them with slim-line trousers. It was our one and only fashion shoot, and we did it ourselves.

The photography budget just covered two young models. Everything else was up to us. David gave us permission to photograph at the China Club. Being a keen amateur photographer, my colleague Tailor Chu had dozens of cameras, lights, and everything else we needed for a *Vogue* shoot. We had a fantastic afternoon and the results, although nowhere in the Mario Testino league, were stylish. I don't know what we thought we would do with them, but it gave the office and design production team an enormous morale boost to see all their efforts come together.

During my time, the new French owners decided to have another go at New York. A store was found on Madison Avenue. David designed the interiors, and I had to style everything for the launch. There would be no big deal, such as when the original store opened. (Back then, there had been a media frenzy, streets were blocked, and police had to control the chaos.) A crazy system governed budgets in these large conglomerates. Allocations for travel and accommodation were determined in Paris, so we travelled first class and stayed at five-star hotels. But David had blown his decorating budget, so there was no more money to spend on styling the store. In my opinion, lots of things needed finishing, but my every suggestion was greeted with a flat "No".

When I asked who was going to do the window, I was informed that it was me. When I asked how much I could spend, I was told that my budget was zilch! With Christmas nigh, I was gobsmacked. A festive window was the most important one of the year! My hotel room was costing US$800 a night. I offered to move to the WMCA to save some money and fund a Christmas window. That was refused. Then I proposed a fabulous design using plastic bamboo and gold spray paint, which would cost only about $100. Even this was refused. I was just going to do it anyway, using my own money, but I decided it would set a dangerous precedent. Where would I draw the line? In the end, I scrambled around in the basement and somehow made the window look festive and quite stylish.

Even the Duchess of York was impressed. She was a good friend of David's and was in New York. David had told her the story of how Mark and I had started our business with her famous bows. Because she figured so prominently in this tale, she wanted to meet me. So she dropped into the store to say hello, trailed by a large entourage, including big burly bodyguards. I thought she was most charming and I was delighted when she commented favourably on the Christmas window as she left. Years later I met her again and she came right up to me and said "Hello Gregory".

Although David and I didn't see eye to eye, and I found him demoralising and cruel, he could be extraordinarily generous. One day I expressed interest in some of the artists in his extensive art collection. The very next day, an expensive coffee table book featuring many of these artists appeared on my desk. Another time, when Mark was visiting me in Hong Kong, David gave us his beach house for the weekend.

David Tang was granted a knighthood but sadly passed away far too young to enjoy his acceptance as the quintessential Englishman he had always aspired to be. Although my interaction with him was challenging, my admiration for him remains undiminished. He was a man of vision and exquisite taste.

35

The Screensaver

One day, when I was working in Hong Kong, I had an appointment with one of our fabric suppliers. As it wasn't normal procedure for a supplier to visit, I was surprised when an old Chinese gentleman was ushered into my studio. Because he had made the overtures, I had assumed that he would be a young, go-getter type. Instead, in shuffled this cartoon character of a Chinese elder, with a battered old sample case under his arm, bowing, scraping and kowtowing.

At this point, I should describe my studio. I had appropriated a narrow slice of Shanghai Tang's open-plan office by building a partition wall across the window. In the process, I had stolen all the natural light. Unfortunately, it took me ages to twig to how much my colleagues resented this. They had to arrive in the dark and leave in the dark! Anyway, along the partition, I had a high desk. Under the stolen sky, I had a long table with a chest of drawers underneath. The old gentleman placed his sample case on the space that I had cleared for him on the table while I turned my back on the desk, waiting for him to present his range.

Behind me were my new computer and usual working mess. This was my first computer, and I was not savvy about its workings or settings. Tommy, the "IT man", had set it up. Then I had added a personal touch by installing my own screensaver – a painting by Maxfield Parrish, whose idealised paintings and illustrations epitomised the golden era of early twentieth-century neoclassical imagery. I was a big fan of his work. The painting I had chosen was of a nubile youth on a boulder by a gurgling brook in the shade of a magnificent, autumnal oak tree. He sat clutching his knees, modestly hiding his nakedness with perfectly sculptured arms. I had come across this image on a "free" screensaver website with an obvious bent to the homoerotic. While the Maxfield Parrish image was definitely of the biscuit-tin variety, others on this site could only be described as sadomasochistic.

Anyway, old Mr Chen started to show me the selection of brocades, satins and traditional Chinese weaves that exploded from his tiny valise. All the time, he kept looking over my shoulder. After ten minutes, he became more agitated – as did his presentation. The fabric samples flew past me faster and faster, some cascading to the floor. And he would grab each sample card back from me well before I had been afforded the chance to ask about the available colours, content or price. All of a sudden, he gathered up every sample, shoved them back in the old battered case, and screamed, "Not for you, not for you," before running out of the office.

I was dumbfounded. Only when I turned back to my computer could understand what had taken place.

When I had chosen my screensaver, I had inadvertently selected not only the romantic Maxfield Parrish scene but all of the other images as well, in rotation. When the screensaver kicked in, they had appeared, one by one, in a slide show. I didn't regret the choice I had made but innocent golden youth had morphed into a somewhat different male figure – sinister, leather-clad, hooded, oiled, shaved, pierced and tattooed. A photograph by Robert Mapplethorpe! This shadowy macho figure was clutching what looked at first like a baseball bat. To my horror – and obviously to that of the recently departed vendor – it was not a baseball bat but his engorged and glowing reptilian appendage, ornamented with metal studs, rings and leather strapping. The following slide was doubly shocking: two figures in most compromising positions, one on his knees.

I panicked and immediately shut down. What if my rather prudish assistant should walk in and spring me? I couldn't ask Tommy to fix the problem because he was convinced that I was straight. He was always offering to take me out to girly bars in Wan Chai after work and played terrible tricks on me, thinking that I shared his interest. Sometimes I would open my computer in the morning to find images of the straight variety that were just as graphic as those on the illicit gay slide show that had driven poor Mr Chen to flee for his life.

For some reason, everybody else in the office was antagonistic towards Tommy – I was the only one who was nice to him. The truth was, he should have hated me because I had stolen half of his office, condemning him to a tiny envelope, where he sat like a mouse squeezed into a corner. My door had once been his desk! He would sit there at his computer, supposedly concentrating on some technical glitch in the office system. Unfortunately, he had one of those diffusing glass screens on his monitor to reduce glare from the flood of light he had once enjoyed in his former office. In the tiny gap between screen and monitor, I could see a reflection of what he was doing. Most of his day was spent playing solitaire or selecting pornographic images to shock me with first thing each morning!

When I first arrived at Shanghai Tang, I certainly encountered some resistance. The head designer I had replaced was a Chinese girl who was adored by all, and the two assistant designers promptly tendered their resignations in protest. I was the third "Gweilo" in the office, after John and the accountant. Everyone else was Chinese. I didn't understand the Chinese sense of humour ... or lack thereof. Things got really bad when I put a sign on my door as a joke. It was a warning not to enter without a passport (or something along those lines), and it nearly caused the whole office to resign.

I think they regarded my tiny studio as occupied territory and me as a foreign invader. I fought a daily battle with insurgents from knitwear, rebel forces from the sample department, and dissidents from homewares. No one was cooperative, and I found it extremely hard to get things done. I am sure quite a bit of sabotage happened behind the scenes: my designs would arrive looking nothing like the sketch, technical working sheet or even the concept; colours and fabrication would be way off; size and fit, too, even after exhaustive fittings. What to do?

Valentine's Day was upon us, so I went out and ordered a single red rose in a specimen vase for every girl in the office. Now, a single red rose was quite an expensive item in Hong Kong on Valentine's Day, and there were more than twenty-five girls in the office, but my gesture was worth every dollar. From that day on, I had them eating out of my hand. One single girl in her late twenties, who had never received a Valentine in her whole life, cried all morning. Years later, I heard, the dried long-stem bloom still sat on her desk. From then on, I had a marvellous relationship with all the staff, and I spoilt them rotten. They came to me with all their minor grievances. Being a soft touch, I almost ended up as a union boss, sticking up for them in disputes and mediating petty battles.

By tradition, the executive staff took turns to buy "morning tea" for the whole office on Fridays. Usually, people would order something like a coffee and a small bun. Not when it was my turn! People ordered complete meals. The amah would return laden with steaming plastic containers and things tied with string. Multi-layered drinks, jumbo-sized fruit shakes in frosted glasses, iced slushies and pots of tea would finish it all off. An air of contentment would then mix with the lingering aromas in the office. Everyone would come and thank me personally, some enthusiastically but most hesitantly – modesty and shyness being characteristic of their nature. Again it was worth the expense. I never put up a protest because my generosity was rewarded in manifold ways in the long run.

I loved the little custard tarts they make in Hong Kong. It seemed every fourth shop was a bakery, and I would follow my nose like Goofy in a Walt Disney cartoon, floating through the air on the wafting smell of the delicious little gems, drifting through the door just as they emerged from the oven. They would hardly have time to cool down before I popped one into my mouth. I would buy four dozen at a time to take back to work. You could smell me before the lift arrived, and word would be out. Tommy had an extra sense beyond the snout. He would arrive first – just as I was untying the string on the greasy, steaming boxes in the tiny kitchen.

"No, Tommy. I don't want to go to an XXXX DVD shop after work. I don't need any more tarts. There are enough here to keep me happy." Off he would swagger, giggling at the prospect that one day he would win me over. In the meantime, he would settle for a sweeter tart … of the custard variety.

36

The Dress that Never Was

This is the story of a little boy and his dreams. He lived most of his life in a dream; his daytime dream was a pleasant one, his sleeping one was a world mostly of beauty and fantasy but on occasion it was dark and frightening.

As a child I had a recurring nightmare. It would wake me, and I would take off sleepwalking until I found myself standing by my grandmother's bed. She would sense my silent presence and wake up, then gently lead me back to bed with comforting words and cuddles.

I can vividly remember this dream. I was walking and constantly glancing behind me as I knew I was being followed. A tiny chicken, like those little ones made out of yellow cotton wool on cheap Easter eggs, was in stealthy pursuit. It was wearing a bonnet and carrying a basket; it would reach into the basket and throw tiny pink rosebuds on the ground in my wake. The ground was the deepest red, an unforgiving harsh red like the desert at the fierce heart of Australia. It was a vast, bleak panorama with an endless horizon and nothing to break the desolation until it joined the sky. This canopy was the deepest, sharpest turquoise,

250

and on I walked. The rosebuds turned into worms, which then wormed off to the horizon. There they morphed into giant columns, which then broke into sections and crashed to the ground in clouds of red dust. Then they slowly formed into ranks and rolled after me until there I was, in a lather of perspiration, at Nanna's side.

I gradually grew out of this dream, and for many years I didn't have it. When it did return to haunt me, it would only be at times of great emotional turmoil. After years of remission, it came again, and it was just as unsettling as I remember, except that there was no Nanna to make it go away.

Looking back over the events that caused this re-emergence of a childhood nightmare, I can put the whole episode into perspective and laugh, but at the time it was a traumatic experience. I think it blew out of proportion because of another dream that I thought was coming true. As I often say, Hollywood is to blame; and once again, I can point the finger at that shallow world of dreams and illusions that have coloured and shaped my entire life.

The Academy Awards is an annual event in the Hollywood calendar that celebrates achievements in the movies. From my lunchtime TV days to the present, the glitter and glamour of this event have held me under their spell.. For years I somehow imagined winning one. How, I don't think came into the equation; I would just get one! That dream gave way to the thought of at least going to the awards ceremony one day, and not in the bleachers but on the arm of some glamorous movie star. Every year I would think, as I would watch the cavalcade of stars walk down the red carpet, "I could make a better dress than that."

I was suddenly, surprisingly, given the opportunity, and I think I did do just that. I felt I made a dress that could be proudly walked down that same red carpet.

Although this part of the dream was realised, to say it was a dream come true is as far removed in the galaxy of my ambitions as those stars are from my dreams of joining them. It was on my very last day after nearly two years working for Shanghai Tang in Hong Kong, in the midst of trying to leave and tidy up last-minute problems, that this nightmare began.

The dippy PR lady (an absolutely delightful and charming person but dippy all the same) was contacted by Sony Music Corporation to make a dress for one of their top stars to wear at the Academy Awards. Coco Lee is the Madonna of Hong Kong and that part of the world. She had sung the title song from the film *Crouching Tiger, Hidden Dragon* and, as it was one of the five nominated songs for an Academy Award, she would sing it live to hundreds of millions of people at that year's Oscar presentation. The child in me with the stars in his eyes said, "Yes, I'll do it", although the logistics seemed impossible. I was leaving Hong Kong for good in two days and was having a holiday in Italy on my way to our annual visit to the prêt-à-porter collections in Paris. How can I do this? It was a chance to be there, if only on someone else's back.

I struck upon the idea to get my darling Rosangela, who lived just outside Milan, to help me. I had intended to visit her for a few days and, if she was willing, we would make the dress. It would be just like old times when she was my right-hand girl in Melbourne. We made many of the best dresses of my career in the years when she worked for me – those heady days of glamour and extravagance in the 1980s.

Rosangela was delighted at the prospect, and it seemed a perfect solution. An appointment was made to see Miss Coco Lee. I had never heard of her and had no idea what she looked like. I didn't even have time to go to HMV and look at one of her albums; however, I guessed "Chinese" and hoped for the best.

I had an idea that incorporated a dragon in a negative image superimposed on a tiger background. The body of the dragon would be all beaded in paillettes and embellished in flat cock feathers to look like scales ... just something as a starting point, having no idea what she had in mind.

As well as the associated challenges of packing up my office, I was having a terrible time packing up the apartment. Although I had tried not to buy much during my tenure in Hong Kong, I had somehow accumulated a lot of stuff. To relieve the tedium, I would visit HMV and buy a CD or two, and I suddenly had at least one hundred. This, to my surprise, was the same for VCDs and, it appeared, DVDs, which I would buy on impulse, as it was sometimes cheaper to buy one than rent one. Unfortunately, I would often arrive home with a new film to find that I already had it. I bought *Evita* four times, *Gone with the Wind* twice, and *Lawrence of Arabia* recorded on someone's dishwasher. I should have known the quality would match the price.

Mark had contacted the local branch of our shipping office to facilitate the evacuation, and they had, in turn, rung me. They had rung me "twice", which at the time did strike me as odd – having the same conversation and conveying the same information "twice". I just thought they were being thorough.

The charge to come and pack up my (meagre) possessions was exorbitant, so I decided to do it myself and collected cardboard and boxes and bought miles of bubble wrap and tape. Georgina and Wendy were in town for a few days, initially to collect me on the way to Europe, but they decided to buy from Shanghai Tang for their "little money" business, and I was the introduction. Thank God I had dissuaded them from staying with me, as the flat looked like a war zone. Having the girls in town had thrown me behind schedule in the packing department, but I had to get it done and had arranged a pickup with the shippers for the same day as the appointment with Coco Lee. There seemed to be plenty of time to do both – until Coco's production machine changed the time to coincide exactly with the time of the pickup.

I rang my contact and requested to change the pickup time, at which point they informed me they had no such record of the appointment. There is no use arguing with the Chinese over the telephone, so a new time was made for later that same day, giving me time to pack and seal up the last of my Hong Kong booty. Armed with the rough sketch for Coco, I made my way to the Grand Hyatt Hotel, where she was holed up in the penthouse. Judith and Tailor Chu were to meet me there to assist in taking notes and measurements (and of course Miss Dippy, being PR, had to be there as well).

In the manner in which all future meetings were arranged, a series of calls (on Coco's sister's mobile telephone) had to be made before we could be admitted: one from downstairs, one when we reached her floor, and one from outside her room. We were finally ushered in to a massive suite to be confronted by a huge table of half-eaten food. Having not had time for lunch, I couldn't help but cast my eyes over the feast, but it was all junk, and everything had a bite out of it or a spoon or fork stuck in it. Another thing struck me as peculiar: several large floral arrangements were placed strategically around the salon's perimeter. They were garlanded with bottles of Chanel's "Coco" perfume like some strange Christmas tree. The reason was to become clear to me later when I found out she was under contract to Chanel as their ambassador in the East.

We were introduced amid a flurry of effusive kisses and gushes, and we all shared our excitement. I went on a bit too long about how I loved the film (having seen it six times at that stage). She loved my sketch initially but then expressed her ideas, which incorporated a desire for bigger tits. As she is not very well blessed in that department, this I thought not a bad idea. She then went on about her spotty back, and she had to be covered, but she had to be sexy and would like to look like she was wearing nothing.

As I had based my design on a version of a traditional cheongsam, it had a high, tight mandarin collar.

"No, no!" She had a terribly sensitive neck and couldn't wear anything that constricting.

We took the measurements, and the demands continued; she wanted it split up to God on one side, no sleeve, no this, no that, and a few other specifications. Although her figure was lacking above the waist, she made up for it below; she had a rather big bum and hips. My design was black from the torso to the hem, which I thought was a winner, as it would have disguised these tragic proportions.

No, she didn't want black. She favoured champagne as a colour; I don't know why the defence system that I had developed from over thirty years of dealing with difficult women didn't kick in and warn me to back out then and there. Those stars in my eyes must have blinded my survival instincts, and three fittings were arranged, and a plan of logistics was projected. The ball was off and rolling. It was all rather opportune: I would have a week in Milan making the dress with Rosangela and meet Coco in Paris the following week for any adjustments. As mentioned, I can put together a dress for anyone with only one fitting of a calico toile and minor tweaks.

Often, clients would come for a second fitting and take the dress home with them. I remember one client ringing me in disbelief: something must be wrong, she wanted to bring the dress back to check it. She did, and it was still perfect.

At 1 pm, in the middle of the appointment, my phone rang, and it was the shipping company. They were outside the apartment building to pick up my goods. Incredulously I told the driver that the appointment was for 4 o'clock. I asked him to wait and I would contact his office. I rang the contact I had been dealing with, and he confirmed that the time was indeed later that day at 4 o'clock. When I told him that a driver was there, he said he would ring me back. When he did, it was to affirm that it couldn't be *their* driver as he had spoken to him. I thought I was going mad. I gave him the telephone number of the waiting driver and asked him to sort it out. I felt I was dealing with two separate companies. When he finally rang back, it became clear that this was almost the case. They had two different divisions, Air and Sea, and I was speaking to people from both and making contradictory arrangements.

Could I make it within half an hour? If I could, the driver would wait, and the two divisions would sort it out later. I was done with the Miss Coco Lee Factory, so I rushed back to the flat thinking of how I was going to finish the packing while the driver was loading it onto the truck.

A local munchkin was waiting and was just a tad crabby; somehow, you don't need to speak the lingo to pick up on these things. I managed to get the rest packed while he struggled to get the boxes onto the truck, the deceptively small ones being the heaviest as they were full of books. One way or another, I got it all done, following him down in the elevator still taping the last box.

I sat down in a mountain of mess and drank the last of the Glenfiddich, still not fully cognisant of all that had happened during the previous twenty-four hours. I had made the decision to finish working for Shanghai Tang, and I felt good that I was leaving Hong Kong on a high note. But I was somewhat deflated when I opened a cupboard in the dining room and found it full of winter clothes. I wished that, as well as an air and sea division, my removalists had a Star Trek division so I could just zap them off into space and not have to worry about how I was going to get them home.

I got rid of most of the rubbish and got doozied up for my last night out at the China Club. One of the best things about my stay in Hong Kong was the privilege of eating at this private dining club whenever I wanted. I took advantage of it, and whenever I had visitors in town, I would take them there. It was conceived by David Tang and is one of the most beautifully resolved interiors, faultless in its execution. The Club is in what were the executive rooms of the Old Bank of China. David had maintained the atmosphere of that elegant period of the 1930s and infused it with the most important collection of contemporary Chinese art. It is a showcase for his exquisite taste and sense of humour, evident in the many light-hearted touches of whimsy throughout the three floors of splendour. The food is also the best, or at least the food I enjoyed most while in Hong Kong. The service is brusque yet attentive.

There were often musical entertainments at the Club. My favourite was a woman in her late fifties singing strange songs from Chinese opera with a few 1930s melodies, her pièce de résistance a rendition of *Home on the Range*. She was always gloriously attired and never without a tiara and long white gloves that reached above her elbows.

Georgina, Wendy and I had the most enjoyable evening talking over old times and looking forward to the next few weeks in Europe. We were anticipating a visit to India on our way back from Europe, and most of the evening was spent discussing the itinerary. The girls had started collecting toiletries from the hotels as they had heard the beggars really appreciated a good body moisturiser and facial toner. They wanted to be prepared for the grateful hordes they envisioned would swamp our vehicle as word got out that two ladies bountiful were dispensing largesse as they took in the sights of the drought and poverty-stricken country. I was in a good mood as I was enthusiastic at the prospect of what the next month might bring and didn't want to dampen their charitable enthusiasms with a reality check.

The next day Tailor Chu started on a toile, and we had the first fitting with Coco at the Hyatt. She seemed extremely modest, and at first we had difficulty removing the various towels and robes in which she was embalmed.

Tailor Chu was the most brilliant cutter and tailor I had ever had the pleasure to work with, and the toile fitting went very well. In my opinion, it fitted perfectly. Coco was not satisfied with the shape we gave her and restated that she wanted Hollywood tits and gestured with her hands the tits she dreamed for. Can do, but I would need another fitting that day at 6 o'clock, so the Lees re-scheduled their afternoon, and we arranged to meet at Shanghai Tang's fabulous flagship store in Pedder Street. I went out immediately in search of a larger underwire bra that we could build in to the dress to achieve Coco's aspired-for bust. I found a triple x cup bra at a very expensive lingerie shop, and Tailor Chu cobbled it into the toile. He was mumbling and grumbling the whole time and, although I didn't know what he was saying, I wholeheartedly agreed. The 6 pm fitting went quite well, although Coco looked like a Chinese May West.

Even she agreed that Hollywood was not ready for these bazookas, so I told her not to worry about them, as tits were my specialty.

I turned the key of the door and my back on Hong Kong and, as I sat down in the Cathay Pacific lounge, I drew my first deep breath for days. I was upgraded to first class and, remembering their service and the library of films from which to choose, I was eager to board the plane and start the next chapter of my dreams, including the specially created Oscar for best dress.

At the airport in Milan I was greeted by Rosangela, who drove me through the countryside to her small village of Besate. The bare winter fields were blanketed in snow and it was a calendar picture-perfect welcome. We caught up on all our news and could barely hide our excitement about making the dress. The next day we went into Milan to look for fabric, and although I couldn't find what I had in mind, I found something even better. At Balchuchero, I found tiger-printed satin and champagne beaded chiffon that was perfect for the dress, a vision of which had suddenly come to me as I spotted the fabrics on a shelf high above our heads.

The next few days were spent cutting and working on the dress in the attic sewing room of Rosangela's charming house. Although she had a dressmaker's dummy, Coco was so tiny that the stand was too big. The dress was cut on the bias, and I could figure the variances of give and take, so it came in handy to at least drape it on to get a feeling of form. The dress was made in three pieces, one being the strapless Hollywood tits bit worn over the tiger skirt, over which was worn a see-through beaded sheath. Before the seams are sewn, the beading is smashed along the joins and these are re-beaded after they are sewn, so they become invisible.

I became an instant celebrity in the village, and my excursions to buy the right-coloured zip, then to the hardware store to buy a punch to break the beads along the seamlines of the chiffon overdress, were a subject of much discussion. The real talk of the day was my visit to the pharmacy, where the village's only photocopier lived. I had a drawing of a tiger's head that I was going to bead onto the tiger satin skirt and I had to blow it up many times to get the proportion that I needed. As I worked on the floor in the middle of the shop, I had a captive audience; the townsfolk were fascinated. Nothing as exciting had occurred since the Americans rolled through the town in tanks at the end of the Second World War. The village was suspended in a time warp, and most of the population was made up of elderly women; Rosangela was about the youngest resident.

We finished the dress, and we were both pleased with the result. Wanting to see what it was like on a real person, Rosangela invited the petite daughter of a friend in a neighbouring village to come and try it on. She was about the same measurements as Coco but shorter, so we propped her up on a pile of magazines and stood back to admire our hard work.

I had had the most wonderful week with Rosangela. She had cooked me delicious food for breakfast, lunch and dinner; we had our music and were doing something together that we both loved: creating a fantasy. I had planned to obtain tickets for La Scala on the black market and to take Rosangela to show her my appreciation for my time in Besate but, as my lowest negotiations were A$1,500 a ticket, I changed my mind and invited her to join me in Paris the following weekend.

Having bought her plane ticket and finally found mine under the bed with my passport, I left for Paris happy and confident that I had achieved what I had set out to do when I departed Hong Kong. Being by myself, I didn't have the regular room that Mark and I have at the Hôtel Grand Powers, our Paris home-away-from-home; I had a smaller attic room. Proudly, I hung the dress to get maximum display and I took a walk along the Champs-Élysées before going to bed.

I love Paris for no reason other than that I feel very comfortable just being there. It is like I have always known it. I rang Nancy, Coco's sister, and received the usual instructions on how to convene for a final fitting. It was the usual knock three times and secret password subterfuge, and I set off for the Paris Hyatt. Of all the beautiful hotels in Paris, I can't imagine why anyone would choose to stay there. It is a five-star hotel but has not one ounce of style or character – when every other Paris hotel, two stars and up, just oozes it. Knowing what I do now, I figure she would have screwed a deal with Hyatt hotels and most likely stays in them for next to nothing for the privilege of their having her as a celebrity guest.

In the lobby, I saw Nancy. She shooed me away and indicated that I should blend in and wait behind a pillar. Coco was having tea with a very chic woman, so I sat and waited as instructed. As this stage of the game played around me, I was not yet aware of Coco's obligations to Chanel. The woman she was hiding me from was the Chanel ambassador looking after Coco during her Paris visit. Nancy apologised when the woman had gone and, with her eyes rolling up into her head, she conveyed her frustrations with the constant attention. She said she didn't want Chanel to know every little thing they were up to.

We went to the anonymous suite they had taken, and once again I was greeted by a wash of déjà vu: another huge table of half-eaten food, this time croissants and Danish pastries, fruit platters and other breakfast delights. It was fairly late, so either the staff were slack or the star was not long out of bed. I also noticed little bundles of absolutely hideous knitting on chairs and the ends of beds. It turned out to be the handwork of a far more evil woman than my first thought (that of Madame Defarge).

Coco slipped into the dress, and it fitted perfectly and she looked lovely – elegant but still sexy as the dress had an allusion of nudity. The subtle enhancement to her shape made her body look well proportioned and natural. The woman knitting was introduced as Coco's mother, and she started whining away in Chinese. Then all hell broke out, and they squabbled back and forth, completely ignoring me. I had a feeling that spotty backs and tits were the topics of controversy, but I was only guessing. After a while, I was let back into the know and mother (the Dragon, as I would name her) told me the dress was not sexy enough for Hollywood, and she wanted it backless, frontless, almost topless, the slit cut higher, and so on. I was more than taken aback and, like a fool, said that I could turn it around to be all those things. Having borrowed some nail scissors, I started cutting up my beautiful gown and, in a few minutes, had pinned together a completely different dress that seemed to please them all. I arranged another fitting in a few days and left the hotel in a daze, not fully cognisant of what had just taken place.

The next four days were spent making this new dress. I had no access to a sewing machine, so I made it entirely by hand. There was an ancient machine in the basement of the hotel that was used to mend linen, but it had only one needle the size of a crowbar. I tried to buy another needle to fit it, without success. The laundress was most impressed with my efforts; once again, I was the talk of the day. All the maids were involved and picked up all the pins and beads that I managed to spread from one end of my room to the lift and beyond. Meanwhile Georgina and Wendy had arrived and were wonderful support and encouragement.

During the next fitting, the Chanel people arrived. I was shoved into the bathroom, along with Coco wearing the remade dress, for what seemed like hours while the sister and the Dragon tried to get rid of Chanel. Not a great deal to talk about, Coco primped and preened to the mirror and practised being natural.

Eventually we were released from the bathroom. The Dragon lady didn't show much appreciation of my new creation and wanted it lower at the back and narrower at the hem. I had already narrowed the hem to nothing as it was, and I refused to comply. Coco and Nancy said they loved it. Coco motioned a few stage gestures and poses and seemed comfortable. Although I preferred the original dress, number two was still stunning. The Hollywood curves looked natural and I thought it was striking enough for the occasion without too much razzmatazz.

Another friend, Jennifer, was in Paris doing a shoot of vintage Chanel for her fashion pages in English *Country Life* and thought it would be a great idea to do a small story on Coco and the dress. This proposal drew a sharp negative response and met the same fate as had the suggestion of doing some PR shots for Shanghai Tang.

I had asked Coco if she could get me an entrée to the Chanel Show the next day, and she said she would try to arrange it. Chanel is the most sought-after show in the ready-to-wear calendar. Because I was working all day, I had to miss several of the shows that I usually attended with Georgina and Wendy, so if I could get to see Chanel it would be a bonus.

I was instructed to leave by the service elevator in case I ran into the Chanel entourage. I was only too happy to play along with the intrigue, thinking that it would be my dress up there on stage, not theirs. All this time, I was emailing a core group of friends about the continuing saga. It was fun getting their responses from all over the world. At every unfolding twist, I would click on Send All and transmit the daily drama to every corner of the globe.

Coco came through with the ticket. I had a quite good seat in the same block as hers. She, of course, was in the front row with numerous stars, including Gerry dippy-do and Carole Bouquet. I was quite surprised at the star treatment Coco received and was impressed when, at the show's finale, she was swept away to be greeted by The Kaiser Karl (Lagerfeld) himself at the end of the catwalk. I got a faint glimmer of recognition from Nancy, but Coco stared straight through me. I expect that is her perception of how a star such as she should act. The three of them, Dragon included, were done out head to foot in Chanel. I must admit they all almost looked as if they had a bit of class. I wondered if there would be a knitting bag in next season's range; Chanel had just about everything else, including a sleeping bag. This was modelled by a rabbit of a young man with one bare skinny leg sticking out through the zipper. I thought this was the most bizarre display I had seen in many years, but it did raise a smile. I had to give Karl points for that.

The dress was near completion and I felt as though the ordeal was almost over. Rosangela arrived from Italy and was upset at what had happened. But, as I was worn out physically and mentally, she took charge of things and completed the hand sewing that was yet to be finished.

Coco left for rehearsals in Los Angeles the day after the Chanel show, and I had arranged to deliver the dress to Nancy on the Monday. Rosangela and I had a beautiful day just walking around Paris and lunching in the Tuileries. I had kept a ticket that Jennifer left me for a parade at the Carrousel du Louvre, and Rosangela was very excited to be going to a show in Paris, a dream come true. We had some delicious dinners and caught up with some mutual friends. We even managed to go out dancing, if you could call it dancing. We went to an amazing club, Barrio Latino, where there was a queue a mile long but somehow we were ushered straight in and didn't have to pay. It was so packed with drunken revellers that I felt more like a squirming sardine than my usual Fred Astaire. It was an inexpensive evening because, even if we had wanted to get a drink, it was impossible to move and try to get to the bar. When we spilled out into the crowd and faced the daunting task of getting a taxi, I was lucky. In the distance I saw a cab with a hand paying the driver from the back seat, so we ran and beat the other thousand desperadoes to the prize.

On Sunday, for some reason, I decided to ring Nancy and deliver the dress then, instead of the next day. She answered the telephone with a tone of reluctance and said she couldn't talk as she was going through security at the airport. In disbelief, I asked why she hadn't told me she was leaving. She said she would ring me back. That was the last time we ever spoke.

I felt like I had been hit by a demolition ball. After all that I had done, I could not believe that they didn't have the slightest consideration for my feelings. It suddenly all became clear. They never intended for Coco to wear my dress; what an absolute chump I had been to be chewed over and spat out. It was the complete lack of manners that stunned me. How could anyone be so rude? If it were me, I would have at least carried the lie through to the end.

Rosangela came back from her show elated and happy, so I didn't tell her, but it only took a few minutes for her to figure out that something was wrong. She, too, came down with a thump, and we both felt totally dejected and disillusioned; it gave the meaning of *Down and Out in Paris and London* a whole new twist.

I woke the next morning with a steely determination that I wouldn't let the tale end there; they were not going to get away with it. I contacted Hong Kong and got Dizzy onto getting their Los Angeles address. I would conclude my part by delivering the dress, although I knew Coco would never wear it. That was the reality but, still starstruck, I imagined that, once they saw it, they would do a two-fingers-up to Chanel and wear it after all. Rosangela was, I think, more upset than I was and her wonderful weekend ended on a sad note, so it was a teary farewell as she departed for home.

That night I was walking back to the hotel feeling as low as I can ever remember. It was raining. I was getting wet but I didn't care. I passed a clochard – a street person, a woman (a clochette?) She was bedding down for the night in a shop doorway and was surrounded by Samsonite suitcases of varying sizes and colours. They were tied together with rags and rope and pantyhose. The scene reminded me of *Bonanza* or some other western in which the settlers formed a camp for the night, the wagon train (in this case Samsonites) forming a wide protective circle to shield them from a midnight attack of savage Apaches. The only thing missing was a big fire in the centre – the one thing she would appreciate, as it was freezing.

Seeing this wretched woman with her whole life strung together in moulded plastic on wheels gave me a reality jolt. Here I was, bemoaning my lot because some spoilt popstar brat had toyed with me over a silly beaded dress. How ridiculous to be upset by such nonsense when, all over Paris, all over the world, people had nothing: no shelter, no food, no future. I had everything. It was a jolt that brought all things into perspective. Suddenly, my anger and my depression vaporised. I went back to my warm, welcoming hotel and, as I lay my head on the feather pillow, I thought, "How does she manage those suitcases?"

Apart from a few tears in the back of the taxi talking to Mark on the mobile phone back in Australia, I was in an optimistic mood as I headed for London. On my arm was The Dress that Never Was, as I called it from then on. In my mind was a desire for an ending.

I got the address from Dizzy, who seemed not to care about the situation and actually justified Coco's position. Sure, she was obligated to wear Chanel under her contract, but it was no excuse for the deception and the shameless lack of consideration I had been shown. I packed up the dress and Federal Expressed it to LA, having included one of my better notes. If they didn't feel some remorse, reading my words in a gracious if somewhat caustic summing up of the whole episode, then they lacked any soul whatsoever.

I reunited with Georgina and Wendy, and we set off to meet Mark in India. Our trip through India was a fantastic, cathartic experience.

The whole Dress that Never Was faded to a dull ache, and I didn't think about it until the day of the awards presentation.

We had expected to be far away from the Hollywood razzmatazz, but that evening we were staying in the most incredible Palace hotel with a satellite dish, so we sat up and watched the ceremony with mixed feelings and some trepidation. My "Send All" group around the world were watching as well. One reply described the Chanel dress as "a bloodbath of red sequins". Chanel had built some prerequisite tits into the dress and the highlight of the whole evening was when Coco Lee turned one way and they stayed where they were! It was a case of sour grapes, but I genuinely believed my dress was better than Chanel's. It was over, and it was an invaluable experience, another lesson in the schoolroom of life.

Actually, it wasn't quite over. Several months later, I had a message from Shanghai Tang that Coco had returned my dress. I had asked her to do so if she didn't wear it. Included was a note, which was forwarded to me. It was on a page torn from a notepad and was written in pencil in a very childish hand. In it Coco graciously thanked me for making such a beautiful dress and hoped I understood her position and why she couldn't wear it. Well, yes, I understood her situation and my position in the scheme of things. Another beaded dress is not such a big deal or an important contribution to our world, but the one great lesson I learnt is to have faith in and follow your dreams, even if they don't come true.

I will never forget the looks on the faces of those Indian villagers as we drove off in our air-conditioned minibus. Some of these villages only had one well or one tap; I don't think hair conditioner was a must. The ladies bountiful had given out their shower caps, moisturisers, body lotions and hair conditioners and the recipients were bemused, to say the least. I thought I saw a mother with a tiny baby in one hand and a bottle of bright blue skin toner in the other, contemplating whether to give the infant a drink; it looked most refreshing!

The End

37

Good and Evil

Now that I'm happily retired, I have had time to reflect on my life and the threads running through it. I will share some confessions and reflections in the following few chapters, starting with the most basic tussles: good versus evil. What have I learned? What passions have stayed with me over the years?

When I was a child, Sunday night was great for television. At 5.30 pm, with great anticipation, we turned on Channel 7 to watch *Disneyland*. I say anticipation because you never knew what "land" the week would bring. Fantasyland, Frontierland, Adventureland or Tomorrowland? I dreaded Frontierland – all those dusty cowboys and Indians and moralistic fables about Daniel Boone or Davey Crockett bored me to tears. Adventureland wasn't much better – big, brown bears scooping up salmon lose their appeal after the umpteenth viewing. Tomorrowland sometimes caught my attention, but Fantasyland was the territory I most looked forward to. It had cartoons, and I have always enjoyed a good laugh.

Goofy was my favourite cartoon character. He was such a jerk.

Nothing sailed smoothly for poor Goofy, and I found the frantic wail that accompanied his current dilemma so amusing. Goofy also gave me my first valuable lesson about good and evil – a simple parable ingrained into my psyche. On one of his shoulders stood an angel and on the other a little devil. The little devil was constantly prodding Goofy with his pitchfork and trying to goad him into performing some heinous act, while the angel on the other shoulder would try to talk him out of it. More often than not, the devil won. Of course, Goofy would then land in all sorts of trouble. In the end, he would see the error of his ways and repent, the angel would lecture him, and we both learnt an important lesson.

My life has been – and still is – a terrible struggle with those two epaulettes. The devil is always trying to get me to do things I know are wrong. I fight and ignore him, listening to the angel's judicious advice, but it's a constant battle. My most trying test is to hold back from shoplifting. My brain automatically goes into thief mode in any shop – be it the milk bar, hardware store or Tiffany's. I case the joint. I check escape routes, staff positions and video surveillance. Lastly – and least importantly – I look for something suitable, desirable and possible to purloin.

I haven't surrendered to this temptation since I was caught at the age of fifteen, but my desire to shoplift is as strong today as it ever was. With my father a policeman, I can't begin to tell you how terrible the incident was at the time. As luck would have it, I was caught by one of my father's mates. He let me off, allowing me to go home on the condition that I told my father of my own volition.

꧁꧂

I don't think it was a suicide attempt. But, somehow, I ended up getting off the train before it stopped, in the process removing the sleeve from my very best new camel-hair jacket. Walking home, I was distressed. How was I going to bring up the subject of my transgression?

Celia saw the bloodied sleeve hanging off me as soon I walked in.

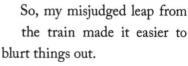

So, my misjudged leap from the train made it easier to blurt things out.

"What happened?"

Out it all came in a flood of tears.

I don't think the punishment was all that severe at the time. The lecture was bad enough, and they probably figured that my state of distress and sleeveless jacket were enough for me to learn my lesson.

I blame my best friend at high school, Stephen, for giving me the taste for the fine art of shoplifting. As mentioned, he was constantly wagging school, and occasionally I would miss a sports meeting or cross-country run and follow him to the city. He was mad about music and would trawl the second-hand record shops looking for bargains. The first album he made me slip into my school satchel was Frank Sinatra's *A Man and His Music*.

To this day, I can't listen to that record without blushing and watching my back in case the big fat salesman who was wedged behind the counter at John Clements should tap me on the shoulder. Thank God I got caught at a tender age. With that ever-present devil prodding me, who knows how far my criminal career would have taken me?

How much better would the world be today if all would-be leaders had loved Goofy the way I did in my formative years?

Or even Mickey Mouse.

38

Cars

I never wanted to learn to drive. However, I am terribly glad that my father – in his quest to make me an all-round "man" – used to drag me under protest into our Valiant with the yellow L plates to teach me. I absolutely love driving now and will be forever grateful for his excellent instruction.

The Valiant had a manual transmission with a column shift. Although I haven't driven a car with such an attachment since – I have always driven automatic cars – every now and then, in a Pavlovian response, I try to change gear with the column shift. The car we had before the Valiant was a big, old 1940s black Dodge. I was embarrassed by this car, as it was old and not sleek like the cars in the magazines. How foolish I was not to see how classy it was. It had beautiful leather upholstery, and there was so much room in the back seat, you could have a party. In the days before seat belts, it had a leather strap across the back of the front seat to hang onto in case of emergency.

I would sit in the back with Nanna. I remember the smell of her 1940s chubby black fox coat as I would snuggle into her arms and drift off to sleep on the drive home from Ferntree Gully or on the way home from a party or a ball. My parents often took me to such evenings, and I think that's how I forever set my time clock when I was little – I am definitely a night-time person.

We often spent Sundays with Auntie Elene and Uncle Brian at Ferntree Gully. I would love to go because you had to go up Toorak Road on the way. The highlight was going past "Magg", the haute couture boutique owned by Dame Zara Bate in the Toorak Village. Magg was a competitor to Le Louvre, although I wasn't aware of Le Louvre at the time. I would get very excited just after we passed Chapel Street, begging my father to slow down at Williams Road so I could catch a glimpse of the windows. Of course, he would speed up, and all I ever saw was a blur of some fantastic silk fabric or sparkling beading. Dame Zara had two Thai temple dancers' headdresses, one in each window, and an exquisite gown somehow suspended from these exotic, glittering, gold curiosities.

A few years have passed since one of my favourite clients, Marie O'Brien, died of cancer. I was making her turbans with matching shawls while she was going through chemotherapy. I was visiting her house, having been there only once before and many years back, when I was reminded of this Toorak Road memory. She had one such Thai headdress in her entry. When I told her my childhood story, she said I must have it. I made three polite refusals before gladly leaving with it under my arm. She was delighted, as her family had always hated it. It is a very fine example and lives in our bedroom, where I think of her often when admiring it.

I am sure my father only got rid of the Dodge because of me. Everything my parents did seemed to be an attempt to please me, and they were all aflutter the day we got the new Valiant. Mum had somehow contrived to get me into the front garden so I could see Dad turn it into our driveway. It was a total surprise, and I was thrilled to pieces that we had the newest car in the neighbourhood. It was not what I aspired to, but it was new, white, sleek and pointy – as opposed to the Dodge's heavy, clumsy, black, curvaceous form.

On our weekly school excursion to the Footscray public library, I never spent time in the children's section but would gravitate to the magazine racks in the adult's book room. There I would pore over the glossy imported journals, *Réalités* being my favourite, as mentioned, because it had full-page ads for Cartier, Harry Winston and Graff. These pages displayed glorious necklaces of pear-shaped diamonds, emerald earrings the size of golf balls, and sets of bracelets in rubies, sapphires and more diamonds.

Having had my fix of jewels, I would then scan the other American magazines for cars like Studebakers, Mustangs and – my top choice – Thunderbird convertibles. White, with aqua upholstery, they were always photographed on some rocky outcrop in Death Valley, with a beautiful blonde, her hair blowing in the wind, and one of those cartoon-character-handsome American men with a chiselled chin and a check shirt open to the waist. Whether it was the car or the driver I lusted after, I hadn't yet figured out. I knew I definitely aspired to more than a Valiant, but it was at least one up on the old GAL 147.

My mother had a little Austin A40, which was baby-poo yellow and would tootle along at some unknown speed, with the speedometer flashing from 0 to 100 no matter what speed you were travelling at, even in reverse. I always felt like I was driving the nose of some Moomba float and would beetle along looking for my lost face. Mum's next car was the famous Bluebird, a Morris Minor that I drove for years until I bought my first car. I have a terrible fear of steep hills and still go to pieces if I have to reverse anywhere, which I put down to an awful day spent at her wheel.

I was always big at shooting my mouth off and had promised a group of friends that I could borrow the Valiant any time I wanted. A picnic was arranged for one Sunday. When I asked if I could take the Valiant out that particular day, Mum and Dad declined because they were going somewhere. I was expected to join them but somehow got out of it. Without telling them, I decided to take Bluebird on the planned picnic. My friends were disappointed when I rattled up in the old blue Morris

Minor. The mystery destination was Mount Macedon. My heart skipped a beat, but I bravely set off regardless of the warnings that were pounding in my head. "*Mount* as in *mountain*." I had already lost too much face by letting the group down with the carriage, so I couldn't renege at this late stage.

All my worst fears came true halfway up the mountain. It was a steep climb, and the road was fairly narrow. There was a vertical, ferny rise on one side and a drop to death on the other. Suddenly, Bluebird just gave up the ghost and conked out.

Panic. Foot on brake, with a handbrake start to get her going again. NO brakes! Nothing. What to do? Well, no choice as she began to roll backwards.

She started to pick up speed, and I couldn't think of what to do to stop her, other than backing her into the ferny rise. That

stopped us all right, but with such impact that she looked like a wombat burrowing into a hole. We somehow extricated her from the bank and, as we didn't have much more than a mile or so to go to the bottom, I made the others walk. I nudged her down the mountain along the bank, on my way disrupting quite a few protected species of fern and native flora, not to mention a layer or two of duco. When we reunited at the bottom of the mountain, we all had a nervous laugh.

One of the group, Alison McMinn, was concerned to see if the farm-fresh eggs we had bought on the way had smashed, as they were in the side of the boot that had taken the maximum impact. The four of us lifted the boot at the same time. For some unknown reason, we then all let go at the same time, thinking someone else was holding on. The boot came down with a loud thud on poor Alison's head, rendering her blotto. When she came to, we counted the eggs. We had thirteen, including hers – a huge, blue double-yolker.

Because I spent all my money on antiques, I didn't buy my first car until years later. I was working for Le Louvre, and Georgina thought it was about time I had a car more suited to my station as the designer for Australia's premier haute couture salon. We started looking in the papers for something cool and came across a Lancia Flavia for what we thought was a bargain price: $13,000.

I had a bit in the bank, Georgina gave me some cash towards it, and I borrowed the rest from my mother. The vendor gave me such a sales pitch. All the cliches – its prestige, the fact that she was only one of three in the country, and a spiel about the designer (Pina Ferraro). Georgina and I loved it. It was sleek and had genuine leather upholstery and a great sound system. But "lemon" does not come anywhere near a description of this car. From almost the moment I drove it away, things started to go wrong. It was so beautifully designed, but everything was put into place for purely visual reasons. To do something as simple as change a spark plug, the whole motor had to be disassembled – the spark plugs were placed out of sight under the engine for a reason only known to the madman who designed it.

Every time this car went in for a service, it cost hundreds of dollars, even to change the aforesaid spark plugs if they could find them. Georgina was fantastic. Perhaps it was out of a sense of guilt because she had been a major factor in its selection, but most of the time she footed the bill or a major part thereof. It got so bad that the car needed thousands spent on her.

I got an itemised quote for all the new parts required to get her back in order. I was going on my first trip to Italy and got it into my mind that I would buy all the parts there as it would be so much cheaper. What a brilliant idea! When I got to Italy, I thought I would see many sisters of my Lancia Flavia stylishly flying along the autostradas and chic inner-city streets of Milan and Rome Not one! I think only four were made and three of those were sent to Australia. As for the fourth, I did see it from a speeding train on my way from Florence to Rome. It was a rusted-out wreck abandoned in the middle of a field of red poppies, a blot on the glorious landscape and not a good sign for my dream car's integrity.

With much investigation and a great amount of trouble, I fronted up to the Lancia spare parts factory about 80 miles out of Rome. It was all going well as I made my selection with the help of the manual that I had brought with me. The necessary parts were circled with a green Texta. Although the storeman couldn't speak any English, he was tireless and would go off into the depths of the warehouse with the manual and return with the next item – a clutch in a wooden crate or a carburettor wrapped in heavy blue plastic. I thought I was doing terribly well, jotting down the prices and getting quite a big pile of spare parts on the counter. It suddenly occurred to me: How was I going to get these back to Rome, let alone home? I picked up one of the smaller parts and found that it seemed to weigh a ton. I then started to total up the bill and it came to well over $1,500 – money I didn't have.

Oh my God, what had I done?

Grinning from ear to ear, the storeman came back with the last item I had earmarked.

"Eccola. Finito."

I then committed one of the most cowardly acts of my life. I grabbed the manual and circled another part, something I hoped would send him far into the depths of Never Never Land. With a look of disbelief that I would want a fuel tank "to go", off he went – and so did I. I had made my way there by bus, and the stop was some distance away. I ran like the wind, all the time looking behind me, hoping I wasn't being chased by an irate storeman brandishing some spare part that could double as a weapon. I often wonder what he thought had happened.

The last straw came when she tried to kill me. In scorching weather, the accelerator cable used to expand and get stuck. I was going through a nervous breakdown, having just been dumped by my first real boyfriend, and wasn't thinking all that clearly. One hot day, it happened, and she just took off. I didn't know what to do and just went with it, speeding through red lights and school crossings, down one-way streets, all the time just trying to keep control. After almost clipping the heels of an expectant mother with a toddler in a pusher, it finally occurred to me to turn the engine off to stop the car, which I finally did. I let her cool off and crawled home, determined that she had to go. I was extremely shaken.

I swear what happened next is the absolute truth. I poured a very stiff drink and sat down at the dining room table with a pen and paper to compose an ad to place in the following week's "Used Cars For Sale" section of *The Age* newspaper. The doorbell rang, and I answered. There at the door was a man holding his card.

"Does that beautiful Lancia Flavia belong to you?" he enquired.

He had been admiring it for months.

"If you are ever interested in parting with it, give me a call."

I had to stop myself from offering *him* money. It was the quickest deal in the history of the motor trade.

I decided I needed something more reliable, something with a bit, but not too much, style – something new. I settled on a Honda hatchback. It was very zippy and hardly gave me a moment's trouble. What I liked most of all was how, when I would come down in the morning to the street where she was parked outside number 6, her windscreen wipers were never curled up as if someone had taken a giant eyelash wand to them; there wasn't a key scratch down the length of the passenger's door; the tyres were still inflated; and the badges and hubcaps were exactly where they had been when she went to bed.

She was just an ordinary, everyday Honda and not some fancy, only three-of-a-kind, imported job that inspired envy and brought out the worst in some passing midnight yobbo's limited imagination. She served me well for years, but I treated her cruelly by thinking I was doing the right thing and lending her to my younger brother for a couple of months while he was going through one of his bad black-sheep periods. When I finally managed to get her back, he had almost destroyed her. The final indignity came when Mark sold her – she was so unroadworthy that she had to be towed away.

My next car was my ideal auto. At the time, had anyone offered me a Rolls-Royce in exchange for this classic English 1969 Rover 3.5 coupé, I would have dismissed them with a hand gesture similar in style to the royal wave of our dearly departed old Queen Mum. That car cost a queen's ransom to keep on the road, as she was old, and her parts, like some of mine, were worn out. Mark lavished much time, money and loving attention on her. As I am impossible to buy a present for, he gradually brought her back to glory for several birthday and Christmas presents over the years.

There were no more than three on the road. When passing the others, one would acknowledge – with a subtle raising of the little finger or nod of the head – that we were indeed a discerning few. She was a petrol guzzler, and I lived in fear that, some grim day in the future, environmental zealots would ban these cars from the road. Although it broke my heart, I finally had to part with her, partly due to issues with my health but also because she wasn't getting the attention an old girl like her deserved. A friend who deals in exotic cars made the farewell as easy as possible. He found a home for her with a collector who restored her and will love and treasure her.

Mark and I have always had Saab convertibles, which are fantastic cars. Unfortunately, the company made them too well and became unviable. We bought our last one on the day before they announced they would no longer be producing them.

Now, if you had ever told me that, one day, I would drive a Holden, I would have promptly told you in reply, "That will never happen." Because I had trouble getting out of the Saabs (we had one in Noosa as well), I decided to buy a small SUV to run around in. It cost "nothing" and is fantastic. Although my love for the Rover will never be matched in my affections, I have to say I love this little car. My only gripe is that I can never remember where I've parked it in those big multi-storey carparks. I can be seen pointing and pushing my keypad at three other cars, at least, before I hit home. I think I've sorted that problem now, as I take a photo.

What's next? Driverless cars? I have to admit that I like the idea, as my distance judgement of bollards, gutters, columns and indeed the other vehicles in carparks nowadays is questionable.

39

Decorating

Although my primary preoccupation in childhood was dressing Teddy, the other creative outlet that has carried through to my adult life has been a dedication to the art of home decoration. From as far back as I can remember, I was constantly arranging furniture, shifting objects and accumulating goods to embellish my environs. I am the original lay-by queen. For those not familiar with this term – in our current era of instant gratification – a lay-by was a method whereby you could secure a purchase by putting down a small deposit and could pay it off in instalments agreed upon by the seller. My first major lay-by was an Edwardian/Art Nouveau mirror, which I still own and still like as much as the day I first saw it. It cost $15. I was thirteen or fourteen, and my pocket money must have been stretched to its limits.

My days of being a serious decorator started when my younger brother, Edwin, was born, and I was allowed to move into the bungalow out the back at Hobbs Street. Having been painted at the same time as the living room, the bungalow was also olive green, with a tangerine feature wall – but not for long. When Mum had decorated the house, it was in the latest "modern Scandinavian" style, influenced heavily by the glossy pages of *The Australian Women's Weekly*. It had a carpet that defies description, but I'll try. I always called it the "Colorado Rapids". It had a grey background and swirls of every other imaginable colour – I suppose the logic being that it would need to pick up and match something in any room in which it was laid. If you made the mistake of looking at it as you walked up the hall, you would finish up quite dizzy by the time you made it to the lounge room. I hated it with a passion.

I must have been very persuasive, bossy or unbearably precocious, but, at the age of eleven, I talked Celia into a very ambitious plan to redecorate number 13. Our budget didn't extend to new carpet, so I devised an idea to dye it. Mum went out and bought tons of chocolate-coloured Dylon dye. We made up big buckets of it and, on our hands and knees, started with a sponge at the front door and slowly hand-dyed the Colorado Rapids. Down past cataracts and a swirling eddy or two, we finished up at the whirlpool by the back door. You could still see the swirls and eddies, but they were all now multi-tones of chocolate brown.

We painted the olive-green living room with the tangerine feature wall a pale sandy beige and bought a three-piece leather-look lounge suite with beige inserts and cushions. I replaced the "Aboriginal-inspired" printed curtains with a plain scrim. A large chocolate-brown Indian rug tied it all together, and I think it was brilliant, even looking back on it today. Mind you, that original 1950s room, as decorated by Celia, is the hot look of today. However, I didn't like it then, and I don't like it now!

I moved in to the bungalow and the décor changed every week as the furniture was pushed from one corner to the other. It had a polished wooden floor, and there was a grid of tracks where I had shifted things backwards and forwards. Although I loved to have things looking themed and preened, I was not that good at keeping them that way – "untidy" was a mild description of how I could finish up. The funniest thing my father ever did was come into my room one day (as I was lying on my bed reading my latest copy of *Look and Learn*) and proceed to hammer five very long nails into the floor. Not anticipating any questions, he answered one anyway. "That's so you can hang up your clothes." I still get a chuckle thinking about it.

I had many different looks in the bungalow. One, I was made to paint out immediately, although I couldn't see what all the fuss was about. I had just discovered Salvador Dali and embarked on a very ambitious mural in a surrealistic manner. It took me days and days of constant work, and it featured a large female nude whose left nipple was the light switch. No one was allowed to see it until it was finished, and I timed the unveiling for one Sunday when we had visitors for lunch. I invited them all out the back and, as I opened the door, I flipped on the nipple and was surprised at the look of shock and horror on the faces of my attendant party. Dad was not at all amused at my efforts and closed the door very dramatically. He made me paint it out the very next weekend.

Still, on to bigger and brighter things. One of my favourite looks was during my Egyptian stage. My bed was pure Cecil B. DeMille. I had

a purple bed that was engulfed in curtains made from orange hessian with a purple, keyhole-pattern border. For over the bed, I made a canopy of giant paper roses. It was like an Egyptian royal barge. I would drift off down the Nile as if in a trance, the soothing rhythm of the beat of hundreds of slaves rowing in time to ancient drums sending me back to a time long forgotten – or at least to the 1934 Claudette Colbert film version of the life and times of my favourite queen, Cleopatra. Actually, the soothing rhythm of the slaves was the soundtrack to the Elizabeth Taylor/Richard Burton version, which was the most terrible and turgid soundtrack ever put to film. However, I was entranced by everything to do with the film and would torture myself and anyone else I could trap into listening to it at every chance.

"Listen to those oars."

I was always keen on mood lighting, and red globes and chiffon-draped lamps were often a feature. The bungalow was like a stage set constantly evolving as this week's fantasy outshone the last. I think Celia grew tired of surprises and shocks. Like a donkey with a carrot, I was offered a budget to redecorate. However, the contract came with conditions such as a "tidy" clause. I was very excited and headed straight to the wallpaper department at Georges, Melbourne's most prestigious store. It was renowned for its decorating department – no Toorak matron worth her salt would go anywhere else.

Wallpaper was very much in vogue, and it is amusing to see the recycled interest today among young trendies, who are rediscovering the very same prints I would pore over for hours at a time. I loved the Art Deco/Pop Art images printed in black flock over silver foil. I was desperate for one called "Bathing Beauties". It was a composite of nude females, one of them being Cleopatra. Unfortunately, my budget didn't go that far, as I had to buy carpet and built-in robes. I settled on a Chinese print, which was subtle but luxurious – at certain angles, the touch of gold would glint, especially in candlelight. A carpet shade called "Burmese Gold" was chosen, and I had one wall of floor-to-ceiling sliding louvre doors forming a walk-in wardrobe. This was particularly handy for keeping up with the "tidy" clause. Later on, it was also convenient for popping a naked man out of sight should Nanna just drop in to say goodnight. You could just sweep up an armful of dirty clothes, and they were out of sight. Same with a naked man, except you would swoop up *his* clothes, throw him in and tell him not to breathe.

When I was eighteen, Celia upgraded from number 13 Hobbs Street, Seddon, to 60 Elizabeth Street, Newport. One of the reasons was so that I could have a real bedroom in the house, like normal people. No way! I had only just discovered the delights of sneaking in midnight callers and didn't want anything to dampen my newfound enthusiasm for nocturnal delights. Thank goodness, number 60 had a bungalow, although it was in a derelict state. Dad wanted to pull it down, but I was insistent that it would do me fine with a lick of paint. We put in some double glass doors to let in more light, a wall of my famous neat-and-trim "hide-a-man" louvre doors, a large cutting/sewing table, and a pseudo-Tiffany light. I was once again the king of my domain. I didn't leave this cosy nest for far too long after I had well and truly spread my wings. After my father's departure, I couldn't leave Celia until she was strong enough.

I was very good at house-sitting, and it was during one house-sit that I "inherited" my Avoca Street flat in South Yarra. I had been minding it for Bruce Finlayson, who was a very talented costume designer. When he landed an offer to stay in Hollywood that was too good to refuse, I decided to stay on at Avoca Street and that was when I asked John Potter if he would like to share it with me. My tenure was precarious as Bruce had told other people about his decision. One lot even turned up with a moving van full of furniture. However, possession being nine-tenths of the law, I was there to stay and did so for the next twenty years. I finally had somewhere of my own that I could decorate as I pleased. I was a tyrant – everything had to be my way – and I am forever ashamed of the shabby treatment poor John received over the years in which we shared number 6.

My first major purchase was an early Australian armoire made out of a variety of Australian timbers. I have always had a passion for inlaid wood, and this cupboard was the first piece I ever bought. I was looking in a shop in High Street owned by Peter Day. Down a long corridor, a door was slightly ajar, and I could see just a fragment of this marvellous piece of furniture. I took off to have a closer look and was tackled (literally) halfway down the hall. Peter lived out the back, and that area was out of bounds. He wouldn't even show the piece to me, and he virtually threw me out.

Months later, he rang me out of the blue and said he was going overseas, and the armoire was for sale as he needed the money. Although having only seen a mere glimpse through the crack in the door, I knew I must have it. I asked the price and agreed to it. It was $600, the exact amount of my life savings. I lined the inside with mirror, and it became my dress shop during the years when I worked from Avoca Street with the front room as my salon. In the heady days of the 1980s, when Lord McAlpine was frenziedly buying rare Australian furniture, I was offered $30,000 for it. But I couldn't part with it. I never get tired of looking at it and it is a constant source of pleasure.

The interior of number 6 Avoca Street was beautiful, to which the pages of a 1980 copy of *Belle* magazine will attest. I hand-painted faux-marble columns to frame the windows, which in turn were swagged in billowing silver gauze. Polished boards showed off my increasing furniture collection, and two glorious kilim rugs added a final (ethnic) touch of colour and warmth. I started with a large paper lantern as the centrepiece of the main room and, through a series of random events, finished up with one of my most treasured possessions: an Empire-style chandelier.

I believe that my taste is innate but a great influence on my style and appreciation I would attribute to Lillian Wightman, who was one of the most stylish women I ever met.

When my mother decided to remarry, I orchestrated to hold the wedding at Avoca Street. Miss Wightman was between houses, and I asked her if I could borrow a very pretty, black, wrought-iron French chandelier that she had packed up. It had pink rock-crystal drops and would add a certain elegance to the room. When the room was filled with people, the only thing you would see would be the chandelier and the tall arrangements of flowers I had planned. It was a beautiful party.

Come the time when Miss Wightman asked for the chandelier back, a chain of events resulted in some good fortune: acquiring another chandelier, which would become my favourite. Miss Wightman was once again following in the footsteps of Dame Mabel Brookes. Previously, she had bought Elm Tree House from the society doyenne and, now that Dame Mabel had built a house on the Mornington Peninsula, Miss Wightman was moving in to her old apartment in Amesbury House, a South Yarra building of only six apartments with the sort of reputation that comes from such an exclusive and prestigious address.

Miss Wightman was about to give the apartment the new broom. I had been through it a couple of times and remembered it full of Regency-style "plastic chandeliers". They were quite stylish. You would never know, in the right setting, that they weren't the real thing. As I had to return her pink crystal chandelier, I asked Miss Wightman if I could have one of the "placky" ones before they went to the tip, as anything would be better than going back to my paper lantern. She said, "Of course", but then thought for a minute and offered me Dame Mabel's old chandelier, which had been included in the sale. Miss Wightman thought it was a terrible old piece of junk. It had gone to Leonard Joel, one of the leading auction houses specialising in fine furniture and art.

"Just go down and tell them I said you can have it."

I went and received a negative response. No, I definitely could not have it!

When I told Miss Wightman, she ruffled and told me to get them on the phone. I was hovering quite close to her as she spoke with Joel's. They told her that this piece was quite rare and worth a considerable amount of money because of its provenance. I watched her pale complexion lose two tones and I think I managed to squeeze out a tear.

She took a deep breath and said, "I said my young man can have it, and he can."

I returned to Joel's to retrieve it and was greeted with much disdain.

However, one of the kinder gentlemen commented on how fortunate I was to acquire this piece and gave me a brief outline of its history.

Dame Mabel had a passion for Napoleonic memorabilia because her great-grandfather, Lord Balcombe, had lived in the house next door to Napoleon during his exile on the island of St Helena and had become a good friend of his. The English didn't want Napoleon to have any friends, so they encouraged Dame Mabel's great-grandfather to leave the island, apparently in no uncertain terms. He came to Australia, and later the family built a house on the Mornington Peninsula called "The Briars", which is now on the National Heritage List and a popular tourist attraction. He brought this chandelier with him from his previous home, where Napoleon had most likely dined under its soft glow. It hung in the dining room at The Briars.

It did indeed look like a terrible old piece of junk. When I got it home, I thought it had topaz drops. After getting at it with soap and hot water, the colour drained away – the residue of many a smoke-filled soiree over the years when Dame Mabel reigned among society's leading hostesses. I guess President Lyndon B. Johnson may have supped under that chandelier as well. Later, I had it semi-restored, bringing it back to somewhere near its original condition. It still had the authentic candleholders, and the old gentleman who came to collect it, being one of the last of his trade, recognised it immediately. He told me Dame Mabel was always adding or taking things off the chandelier at her whim. It is still far from how it should be, but it is charming, and I love it. I often think about all the history that has passed beneath its elegant form in all the years since it hung over Napoleon's defeat.

I believe no room is dressed without a chandelier. My next favourite one is an Italian job from the 1940s. It is pink crystal as well, and it looks like a Spanish galleon in full sail. I purchased this one when Mark and I bought our first property.

With our first big profits from the Fergie Bows, Mark and I were in the market to buy our first house together. He was living in a modern townhouse in Parkville with central heating – one of the things that cemented our relationship. Avoca Street being like an icebox in winter, I spent as much time at Parkville as at South Yarra. (It was Mark's cousin's company's flat, and they had furnished it in a style I could only describe as "early Fred Flintstone". I'd needed to do a bit of redecorating to make it habitable. Piece by piece, I had gradually got rid of the look. No one had seemed to notice or mind, and I had soon made it much more stylish.)

Anyway, we were out looking at prospects to buy when we drove past an auction about to take place. We had a quick run through and bought it, not thinking about any of the things you should do when buying a property, like "stumps" or a freeway confiscating the backyard for an access ramp. In an ironic twist, the day we took possession was April Fool's Day, 1985, and the local newspaper put in a front-page story with just such a scenario. Our faces dropped – until, in disbelief, we read it a few more times and got the joke. Apparently, one poor pensioner in the old people's home nearby had a nasty turn as he failed to appreciate the joke. The story caused ructions in the local press for weeks.

With a budget of $30,000, I achieved a wonderful result. The "stumps" had indeed gone, so I put in a new floor. I used chipboard set in an inlay of timber with a large diamond pattern. When I had bleached and polished it, it looked for all the world like the finest Carrara marble. I didn't know about things like building permits or engineer's reports, and I knocked out every wall I could, much to the consternation of the builder. He said it would fall down and was quite surprised when it didn't.

The place was now full of light and looked fabulous. It had been a Victorian house, so it had very high ceilings, but every trace of period had been savaged in the 1950s. The original bay windows had been replaced with the narrow sash type that was popular at that time. New windows didn't come into the budget equation, so I made a feature of them by adding internal shutters and trompe-l'oeil painted swags. We found a funny 1920s lounge suite in Echuca, of all places, and I re-covered it with 1940s men's-tie fabric in burgundy and grey.

I resuscitated the old kitchen, hiding it behind a curved wall of marine plywood, which I stained to match the floor. It looked very stylish. I had two pieces made out of the same ply: a dining-room table and a half-elliptical wall shelf to serve from. The whole thing looked a million dollars. The pièce de résistance was the chandelier. At $6,000, it took a big bite out of the budget but turned the house into a celebration.

I was constantly giving decorating advice to clients and even to one who had embarked on a career in the field. I always thought it a hoot that I would decorate her house for nothing, and she would charge a fortune to do the same for others.

Taste is such a subjective thing. Often, I would work on a house to find all my hard work ruined by the client's whim to contribute. I was working on a large double drawing room in a Victorian mansion, and it was all coming together beautifully. I had found a huge 1930s kilim that filled the room. It was all chocolate and pinks with giant, stylised roses. We had made several seating and conversation areas and a study in a corner. One day, I arrived, and there was the most grotesque dining-room table filling the two rooms. It must have seated twenty, at least. The client had pushed everything else up against the walls. The deco carpet got lost and I gave up. I decided to keep my taste to myself and concentrate on what I did best: frocks.

I had made Mark promise that we would never sell our Clifton Hill house, as I loved it, but one day I came home to find an auction sign on the front fence. We were having trouble with the mad family next door. There can be nothing worse than bad neighbours.

When Mark and I bought this house, it had a small backyard. It was all concrete, fence to fence. I gave it a faux Tuscan makeover with pencil pines in large terracotta urns along the boundary with the neighbouring property. I cut lines into the concrete so it looked like giant paving stones, then I built a cyclone wire fence and grew vines and climbing geraniums behind the row of pines. It was very congenial – something I couldn't say about the neighbours. They were Maltese and volatile. They never spoke in normal tones but screamed everything at each other. One day we came home to find that they had cut off the tops of the pencil pines and sliced my glorious green wall from the cyclone fence. Lying on the ground, it was no longer a wall but a withering carpet. I stood there in a state of shock and disbelief. I could once again see into the neighbours' kitchen. When they saw me, the old mother-in-law came out onto the back step and screamed, "If you want green, go live in the jungle!" It was time to move on.

Soon we were looking for somewhere to live, and serendipity played a part yet again. This was at the beginning of the 1990s, just after the property crash, when a lot of developers sent many a bank into a spin. Mark came across a neglected 1950s Lutheran church that nobody wanted. I hated it when I first saw it and he had to do some swift talking to get me to look inside. Within two minutes, I saw the whole thing – a vision very much as it is today.

Mark made an offer to the bank, who had foreclosed, but they figured it owed them a million dollars and refused, putting it up for auction. No one was interested. The only bidder was the old codger from across the road who didn't really want it and was just playing silly buggers – so he informed us later. We got it for the same price as we had offered the bank – nowhere near what they had wanted – and we were content in the fact that we had scored a bargain.

Although no one else had wanted to buy it, every architect in Melbourne wanted to put their stamp on it now, and I would find their cards under the door. Not knowing what I know today, I started a search for one. In many an interview, I would explain what I wanted, often getting the reply, "No, you don't. That's not what you want." Well, there is one thing I can say for myself in my life, and that is I have always known exactly what I wanted, and I usually got it. My final choice of architect was a disaster beyond recall, but the immediate problem was where to live in the meantime.

We looked around for flats. Those that fitted our budget were hideous, and even those we couldn't afford were no better. Our dear friends Bob and Bruce had what had originally been a small stable at the back of their house. I asked if we could move in there for six months while our renovations took place, and they graciously agreed. We did a quick makeover with a slap of paint and new carpet, and I literally squeezed all my furniture in. We spent the happiest two years of my life there. Bruce is one of the world's best cooks and we would take turns at cooking, with me trying all the harder to keep up with him. It was a joyous time; we laughed for two years non-stop. I cried like a baby when we had to leave, and if it hadn't been to move into such a superb residence I would have preferred to stay put in the stables. Things, unfortunately, do change. Bob and Bruce's life together came adrift a few years later, although they remain good friends.

The church became a home, a refuge from the hassle of the busy world, a fortress against the ugliness of the real world, a cocoon. My furniture and the pieces that Mark and I have gleaned from all around the globe sit harmoniously in a simple contemporary setting. I took the roof off the church and made a garden where the congregation once sat. At the end, where the altar was, we built a two-storey dwelling, with a living

area and kitchen downstairs, and a bedroom, a guestroom and two bathrooms upstairs. French doors open the house to the garden, which becomes our dining room in summer.

The design was executed by Paul Fleming and has a Japanese feeling. Some of the rocks weigh nearly two tons. We had a great time riding around in the back of a ute, handpicking them on a country property near Mansfield. Getting them into the garden was a saga in itself. We hired a crane at $1,000 for the day, as that was how long it would take, so they said. We had half the street blocked off, and we were the cause of much gossip and speculation as to what was going on. It took three days in the end because I kept changing my mind about the position of some.

"No, no, you were right. Put it back."

I like touches of whimsy, and my friend Maree has added subtle tricks such as the speaker covers, which are trompe-l'oeil books, the titles of which are jokes at our friends' expense. I must admit that a few friends have fallen by the wayside and have been painted out. The most comprehensive volume is by Georgina, its title being "I Taught Him Everything He Knows".

Another masterstroke at Maree's hand is a suite of Louis XIV furniture, which came from a maharaja's palace. When I bought it, part of its charm was the upholstery. It was in tatters, the gold threads in the cloth all oxidised and the stuffing escaping where it could. I promised the dealer I would never re-cover it. However, it didn't take much more wear and tear to reach the point where it couldn't be saved. So I got Maree to paint new upholstery to look just like the old had been when I bought it. Not without very close inspection can you tell that it is fake decay. I had her place a mouse peeping out from one corner of one chair, another taking a run for cover on a second chair, and a third squashed one on the sofa. (He wasn't quick enough!) Maree also hand-painted our bedroom in the appearance of seventeenth-century Chinoiserie-style wallpaper. It reminds me of her every morning I awake there surrounded by such splendour.

My favourite touch of whimsy – and I know some people think it is in very dubious taste – is my set of tiger cushions. These cushions were the cause of the only real fight that Mark and I have ever had in our many years together. We were strolling through the night market in Penang when I spotted one of those garish carpets that are meant for the wall – "Tigers taking a drink at sunset". It was fairly hideous, and only I could turn it into a triumph. I decided to buy it. Mark couldn't believe I was buying anything so grotesque. It wasn't a huge fight, but words were exchanged. He stormed off, leaving me in stunned disbelief. Undaunted, I bought the tigers anyway and hid them from him for a few years until the right moment. Then I cut them up, rearranged them, and appliquéd them into a different configuration. Voilà! Six fabulous cushions of tigers taking a drink at sunset!

I had always bought hundreds of architectural and interior magazines and have *Architectural Digest* going back to when it was printed in black and white. I continued to buy it even when it went through a suspect period in the 1980s – at the time no one would confess to even opening it, but I bought it nevertheless.

It's interesting to look back at those years of dubious taste – or should I say, excess – in the 1980s/90s. I always find that there is something of quality or style that will show someone's individuality and confidence in their own taste, regardless of what other people think. I think this has been a characteristic I have always had, ever since I can remember. I have never cared what anyone else thinks. As long as I like it, it's okay. There is never a moment of doubt.

I often wish I had questioned some of my decisions in life. But, all in all, I have few regrets when it comes to my sense of style.

40

Other Backyards

When I first left the family home, my backyard at Avoca Street was a poor excuse for a garden as it was too far away to enjoy, being down three flights of stairs. I only went there to put the rubbish out or to shove something into the overcrowded storeroom. Once, my dear friend Daphne was minding the flat when I was away. I neglected to tell her to watch out for the backdoor, which had a nasty habit of locking you out. Realising it was rubbish day one morning, she rushed down to the backyard to catch the collection. Not only was the side gate locked but, when she turned to go back into the house, she found the back door had slammed and locked her out. She was in a terrible dilemma. All she was wearing was a skimpy T-shirt. Nothing else, not even slippers. And what was worse, no make-up.

She knew that my friend Graham had a spare key and decided to ring him as he worked close by. How to scale the fence was the first challenge. She raised herself up to find that the drop to the street was almost 2 feet deeper than on the garden side. Her predicament attracted the attention of a passing gentleman. She assured me that he *was* a gentleman because

he did close his eyes, but I am certain he would have had more than a handful of cheap thrills – as Daphne had, and still has, a gorgeous body. Then she called Graham, who didn't let Daphne get the full story out as he was serving a customer and said he was busy. He nearly fainted when Daphne appeared in the store, a near-naked apparition. How she negotiated her way down one of the busiest, most prestigious shopping strips in Melbourne without being arrested for indecent exposure I will never know.

We built our first holiday house in Noosa in 2000 and named it Palmyra. When I looked out the kitchen window, I could see 27 acres of pristine bush and rainforest, home to a resident family of kangaroos and some rogue deer. (I don't blame any joey that refuses to leave home.)

I gave Mark the nickname of Capability Brown after he created a magnificent tropical paradise – a mixture of natural bush, tropical forest and formal plantings – at Noosa in a few short years. He established hundreds of gardenias, many varieties of palms, a frangipani grove, a myriad of gingers, heliconias, bromeliads and caladiums. Mark created a secret garden, which we named the fairy garden because it had a myriad of secret paths meandering through just about every variety of coleus you could imagine. Not a Hills Hoist in bloom. Of course, our marvellous housekeeper, Beryl, kept the whole shebang running, taking charge of a team of gardeners and doing much of the maintenance herself. One scorching day, lying by the pool, something caught the corner of my eye and I realised that it was Beryl up a ladder, sawing away at a rogue palm frond. She was in her late sixties. I said, "When Beryl goes, I go." As it transpired, she soon passed away quite unexpectedly, and our years at Palmyra ended.

We replaced the acres of gardens at Palmyra for a view. Our new Noosa house needs little maintenance, being perched atop a lofty crest looking down a valley at the distant vista of the ocean. There are weeds – to be expected – and the daily sweeping under the established frangipanis we planted, but no more endless hours on a ride-on mower and loading a trailer with dozens of palm fronds. Our only garden is an inner court in a Japanese-inspired manner with a bubbling brook. And our only kangaroos are terracotta, now resting under a delicate swathe of sacred bamboo.

Will this be our last backyard? Have I got another house in me? My dream house is on a cliff overlooking a wild ocean with the house buried into the hill. Nothing but wild grass as the garden. No backyard at all! I must buy a Lotto ticket.

41

Food & Bev

I love food. I love to cook it. I love to eat it. A saying that rings true for me is, "Some people eat to live, and others live to eat." I am the latter.

Food is one of life's pleasures. I love to collect and read any type of cookbook. I seldom follow them but delight in their culinary variety, immersing myself in their glossy photographs, planning where I can buy the ingredients, noting the weights and measures, and envisaging my skills in slicing and dicing, mixing, baking, roasting, steaming, frying and grilling. As a toddler, I preferred pots and pans to my toys – my mother could leave me happily on the kitchen floor with a cupboard door open, and I would be content for hours. I love to watch cooking programs on the telly and enjoy all the cooks, chefs and pretenders. Much as I admire the likes of Nigella, the "Two Fat Ladies", and the cheeky Jamie Oliver; however, I would never aspire to be in their shoes. After one brief stint in the commercial realm of food and beverage, I have to put working with food ahead of any warnings about working with children or animals. It is just too hard.

Of all the terrible things that Georgina bamboozled me into doing over the years, becoming involved in a catering business was by far the worst. Our mutual friend Louise – that she has remained so is a testament to friendship – was just starting as a caterer, and Georgina had thought it would be a brilliant idea if I became involved.

I was happily sewing away, making my couture dresses and achieving a modest living. I had a very good clientele and more than enough work. So why did I let myself be talked into it? I still don't understand. The idea was that I would be the creative director, in charge of everything behind the scenes. I would design the settings, flowers and themes for the glamorous parties and dinners that would no doubt dazzle Melbourne society in no time at all. It sounded reasonable and manageable. Surely, I could juggle a few table arrangements on the side while making my frocks?

Louise and I formed a partnership. Mistake number one. This meant that I had to put money into the business, matching Louise's investment. It wasn't a great amount, but it was significant relative to what I had, which wasn't a lot in those days. I never saw that money again. No regular wage. No return on investment. Everything we made was sunk back into the business.

Although Louise has gone on to become a well-respected caterer and food consultant, she really couldn't cook when we started – as I was quite surprised to discover. She was also a vegetarian – she hated meat, couldn't bear to touch it. She had no idea how it tasted or should taste. Louise's greatest skill was organising other people to do most of the work, and this included me. With Georgina's networking and bullying tactics, it wasn't very long before charity-driven Toorak matrons were booking ladies' lunches, and flashy property developers from Brighton were planning big, sit-down fortieth-birthday parties.

Our very first big society ladies' lunch was an outstanding success. I wanted to make a good impression, as everybody who was anybody among Melbourne's ladies-who-lunch would be there. In planning the flowers, I decided to invest in twenty honey-coloured glazed ceramic pots on little trays for the centrepieces. At $20 each, I thought they were expensive at the time, but I would get plenty of use out of them in the future.

Louise did a perfect job – the food looked fabulous and was delicious. If I remember correctly, she offered the choice of a light pumpkin-and-sage ravioli or succulent lamb strap for the main course. This was followed by tiny meringues with soused strawberries for dessert. For the flowers, I decided against pretty, using lots of Australian natives, including every bloom from a poor hakea tree I just happened to spot on a midnight drive. I still feel guilty about decimating the poor thing. As I made my escape, I caught sight in the rear-view mirror of what remained, and it looked as if it had been struck by a plague of locusts. But its flowers were a big hit – so much so that, when I went to dismantle the settings, I found that the Toorak matrons had beaten me to it. But not only had they taken the flowers, they had swiped the glazed pots as well. That took care of the profit on that lunch!

Louise proudly only used the finest ingredients and bought all her fruit and vegetables from Marios, the best (and most expensive) fruit shop in Melbourne. Once, we had a big sit-down luncheon party for 100, and the entrée was an avocado salad. The avocados looked perfect: large, glossy orbs like uncut emeralds, each wrapped in pure-white tissue paper. Imagine our horror when we cut into the first one, and it was full of big black spots. Every one we cut was the same – in all three boxes. Louise always managed to stay calm. She never ever showed panic. She saved what she could and arranged the lettuces in a clever artistic camouflage. It was a brave move, but it didn't fool the host.

The invoice was sent twice. No payment came. So, Louise sent me to enquire. The birthday boy wasn't happy. In no uncertain terms, he let me have it about the "Black Death" salad, although he did admit that the rest of the lunch had been faultless. I didn't try to argue with him, or to bargain or justify anything. I just stood there silently until he ran out of steam. When he realised he wasn't going to get the showdown or backdown that he expected, he handed over the total amount. Silence is a tactic I have employed in many situations since. Indeed, I wish I had used it more.

Because we never had resources behind us, we were always looking for ways to save money. My solution with flowers was to cut costs by stealing anything that hung over a fence, grew on a median strip, or was freely available in a public space. My friend Graham was a fabulous spotter and often accompanied me on midnight raids down back lanes from Toorak to Williamstown. I even carried a saw in the boot of my car for large branches, be they armloads of autumnal splendour, spring blossoms or winter silhouettes. Although I never set foot in any private garden, caused grievous visual harm, or damaged the environment (apart from the hakea), my bounty was often glorious. Even so, I am ashamed to admit to this wilful vandalism.

Justice was ultimately served, however, curing me of this disgraceful behaviour forever. I had spotted some blooms that were just out of reach, and I was leaning over a fence into territory normally out of bounds when I lost my balance and fell straight into a huge cactus plant. I propelled myself back over the fence like a rocket, covered in thousands of tiny invisible boosters. I virtually tore off my clothes. All to no avail – the offending barbs had passed straight through and buried themselves sub-epidermis. Luckily, I was within running distance of home and screamed into the house, yelling for Mark to help. I tried a hot bath, thinking that would sweat them out. Then I tried ice packs to numb the pain. Nothing seemed to help. I don't remember when I got back to normal, but I did. Never since – to this day – have I been tempted to steal as much as a swaying weed from over a garden wall!

When we had a big party, I would get up at 3 am to go to the flower market and then work all day. By the time the party would wrap up, it would often be 3 am the following day before I got to bed. As we were a shoestring operation, I found myself having to be more than multifunctional. I would not only orchestrate the visuals but also often became deliveryman, waiter, chef and dishwasher.

I remember doing a big dance party. Mark and a lot of our friends attended, and he thought it would be a great idea to bring people behind the scenes to say hello throughout the night. As they became progressively more drunk, I became progressively more cranky. At 2 am, there I was, making fish and chips, mini-hamburgers and Persian fairy-floss wands, while everyone else was having a great time. No wonder I was testy.

But the crunch was yet to come. The occasion was another huge Toorak party at about the same witching hour. I had worked all day on transforming the house into a magic forest. Gigantic bowers of autumnal branches in tall crystal vases scraped the ceiling. Cascades of vines and flowers spilled out of urns. And a living landscape of moss surrounded everything. I was thrilled with the results. Louise would spring things on you at the eleventh hour. Suddenly, I was to be the chef for this occasion. She had devised a menu that flowed continuously all night. At one interval, she planned to serve deep-fried oysters. I had never deep-fried anything in my life. Surprised at this admission, she looked at me blankly and gave vague instructions. She obviously didn't know how to deep-fry either.

"You heat up the oil and throw them in."

I battered what seemed like 300 oysters (I think there were about 150 guests). When a great deal of smoke seemed to be rising from the deep-fryer, I threw them in as instructed. Instantly, hundreds of oysters became one huge one. They made an unusual noise like *shloomp* as they joined ranks and splattered for a radius of at least 8 feet – sizzling-hot little spitballs, meteors burning everything in their path. I took the brunt of the intergalactic shower, losing much of the hair on my arms and eyebrows.

When the oyster course was not forthcoming, Louise found me, struggling with what looked like some furious, mutinous intelligence that had invaded from another planet. Again, her sense of control clicked in. She told me coolly to separate them and disguise the problem by serving them tossed through a bed of rocket salad. This was easier said than done; they were white-hot. As I didn't have gloves, I inflicted further burns on my poor fingers while trying to execute her orders.

I decided to get out of the business there and then, and I did so over the next couple of months. Louise had committed to do the food styling for a TV mini-series, and I couldn't leave her in the lurch, so I agreed to stay on until shooting was completed.

Glass Babies was a contemporary soap drama revolving around the dastardly doings of doctors, scientists and corrupt businessmen working on an IVF program. I couldn't actually follow the plot, but there were plenty of rich and beautiful characters. We had to style the food and flowers for the many scenes set in glamorous restaurants, country properties and ritzy mansions. I recall one location, which was a romantic dinner for two. They had set it in the Great Hall of the National Gallery of Victoria. To say the actors looked lost was an understatement. I did a huge canopy of white rhododendrons that I had conned a woman in Canterbury to sell me out of her garden. At least twenty years of growth towered 7 feet above the table from a tall column of crystal. It looked fantastic. Louise made a dessert with spun toffee domes over frozen ice-cream bombes swirled in tall, oversized martini glasses.

The scene would have gone well if it had been one take. But shooting took all day, and it became a nightmare trying to please the continuity girl. Louise had left me to it, as usual, and the ice cream kept melting and dissolving the toffee domes. They would either sink and disappear or slide off onto the table. I would have to shift the flowers, change the tablecloth, and make up a new dessert. (Luckily, I had an Esky with back-ups.) It was a horrible day. If only Louise had made a torte!

Nothing seemed to please anyone except the lead actress, who was most impressed with the glorious food. She kept trying to persuade me to cook a dinner party for her!

There was a funeral in one of the final shoots. The director never knew what he wanted. Knowing his thought process, I asked him exactly what he wanted.

"A funeral. It's a funeral. I want flowers for a funeral."

So that's what I did. I made wreaths, crosses, sprays and bunches. I had tonal colours, all colours, ghastly mixed colours. I worked all day. I had just about finished at 11 pm when I got a phone call from the director's assistant.

"He wants an all-white funeral."

Apparently, it was a virgin – a drowned child or one of the embryonic "glass babies" that was being interned the following day – and he decided that it had to be all "white, white and white". Had I read the script further than the six pages I had attempted before being bored witless, I would have probably suggested that myself.

I told the poor girl taking the blast of my wrath at the other end of the phone, "I can't do it. It's impossible. Where does he expect me to get a truckload of white flowers at this time of night?" A large garden in Albany Road did cross my mind, but I had given up all that nefarious business and slammed down the phone. When I calmed down, I phoned her back. She was in tears. I suggested ringing Interflora, who would have the resources and might be able to do it by the morning.

Meanwhile, what was I going to do with a room full of funeral tributes? I could hardly rearrange them into vases because I had cut most of the heads off the flowers to wire them onto different shapes. Suddenly, I had a brilliant idea. Mark and I bundled them into my car and headed off down St Kilda Road, draping them all over an Egyptian obelisk erected to remember the fallen from some world war or Crimean battle. They looked beautiful, and I took great amusement the next day seeing the puzzled expressions on tram commuters and passing motorists as they tried to recall what memorial day they had missed.

That saw the end to my career in catering and the world of TV and films. I know how Kevin Costner felt when he saw *The Big Chill*; all my work ended up on the cutting-room floor. There was a distant shot of the tête-à-tête in the Great Hall, but just about all the effort of the hundreds of hours that I spent on the flowers was cut. The all-white funeral was the only scene where the flowers were in focus – and I must say that Interflora had done a splendid job.

As well as cooking, I adore entertaining, although lifestyles have changed over the years and the type of food I now prepare is very simple. The secret is to buy the very best and not adulterate it. My favourite dinner is roasted poussin. I do nothing but roast it over a bain-marie, which ensures it doesn't dry out. With a salad and maybe some red sweet potato, that is my idea of a perfect meal.

In the past, I have cooked very elaborate dinners, with course after course of carefully chosen elements – the stuff of television series. This is why I still enjoy the art of it all. Sometimes, though, I think that the art goes a bit too far. I was served "Smoke" at one of the restaurants that are the current rage. I had to control myself from hysterics. Not only at the silliness of the notion but at all the palaver that accompanied it. This particular dish had won Dish of the Year and should have taken an extra gong for joke of the year as well. The restaurant concerned had all sorts of other culinary tricks. Every dish featured some nonsense – a smear of abalone cream, a foam of chanterelles, or a chiffon of hand-gathered seaweed. One dish featured lamb that had been poached, roasted, shredded and compacted into a loaf. With the appearance of tinned dog food, it tasted fine but was nothing special, yet it was their signature dish and the most popular offering on the menu. I was bemused to watch other patrons in rapture as they flaked it into their quivering maws.

Ideas are running out. The latest trend, now that fusion is losing steam, is to take ethnic food and give it a modern prefix. Modern Persian, Greek, Lebanese. This trend purports to take good, earthy, robust food and imbue it with a sophisticated "modern" interpretation. What it means is that restaurants can serve tiny portions on fancy plates and charge twice as much.

I tend to cook at home rather than dine out. The food is usually better. I don't stack, smear, foam or chiffon. But, whatever my style of food is called – be it "home cooking" or otherwise – it is prepared with the best ingredient of all – love.

My last meal before the firing squad?

Lamb chops, mashed potato and peas.

42

Yo-yo

I was searching for a CD that Mark had heard in a café. I only had the vaguest idea of what the song was called, the name of the album and the band. I hadn't heard the CD, so I was saved my usually embarrassing rapid exit from the shop when I would ask the shop assistant, "Do you have this?" and proceed to hum, or worse, try to sing the piece in question. (I would always have to flee, as the stunned silence that followed my singsong was so embarrassing.)

This search had led me to a particularly hip music store in trendy Chapel Street, South Yarra. Out in the street, I was already feeling old. As I stood waiting for someone to notice me inside the shop, I felt like a dinosaur that had been defrosted and dropped in 100,000 years later. The music was deafening; for me to think that, it must have been ear splitting. The sales assistants seemed preoccupied or not interested in dinosaurs as I waited by the counter for some attention. That was when I noticed him.

He was most likely nineteen or twenty and decked out in the most amazing outfit. It was essentially a polyester satin ensemble: three-quarter pants, slippery navy satin with broad white-and-red stripes that puckered down the outside leg. A black see-through Lycra singlet was worn under a camouflage mesh T-shirt. This somewhat disguised a black bear-like doormat chest, and a twinkle suggested a pierced nipple. Swamping the lot was a heavy, white satin bomber jacket with acid yellow raised numbers in glowing rubber. It was adorned with dozens of badges, which I presumed to be American College football teams. On the head, the obligatory baseball cap was worn back to front – which, being made out of the one fabric, was relatively simple. It changed colour when he moved.

But it was when you cast your eye to his feet that the true visual treat became startling. He looked like he was hovering on twin spaceships. They were silver and white with orange reflector strips and what looked like blue mercury flowing through clear acrylic tubes around the heels and under the foot. I took in the whole picture and contemplated the state of street fashion. I shuddered at the thought of how this particular strain of it would filter down to the mainstream.

What was even more fascinating than his appearance was what this boy was doing: he was playing with a yo-yo. He was earnest, and he was concentrating very hard on his exhibition skills. Unfortunately, he was absolutely hopeless. I am glad Mark wasn't with me as it would have been the "close your mouth" scenario; I couldn't take my eyes off him. I was transported back to my Hyde Street school days behind the shelter shed at the height of yo-yo fervour. "Around the World", "Walking the Dog", "Swinging the Monkey", and "Rock the Cradle" are just a few of the tricks that come to mind.

Yo-yos were seasonal, and every year Coca-Cola would promote their libation by launching a new fancy model. This always made last year's yo-yo antiquated. This year's was always thicker, heavier, sharper and faster. One year I remember one that lit up as it gyrated up and down on its string. There were usually three models of yo-yos, priced accordingly, and no matter how I would aim, I could never save up enough to buy the top of the range. I was never a champion and still remember how the end of my finger would turn purple when the string would twist and tighten around it as I endeavoured to master all the tricks in the required repertoire.

At twelve, I could have slayed this boy standing before me in the music shop; he was so inept that I thought he must have just got his first yo-yo – maybe it was a giveaway in a packet of chips. He would flip his wrist and launch the yo-yo into a fancy manoeuvre but, to his consternation, connect with the ground; the yo-yo would bounce back and hit something, not infrequently whacking his exposed shins. Nothing deterred his earnestness or his confidence; he thought he was fabulous. You think you've got the picture? Well, you haven't.

This boy was mammoth; I was reed-slim standing next to him. I wondered how such a young man got so big so soon. I thought back to what I was like at that age, and I drew a metaphor between the body and the yo-yo. Looking back, I see now that I have always had a problem with body image. I was skinny for years, but I saw a fat person when I looked in a mirror. At that age, I embarked on a lifetime of "yo-yo dieting". I was 72 kilos for years and worked hard to stay that way. I would weigh myself every morning and every night – and at lunchtime, if anywhere near scales – constantly watching every gain and loss. I have continuously been yo-yo dieting ever since, and there isn't a diet I haven't tried: Dr Atkins, Pritikin, Beverly Hills, the Zone, the Mayo Clinic Diet, the Scarsdale, Grapefruit, Cabbage, The Heart Foundation Diet, Fit for Life – and the worst diet of all time, "The Israeli Army Diet".

I went on the latter on more than one occasion. I remember about six of us being on it once, and we would have dinner parties as we tried to outdo each other in style and cleverness with the different ways to make eight days of torture pass with as much fun as possible. Two days of cheese! We always started with the cheese. The fun part was the buying of dozens of different varieties. I would proceed to slice them, cube them, grate them, and layer them, and for a particular main course, I had a cheese that I would grill until it formed a crunchy crust that I would top with another lighter cheese which would slightly melt. After a light dusting of chilli flakes, it was served in wedges; it was almost a pizza.

On the third day, an early rising meant the first juicy, refreshing bite of an apple, bliss after all that cheese. It was hard to maintain as much interest in apples. I sliced, diced, peeled, cored and carved them into pretty crescents. I fashioned never-ending twists made with the potato peeler (whoever got the longest ribbon won). I baked, pureed and grated. To impress my fellow Israeli Dieting guests, I prepared a gourmet extravaganza, "Apple kebabs on the BBQ". Two days of protein in the form of chicken or steak followed.

The Menu

(A) Steak:

A porterhouse for breakfast, a small eye fillet for lunch and a slab of rump that didn't fit on the most enormous plate for dinner.

(B) Chicken:

A roast chicken for breakfast, a roast chicken for lunch, followed by a roast chicken for dinner.

Day 6: Everyone has breath that would strip paint; this is due to the body producing ketones and it results in headaches and dizziness. At least the salad days allowed for a variety of colours and texture and the hope that the end was in sight. We all professed to have lost kilos and that our pants were dropping off. A yo-yo pattern of loss and gain was established, with the gain just ahead of the loss every time.

As I have grown older, my waist seems to have tried to keep up with my age; at one stage, I thought it might outrun it. Ironically I didn't see a fat person when I looked in a mirror. I didn't see a skinny person either, but I didn't see the truth. A photograph is a different matter, and it was when seeing holiday snaps that the reality hit home. I didn't recognise myself and was shocked.

I can't remember a moment in time when I thought my body was any good; there must have been a flash as it went from anorexic to obese, but I think I missed that. Even at 72 kilos, I looked like a poster for the "Save the Children Foundation". I always have a belly and I seem to have an extra set of ribs that stick out; once, in New York, a store detective

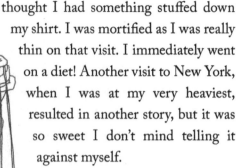

thought I had something stuffed down my shirt. I was mortified as I was really thin on that visit. I immediately went on a diet! Another visit to New York, when I was at my very heaviest, resulted in another story, but it was so sweet I don't mind telling it against myself.

I was doing all the street kids' shops right down "downtown" where all the black dudes buy their gear. An adorable assistant asked if she could help me with anything. I spluttered out a response about being too old and fat for anything in the shop. She held my hand and whispered in my ear in a voice like Miss Scarlett's maid in *Gone with the Wind*, "Wha honey, you ain't fat, you've just got a little tummy." She could have sold me the whole shop.

I have a suspicion that my friend with the yo-yo transports himself on those silver space shoes to that very shop to gear up.

After a very successful bash with Weight Watchers, again, I have yo-yoed to a new high. I am currently doing a keto-style diet with some results, but who knows when that will lose its effectiveness. Will I ever stay at an acceptable weight for me? I know I will never see 72 kilos again, and neither should I; the prospect of being released from the twisted tyranny of the dieter's yo-yo string is a hopeful possibility. Once again, I can look to Sarah Ferguson for inspiration, another chance to change my destiny. She is skinny again, although I think at least a small sleeve wouldn't go astray. She will always be held in my highest esteem; even when *New Idea* shows her in funny zebra shoes with a matching skirt and orange sleeveless top, she can do no wrong. She did it, so can I!

"The Duchess of Pork"?

Not any more!

43

Opera and Ballet

Ever since its release, I had avoided seeing *Billy Elliot*. I just had a feeling that this film about a working-class boy wanting to be a ballet dancer would be too close to the bone. On a plane on my way to India, however, I came across it among the movies on demand and decided to watch it. Once I had started, there was no turning back. It was *my* story.

I don't remember how I came into contact with the world of ballet. Maybe it was through swap cards. I can remember being fascinated with the huge wad of them that Pat's elder sister, Karen, had collected. Swap cards were a big-time obsession with schoolgirls in the 1950s. I think they could be bought from paper shops, and girls would swap them to build up their collections. Karen's stack was so huge that you couldn't hold them comfortably, and she kept them together with an elastic band so thick that it could start the motor of a light aeroplane. Cards with horses were the most desirable, followed by those with kittens, dogs, roses and – *my* favourite – ballerinas.

Karen watched over her cards very closely, as if they were as precious as gold. I had much more access to Pat's bundle, but they weren't as good as Karen's. When allowed to view Karen's, I would shuffle to the ballet sets. She must have had a complete set of *Swan Lake*. All those romantic lovers executing exquisite pas de deux and flying through the pastel-coloured clouds of some kitsch painter's imagination inspired me to make a balletic leap out of my ho-hum suburban world. I wanted to escape into the magical realm that I saw depicted on those swap cards.

The first real ballerinas I saw were in a school concert. Two third graders with giant butterfly wings of painted Japanese silk on extended bamboo poles flitted onto the stage, up on points in flesh-coloured satin ballet slippers. Oh, how I wanted a pair of my own. It didn't take me long to perfect the art of standing on my toes even without the help of wooden blocks (which I only found out later were the secret boost in those slippers). Hanging on to a branch of the old apple tree, I would get up on points and take off, leaping and bounding around the backyard.

When I was ten, I begged my mother to take me to see the visiting New York City Ballet for my birthday. It was the most magical afternoon of my life to that point. They presented a mixed program, with some wildly energetic modern pieces and classical highlights. Excerpts from *Swan Lake* took up the whole second half. The swap cards came to life, and I was enraptured for weeks after.

I wasn't as lucky as Billy, never getting as far as lessons. When

I brought up the subject, my father just stared at me blankly and didn't even answer. About this time, he renewed his efforts to teach me how to kick a football. A star player for Williamstown in the Victorian Football Association, he was a perfect teacher. By the time he had bullied and drilled me, I could kick a football further than anyone else at school. The only thing missing was my desire to do so. No matter how many threats or encouragements I received from the sports master at school, I wouldn't oblige. Occasionally, I would tease the football coach with a perfect goal at a practice session and then refuse to play if I was put on a team. I hated football. It was so rough!

Billy Elliot completely devastated me on that flight to India. I didn't cry. I didn't sob. I convulsed. Luckily for me, Georgina was a few rows back and kept passing with another wad of tissues. I was so spellbound by my life as it should have been that I couldn't move. The flight attendants were puzzled. They couldn't figure out what could make me so sad! The only regret of my life is that I didn't have Billy's courage to stand up to my father stolidly and pursue my dream. I know I would have made a good dancer. On the other hand, looking back now, I realise that my career would have finished early, and I may not have achieved the things I have done otherwise.

Although I missed out on a professional life as a dancer, I have never lost that instinctual need to express myself to music. I have loved dancing all my life. Even today, with my feet begging me not to do it, if the music is right and I have had a few drinks to anaesthetise the pain you can't stop me. In my early twenties, I think I spent six nights a week on the disco floor. Tuesday was the only night we stayed home. Usually, laundry was done that night (not that I have ever done my own).

I love to dance with a female partner. Even though I am gay, I think two men dancing together look ridiculous. I have had many fabulous dancing partners over the years – Cheryl, Veronica, Miss Size Fives and, my favourite, Rosangela. We can dance for hours and hours. I love to fling a girl around a dance floor with her completely under my spell. During my tenure in Hong Kong, I think I nearly killed Judith at a big

Chinese wedding. As we were whirling about, I held her to me at one stage, and her little heart was racing at a thousand beats a second. I don't think she had the chance to ask me to stop.

Most of all, however, I prefer to dance by myself. Just before I left Hong Kong, I went to a club. I had promised to catch the drag act of a friend's protégé, a kid who was giving drag a whole new edge and had such a cute bum. It was "happy hour" – two drinks for the price of one – but all I kept thinking while watching these desperados was, "When are they going to get happy?" Eventually, after an hour or so, everybody did become very happy, including me.

On this particular evening, the club was only gay until 9 o'clock. When they announced the last dance, my painful feet usually held me back from the dance floor. But on this occasion I had lost all feeling after so much alcohol, so I hit the floor and danced with gay abandon, pairing up with a sweet English boy. Then, without noticing, I cleared the floor. The whole room of vicious queens was watching me whirl away with unbridled, uninhibited, unabashed exhibitionism. When the music stopped, I looked around at all the faces and thought, "Oh my God! I am going to be beer-bottled to death." Instead, they broke out in loud whoops and applause. Making the most of my one and only moment of stage euphoria, I swirled and bowed, then grabbed my coat and fled. From that one and only taste of applause, I realise it is a fabulous drug. I can imagine the surge that must pass from an adoring audience to a performer as they are rewarded for imparting their talent.

As with ballet, my love of opera is a mystery to me. Mine wasn't a musical home – we had no music until I got a Pye Black Box for my fourteenth birthday. My only recollections of what emanated from the radio on the mantelpiece are the soap operas that my Nanna listened to and *The Goon Show*, which my father never missed.

The first aria that sparked my interest in opera was in a very camp film from the 1960s, *Modesty Blaise*, starring Dirk Bogarde and Monica Vitti. In the movie, there was an evil lesbian who ran a nefarious crime syndicate from an antique-looking Egyptian Doha. It was all high-tech and computer-driven below deck, but that is a subplot. Up on deck, she would languish around on brocade and silk cushions, barking her evil instructions to the beleaguered crew. She kept a poor, short, fat, bald, ugly, old slave on the end of a rope tied around his ankle. She would push him over the side to bring her a lobster for lunch, and he would almost drown in the process. In a scene of comic pathos, he stands on the deck, dripping and barely breathing, when – before she sends him down again – he bursts into "E lucevan le stelle" ("And the stars were shining") from *Tosca*. Then she tugs on the rope, and, of course, he is lost to the jaws of a passing shark. When I left the theatre, I carried the echo of that haunting melody with me. I had to find out more about it. Hence, I discovered Puccini and a deep love for the world of opera.

Going to La Scala is every opera lover's dream. I could hardly believe it when I took my seat in the second row of the dress circle at that famous venue. It was on my first trip to Italy and I was travelling with a close friend at the time, Marisa Sillitto. With only minutes to spare, she risked buying two tickets at a highly inflated price from a scalper outside the theatre. It was magic, with dazzling production values. The heroine appeared in a carriage drawn by six white horses, setting the standard for the whole evening.

The Italians are shocking. They talk and sing throughout a performance. Having never witnessed such a thing, I was horrified. The woman in front of me kept up a conversation for the first 10 minutes until I couldn't stand it another second. I rolled up my rather large program and gave her not a gentle tap but a very enthusiastic whack. She nearly died from shock. Not another peep was heard from her for the rest of the magnificent performance.

On that particular trip, I was very fortunate, enjoying opera in Florence, Rome and Venice. In Florence, Marisa only managed to get one ticket from a scalper, but she found an usher who, for 10,000 lire, let me sneak in and stand up the back. At that time, it was difficult to distinguish between the 10,000 and 50,000 lire notes – they were being changed around, and you had to know what you were doing. Of course,

I slipped him the wrong note. In those days, 50,000 lire would have bought you seats in the royal box!

Anyway, when the lights went down, he secreted me into the theatre with far too much grinning and head nodding for my liking. It was *The Sicilian Vespers*, a Verdi opera that goes for about five hours. A composer who liked to give value for money, Verdi included a full-length ballet in it for extra audience pull. (Let's not forget that opera was popular entertainment in its heyday, not the elitist diversion it has become.) Halfway through the first act, the head usher spotted me. My man quickly gestured for me to become invisible, so I melded into a column. For the next five hours, I eluded capture – crawling down aisles on my hands and knees, hiding in potted palms, or pretending to be a piece of roman statuary one moment and a fire extinguisher the next. Although fraught with anxiety about being captured, I thoroughly enjoyed the whole thing, the danger of discovery giving the experience an extra excitement.

In Rome, I had another interesting evening, this time at an avant-garde production of Massenet's *Manon Lescaut*. As mentioned, Italians have no qualms about talking and singing along. If they don't like something, they vocalise their feelings in no uncertain terms. To my amazement, they were booing and cursing the conductor, the singers, even the sets (which were the most exciting settings I had ever seen). While enjoying the whole riotous carry-on, I had to contend with yet another distraction: the gentleman sitting in front of me kept running an exploratory hand up my leg. Whacking him with my program would deter him for a few minutes, but he would try again when he thought a suitable time had passed. I don't know what his boyfriend or the people sitting next to me thought, but it just added to the bizarre atmosphere of the evening.

The funniest thing I ever saw onstage took place during that unforgettable evening. The set was all black, with the action taking place in several boxes like colossal TV screens. Portraying the (supposedly) nubile nineteen-year-old nymph, Manon, was a diva aged about sixty and weighing at least 20 stone. She was doing some very sensual writhing, stirring up the passions of several admirers recumbent at her feet. Meanwhile, her tormented lover was having an erotic dream in a box far above. As he reached orgasm, two of the slaves-to-love at Manon's feet ripped away her flimsy gown, and she climaxed simultaneously with a triple high C note that threatened to shatter the chandelier above our heads. Unfortunately, they ripped away the naked body in moulded latex that was supposed to be revealed. Instead, the diva was revealed in a dazzling white corset with more iron girders and rivets than the Sydney Harbour Bridge. Everybody in the audience – along with the chorus, orchestra and principal artists – gasped in disbelief. When the two love-slaves realised what they had done, they let go of the latex body. It then bounced back, hitting Manon for six with a loud thwack. The audience sprang to their feet, and the curtain came down. Who said opera is dull and boring?

Having had enough orgasms for one evening, I declined an invitation to join the roaming hand and his boyfriend for drinks on the Via Veneto and made my way home through the back streets to my humble pensione, clutching my battered program. I went to bed humming the haunting intermezzo, still grinning from ear to ear after such an unforgettable night of theatrical high jinks.

Many a story has been told about seeing Tosca bounce back after throwing herself off the parapets of Castel Sant'Angelo. But I swear I really did see that at one performance. After a tear-jerking farewell to the world, she flung herself to the rocks below. When she hit the Sleepmaker double inner-spring – it must have been the deluxe, orthopaedic model – she sprang back with such alacrity that the stagehands waiting to grab her must have been taken by surprise. Even more surprised, she reappeared with slightly less dignity and even higher than the parapet she had just leapt from.

Although my feet are firmly (if reluctantly) grounded, my heart still soars and leaps like that young Billy Elliot whenever I hear such glorious music. Its inexplicable chemistry – a blending of emotions and sentiment – takes us somewhere else. This elixir of sound motivates and inspires like-minded Billys everywhere.

44

What Not to Wear

Today, there seems to be a plethora of advice about every lifestyle choice – from our cars and homes to our personal appearance. Reality TV has spawned dozens of programs over the years – including *Trinny & Susannah Undress the Nation*, *How to Look Good Naked*, *Fashion Police* and *Extreme Makeover*.

There, before our very eyes, harridans, frumps and raw, ugly ducklings are transformed in less than an hour into graceful swans. We become personally involved, just like their flabbergasted spouses and bewildered children. Our hearts are in our throats when we assemble at the mansion on the hill for the unveiling. We are astonished and befuddled when the victim wobbles down the sweeping staircase in 6 inch FMH pumps. Gone are the fluffy slippers and stretch track pants. There she stands – transformed from a homely homemaker into a slut wearing a red, strapless, backless, satin mini-dress.

My heart goes out to those poor children who have no idea who this woman is! As they suffocate in the cleavage of her new triple Ds, they must be terrified that she is going to devour them. She clutches them like a demented vampire. Her new set of menacing, blinding-white porcelain veneers don't quite fit into her mouth, and her once-modest smile has turned into a manic grin, threatening to take the poor little tots' last gasps. There is a look of wanton lust in the husband's eyes as he is confronted by this creature. She looks like she has escaped from the pages of the *Hooters* magazines that he has been hiding under the mattress all these years. What he's thinking doesn't quite match his comments.

"She is the same Lou Lou Anne I took to the prom. She was always beautiful to me."

His every fantasy is about to come true. He can't wait to get her panties off in the back of the stretch limo, then get her home and have her on the kitchen island. The look in her eyes portends another scenario – "I'm gonna dump this loser by the end of the week."

I have been dispensing fashion advice since I was a toddler. I have outfitted my much-loved, cross-dressing Teddy from the moment I first discovered I could. He has suffered his whole life according to my fashion dictates. After a career in fashion, with all due modesty, I can claim years of experience as an observer of "La Mode". My observation of late? With this universal bombardment of fashion advice, no one is listening.

Looking around, I seldom see a well-dressed woman. Not at the theatre any more. Maybe at a restaurant. A few at the races but not like before. I dressed exquisite women for the whole season. They would have two outfits for each day – one for inclement weather and one for a glorious day as only Melbourne can flaunt. Black and white for the Derby, colour for the Cup and pretty for Oaks Day. It is all out the window now. When I look, I think they have forgotten to put their dress on, strutting the birdcage in little more than a slip.

One piece of advice about what not to wear is White. I say this as it reminded me of my first Melbourne Cup when I wore a white linen Walter Albini suit. I woke up under a seat in a double-decker bus about two hours after the course had closed. The bus had been abandoned in the middle of the members' carpark in the epicentre of a small cyclone of debris and the occasional floral straw chapeau. That suit never recovered, and I learnt a valuable lesson about French Champagne: you don't have to worry that it will run out! Pace yourself!

I certainly don't see elegance in day-to-day life. Not like when I would go to town with my mother or Nanna. Still, monthly and weekly fashion magazines are dedicated to spewing endless advice. They scrounge to assemble page after page of fashion wisdom.

"This goes with that."

"60 ways to wear a tank top."

"The little black dress from $49.99 to $5,000."

"Five basics equal a different look for every day of the month – from early morning golf to a day at the office, 6 pm cocktails, and then on to a charity ball."

The latter amazing wardrobe promises so much with just the change of a pair of shoes and a brooch. You can be hip, chic, elegant, timeless, trendy, dressed to flatter, dressed to impress, dressed for success, and dressed to kill – all for under $150. Over the years, my clients were always asking for this elusive garment. Of course, I could come up with the goods, but it was not in my interest to do so.

Actually, I did produce the goods on several occasions – including for one of my favourite clients, Liz Rice (I knew her through three husbands, but she was always Liz Rice to me). When she was in between husbands at one stage and had a European prince in her sights, I made her a complete travelling ensemble that did all of the above in just five pieces – a jacket, a short skirt, a long skirt, a blouse, and trousers. With sleeves that zipped off, the jacket became a bodice or a vest. Skirts turned inside out. Everything was reversible. The only thing that it lacked was waterproofing. With just the addition of a whip or tiara, it morphed from an outfit fit for riding the hounds to one fit for a gala charity ball. She was away for three weeks and, apart from jeans and sweaters, my ensemble was all she took. Maybe it wasn't as great as I thought, however, as she returned without the royal trophy.

Liz was one of three daughters of a former lord mayor of Melbourne, Sir Leo Curtis. The Curtis family were regarded as Melbourne royalty. An iconic image that always sticks in my mind was a photo taken on the balcony of the Melbourne Town Hall during the Beatles tour – the famous four (John, Paul, George and Ringo) with the famous three (Liz, Ann and Vikki). The three daughters certainly were princesses, and Lady Curtis, their mother, was the reigning queen. Elvie was also one of my best clients, and I could write a whole book about her alone.

I had a lot of dealings with the family during my time at Le Louvre and later when I was on my own. Liz was one of only three clients that I ever threw out of my salon. With gifts and tears, she begged to come back because she knew I was good at what I did. I eventually did allow her back, and we became great friends. Many of my best dresses were made for her. She had special conditions dictating her wardrobe. One was refusing to pay for anything "under the table" – in her mind, if you couldn't see it when you sat down to dinner, it was a waste of money.

When Liz passed away suddenly and far too young, her death prompted a major reassessment of my life. Since I had stopped making clothes, we hadn't seen each other as much in person, but we had regularly phoned and emailed each other. She had been one of the "book club", as I refer to my group of friends who have followed the process of this memoir. The week before she died, we had spoken on the phone and the last thing she had said to me was, "We must get together for lunch before one of us drops dead."

She was a troublesome client, always full of doubt and insecurity, as is often the case with beautiful women. We had many fights over the clothes I made her, the best ones only happening when I got my way. She also expected something that Mark and I referred to as "the 10,000 mile warranty" – her dresses kept coming back for service, repairs and makeovers. Many of the fights I had with clients resulted from this (presumed) warranty clause. They would baulk at any bill – expecting me to spend ten to twenty hours shortening a ball gown into a cocktail frock, adding ruffles to the neckline and sleeves, and affixing a 2 inch invisible panel to accommodate their ever-expanding waistlines, all for nothing. They all did it – I doubt that many of the gorgeous clothes I made in those days remain intact as originally designed and constructed.

"Can you alter this chiffon gown into a mountaineering jumpsuit by this weekend? I'm off to Aspen."

I have one of Liz's dresses, which came back to have the Dynasty shoulder pads reduced (it was that era). I refused to comply, and she never picked it up. It is a beautiful gown – black cut-silk devoré with a design of loose, full-blown roses. It was tight and narrow, with virtually no back in it, and swathes from the shoulders over the bosom that were caught in another wrap around the hips. It had a complete body built into it of nude-coloured chiffon. In it, Liz looked as if she had almost nothing on, except for a drape thrown nonchalantly around her. Of the many dresses I made for her, it was one of my favourites.

In the mid-1970s, there emerged a group of women who had suddenly become rich. To say "They hit the fashion bus before it hit them" is a slight understatement. Most of those girls are all still around, and some fared better than others. Several of them could now be described as among the most stylish women in town, having developed their own individual elegance. A few have become prominent philanthropists and patrons of the arts.

Although plastic surgery and cosmetic enhancement are now the norm, these were not so readily available or so blatantly flaunted back then as they are today. One girl was the first among the group to get breast implants, and she was very proud of them. With little encouragement, she would rip open her blouse and shove them in your face, even suggesting a quick squeeze. Because she was reed-slim, these newly pumped-up bosoms looked like two hard grapefruit on a platter. I was horrified at my first glimpse of them. Although this set hadn't quite made the inner sanctum of Le Louvre, they were willing customers for the ready-to-wear collections – or "little money" collections, as they were known.

Georgina would have a charity parade at the drop of a hat. One of these women had just completed a mansion in the mini-Versailles style and was eager to show it off to Melbourne's elite, so it became the venue for the "Spring/Summer collection" of Little Money. Everyone who was anyone was at this luncheon parade and we couldn't wait to get inside the house. Jenny Ham, a famed Melbourne social beauty, volunteered to be a dresser so that she could have a good squiz. As she gazed upwards to the minstrels' gallery surrounding the ballroom, she bumped into the Golden Harp, knocking it over. Fortunately, I caught it just in time, as it wasn't a reproduction and was quite exquisite. How often the hostess gave a harp recital was a matter for speculation among the hot gossip.

We dressers were very naughty. On the pretence of setting up, we managed to run amok through the entire house while pre-lunch drinks were being served on the croquet lawn. The master en suite was all white marble, with Aphrodite's temple as the centrepiece draped in white chiffon. Several steps led to a bath with gold fittings. The taps were two life-size swans about to attack, their wings in full span and their beaks ready to rip a victim to shreds. The intended prey might have been the dolphin up the deep end. It turned out to be a clever hand-held shower head. I have to add that the bath itself was just an ordinary-sized bath!

After the parade, there was a frenzy to try and buy. The new grapefruits were being flashed around, and I nearly fainted when the recipient of these silicone wonder cones grabbed my hands and held them on the left boob to let me feel what a "real tit" felt like. Much laughter echoed around the minstrels' gallery above. Horrified and embarrassed, I swore not to have anything to do with this woman ever again. Still, our paths inevitably crossed over the years, and we ended up becoming quite friendly. She was brash, loud and just a touch common, but also a genuine, good-hearted soul, and funny. Although she was rich, she never became a client because she would never spend the money. Occasionally, though, I would help her out with alterations and such.

She had shocking taste and usually looked terrible, so no one was more surprised than me when she and a girlfriend opened a "What-not-to-wear" advice agency. (I would have thought one look at the two founders would tell you everything you needed to know at first glance.) As exponents of the *Trinny & Susannah* phenomenon, they invested quite a tidy sum in corporate offices. They were all set to advise the women of Melbourne about where to shop, what to buy, and how to put it all together. Not surprisingly, the business never took off.

In those days, many women told their girlfriends that they had clothes made by me. I still run into women who tell me that I made their wedding dress. I know very well that I didn't, but I usually say, "Oh, yes, I remember it so well. A beautiful gown. One of my best." This I do to save them any embarrassment because, quite often, they will be in the company of an ex-client whose dress I did make. And what does it matter to me?

Anyway, Melbourne's answer to Trinny nearly ruined my career by announcing to an assembled cast of hundreds that I was her couturier. It happened at a large Red Cross Ball, another of the highlights of the Melbourne social calendar. Across a crowded dance floor, she announced at the top of her voice, "There's Gregory Ladner. He's my dressmaker." Something akin to the parting of the Red Sea then occurred. There she stood on one shore, wearing a ghastly, gaudily-coloured polyester-chiffon dress, the grapefruits almost completely exposed. On the other shore of the room, a spotlight caught me with a glass of Champagne and half a sausage roll in my mouth. I got such a fright that I spilled the Champagne and choked on the sausage roll. The parted masses all looked at her. Then they looked at me. Then they looked back at her and the dress. I prayed that the sausage roll would take me then and there because there was no way I'd ever get work in this town again!

She didn't fare so well over the years, divorcing her husband because she found greener grass. But the younger bull in the other paddock eventually did her for all of her money, and she took to drink!

I always knew how best to flatter and enhance any figure problems. Not all my clients were size 8. Indeed, some of my favourite clients were far from it. One, in particular, was about size 22 and I loved the clothes I made for her. She let me do exactly what I wanted. As a result, the dresses were always flattering and quite often avant-garde. Above all, she loved them and wore them till they fell apart – she couldn't pull the 10,000 mile service trick because genuine wear and tear wasn't covered! Unfortunately, we eventually had a nasty falling out. I made her a magnificent chiffon dress that conjured up a picture of Botticelli's Rites of Spring. Hard to imagine in size 22, but it was beautiful. She took off for Europe to get married in it, neglecting to pay beforehand. When she returned years later, we had a very unpleasant run-in in the foyer of the Regent Theatre before she finally settled the bill.

With my predisposition for telling the truth, requests for fashion advice along the lines of "Does my bum look big in this?" can be problematic for me. A direct answer is best avoided. I usually divert the subject by saying something nice about their shoes.

One of my fashion idols was the Duchess of Windsor – she of the supposed "I'd rather be dressed in rags than wear a dress made in Istanbul" line. Her best piece of fashion advice was, "When in doubt, remove one item", be it a piece of jewellery or any other embellishment. Thinking back, maybe that was one of Coco Chanel's sayings, but same, same. I worshipped them both – both very unpleasant characters, but all is forgiven for the cut of a good frock. Whoever said it, I think the advice is an invaluable piece of wisdom. I always suggest checking in a full-length mirror whenever one leaves the house. Obviously, not many people own such a thing any more, judging by what I see out there. So that leaves me with only one piece of fashion advice I can offer them: Do not leave the house at all.

45

My Father

Some people have noted, in reading a draft of this book, that there is not much mention of my father. The book has relied on my memories, and, as I don't have that many fond memories of him, I guess it is no surprise that he doesn't feature much on its pages. What *is* surprising and annoying is that I think of my father every day of my life, except on those days when I can get away with not having a shower.

At Hobbs Street, we had a peculiar arrangement with the shower. The bathroom was relatively small, with just a bath and a handbasin; it looked very smart, as it was part of the refurbishment – all black tiles. The one thing I hated about it was a pseudo leather concertina door that was tricky and which you could never successfully lock. This made my hairdressing and make-up sessions fraught with anxiety, thinking that someone would come barging in and catch me with my eyeshadow wand working its wizardry. Down the hall next to the laundry was a shower room. Very early on, my father taught me to sluice down after my shower to save wear and tear on the towels by having to soak up too much water. I now do this automatically after a shower. No matter how many and how thick and fluffy the towels might be, I sluice regardless and think of him every day. As I was never that fond of him, this is quite a galling thing to go through every time I take my ablutions and it explains why, given any excuse, I will try to get out of going under water.

I was a bitter disappointment to my father. I was not exactly what he had in mind; Edwin, my younger brother, was closer to his idea of what an ideal son should be. Edwin worshipped his father, and that he broke his son's heart so badly is one of the main reasons for my unfailing antipathy towards him. He was always kind and loving, I suppose, but constantly disapproving. "What's he doing now – drawing shoes?"

The blank wall that I met when I so badly wanted to be a ballet dancer was probably the beginning of my distancing myself from him. It established an invisible barrier that, unlike the Berlin Wall, never crumbled. He was not an educated man, and I am sure not a bad man, but when I think of him, all I see is weakness. He fell into the clutches of a younger, simple village girl from the country formerly known as Yugoslavia, leaving my mother for her and starting another family; well, he had started the family before he left – another story.

So although he broke two hearts, mine was not one of them. I couldn't have cared less; I was twenty years old and, as far as I was concerned, he didn't play a significant part in my life anyway. From what I have been able to find out about his duplicitous life, it seems he was entirely under the thumb of the second wife, a downtrodden henpecked mouse, I mean spouse; I can only hope he wasn't happy.

I can never erase from my mind the look on my brother's face when he understood that our father had left. He was only ten years old, and the man that he adored didn't even have the heart to tell him face to face; his explanation was a scribbled letter of four lines. I have it somewhere, and the tears on the envelope are mine, but I wasn't crying for myself. I know that Edwin suffered from this traumatic exit, which is why I have always stood by him. He has been a classic black sheep over the years and caused me untold anguish, but as a baby and a little boy he was beautiful and I adored him. Our mother lavished on him , as she had always done with me, as much luxury as she could afford. She bought the Rolls-Royce of prams for him, and I loved taking him for walks in it. It was one of those huge English jobs, navy blue duco and white detailing, whitewall tyres, white hood and bobble braid fringing. I was so proud of it. It was one boast I didn't have to worry about being caught out on.

My father was a hard worker and always had a job on the side, although when he joined the police force he wasn't supposed to. I could never understand what my mother saw in him – although I admit he was handsome in the rough Aussie mould – because she far outshone him in every way. She was very intelligent, artistic, stylish, the complete opposite of him, but she loved him passionately, and she was all but destroyed when he left.

I say I don't know how she survived, as she wanted to die; but I do know how. I forced her, cajoled her, loved her harder, trying to make up the gap. My father had joined the police force after we moved to Hobbs Street, and I remember being very impressed with the uniform. In those days, it was made from the most beautiful pure wool twill in the darkest shade of navy, unlike the terrible junior navy polyester crap of more recent uniforms. I had an uncanny knack for spotting quality from an early age. It had sparkling silver buckles and buttons that shone like stars. Like everything my parents did, it was presented as a special surprise just for me. I was ushered into the lounge room and told to shut my eyes. When I was told to open them, and I saw him standing there in his new uniform and my mother beaming

with pride. He looked very handsome. I hope I put on enough of a show; I certainly tried to look thrilled.

The fact that he was a policeman has had an effect on my life in that I am terribly law-abiding. I won't even park in places that I shouldn't, and I would hate to think where I would be today with my penchant for shoplifting if it had not been for his sobering influence.

His career came to a halt when he left my mother. I think his actions were frowned upon by the powers that be; one particular superior of his was very fond of Celia, so I will never know if it was some sort of punishment or just a natural hiatus.

Mark can't understand why I never wanted a relationship with my father and have never so much as set eyes on my half-brother and half-sister or their children. I know it is an unresolved issue, and I have tried to deal with it several times, even seeking professional help. I will soften my resolve, but then will recall one of the instances of his shabby behaviour, like telling Edwin to lie and cover his cheating trail. He would take Edwin to the football and only stay for the first quarter and then park his son outside his love nest for a couple of hours. Edwin still feels guilty for his unwitting collaboration after all these years.

In the last years of their lives, my mother and father had made a sort of peace (making me feel like a shag on a rock). He often visited the nursing home where she lived. However, Miss Yugoslavia, found out and banned him from seeing her. He rang my mother from a public telephone box to tell her. Still as weak as piss!

It is easy to sift out the happy memories of my father, my favourite being carried through the hot sand dunes at Seaford as a little boy, being lifted so high in the air and placed on his broad shoulders. It was like flying to heaven. There were many happy times that we spent as a family before he messed up his life and ours. Unfortunately, those memories are tarnished by the bitterness that has such a hold on me.

He passed away not that long ago, and my feelings are not clear; I mainly feel guilt at not feeling anything and guilt at my failure to forgive. I can't do it. I know it's a bad thing, gnawing away at my heart, which still aches when I look back at that sad time. It's all gone, they are both dead, and maybe they are catching up and reminiscing, looking down on me and hoping I can resolve my lingering culpability.

"What's he doing now? Drawing shoes?"

46

Toys

Mark and I were travelling in the countryside in Turkey, where a well-maintained highway system crisscrosses the vast, beautiful land.

Every now and then, in the middle of nowhere, you would come across a set of traffic lights at a roundabout or highway entry. There you would be, stopped by a red light, with not another car in sight as far as the horizon. At one such connection, we did come across another vehicle; a beaten up old ute tore through the traffic lights in a cloud of dust with two little boys bouncing around in the tray. The boys seemed to be having a wow of a time. They were armed with what I hoped were toy pistols, which they aimed at us and fired. Mark commented wistfully, "Remember that, playing cowboys and Indians?" Indignantly, I snapped back, "I never played with guns", as if my gay sensitivities were being challenged.

It was some hours later that the memory came seeping back. I did in fact own a set of fancy silver pistols with white bone handles set with rubies. I must have been about eight years old. The matching pony-skin holsters, decorated with elaborate silver-and-ruby medallions with long, leather fringes, completed a set of vest, hat and stirrups. The cowboy hat had a pony-skin band with the same jewelled medallions. The pistols were cap guns and I much preferred to unroll the ammunition and run a sixpence along the strip and get it all over and done with, rather than load the pistols and endure the tedious, repetitious bang, bang, bang. They were very heavy and the trigger was hard to squeeze, as I remember. I was always dead in a showdown before I could aim and fire. Being given this cowboy set was obviously yet another attempt to wean me off Teddy and his dresses. Undeterred, I somehow jimmied all the ruby settings from the guns, fringes, holsters and stirrups and made Teddy a rather heavy, unforgiving Annie Oakley costume!

All the toys I was given were very much Boys' Toys and they seldom held my attention for long. The ribbon that had tied up the gift often had more appeal. Hours after I had lost interest in a tip truck, the ribbon would be salvaged and find itself either wound around Teddy's head as an exotic turban or wrapped around his body as a skin-tight sheath.

Over the years there were always distant cousins of my mothers who would appear every so often to stay, and I remember that one of these uncles died and left me a Meccano set. For those not familiar with Meccano, it was a model construction kit invented in 1901 and was designed to encourage boys to explore the principles of mechanical engineering. Mine was housed in a beautiful wooden box with brass fittings and comprised a huge selection of pieces. My set had hundreds of bits, perforated strips and plates, bars, angled bits, round bits, wheels, axels, pulleys, gears, cogs, chains, nuts and bolts, all designed to be put together with screwdrivers and spanners. Every piece had its own little spot in the several trays within the box, where one was supposed to replace them after having constructed a bridge, an oil rig or a locomotive.

There were books with instructions on how to construct the suggested models. Till this day I can't follow instructions, be they from IKEA or Samsung, so I got quickly disenchanted with my efforts to construct anything. I soon tired of Meccano and my set gradually disappeared bit by bit. More diligent hobbyists are today still happily screwing and bolting together everything from rockets to skyscrapers out of this system of prefabricated metal pieces, although it is now very sophisticated, having entered the age of electronics.

Having done some research, I gather my set was from the red-and-green era, dating it as pre-war. I wish I had put it under the bed and never opened it. If it was still intact today, in pristine condition, it would be worth a considerable sum.

My very favourite toy of this time belonged to my cousins, Richard and John, who had the most marvellous electric train set. Although I dreaded going to Auntie Norma and Uncles George's, the possibility that the train set hadn't been put away since our last visit was a heady enticement. Auntie Norma was gorgeous and I loved her but she was not the best housekeeper or cook, so the house was always a dirty mess and unless we arrived with dinner the food was awful. She did, however, always have in the freezer a tray of ice cream, which I preferred to Mum's. Auntie Norma's was made with Nestles condensed milk, much to Celia's horror; hers was made with eggs, cream and real vanilla.

The train set was on a scale that dwarfed any other I had come across. It was huge and seemed to weigh a ton, so it sat heavily on the track and would never derail like every other model train did. The engine was a deep royal navy colour, while the carriages were a ravishing

burgundy with gold stripes, and they bore royal insignias. The details were delicious: the doors opened, the windows went up and down and the engine's headlights shone brightly when going through tunnels or under beds. The set had miles of track and, when fully assembled, wound its way throughout the house, making several turns around the living room, into the kitchen, through the family's bedrooms and under the big double bed in which Uncle George seemed to be permanently asleep. There was often mention of night shift, but I thought he was just a lazy slob. I never got tired of watching that train speeding around and around my cousins' house.

As mentioned, I was never mad about my father, but I liked *his* father even less. My grandfather was, sadly, a hopeless alcoholic. Sometimes, after Sunday school, my father would take me to visit him. He was never out of bed and would shamble towards the kitchen, past the rooster that lived on top of the television set and, before saying hello, would grab a cold beer from the fridge. When he finally focused and had exchanged greetings with my father he would cast his eyes on me in all my Sunday best: suede shoes, English Viyella checked shirt, velvet jerkin, long socks and knee-length pants, all in subtle tones of olive green. He would shake his head, mutter something discouraging under his breath and reach for another beer.

I remember how, at this time, my grandfather lived in a ramshackle boarding house in the working-class suburb of Collingwood. Not long after moving in, his affection was directed to the woman who ran it, and it was her room from which he emerged. Some time later, "Auntie Sylvie" would appear in a cloud of powder and perfume, wearing several layers of fluffy chiffon and a matching nightgown under a voluminous housecoat usually trimmed with feathers, whereupon the rooster on Sylvie's TV would spark up, thinking she was his girlfriend.

Even at that young age I could recognise that expensive taste and good taste didn't necessarily go hand in hand. I don't think Auntie Sylvie's lingerie was worn just for our benefit; she was a snappy dresser. I adored her. She reminded me of Belle, Rhett Butler's lady friend of ill repute in *Gone with the Wind*, except she was older and a bit knocked about. She wore make-up not far removed from Cherokee war paint, her cheeks crimson with two bright circles of rouge, her nose pink with powder, her eyes usually a flash of iridescence rimmed with smudged mascara. Her hair was coloured (to be kind), with roots of quite another tone, and permed into a tight curl. She never seemed to have a cigarette far from her cupid-bow lips, which the lipstick sometimes missed by several degrees. She had a voice and a hacking cough that goes with a sixty-a-day habit. She was a jolly, rotund bundle of fun, had a raucous laugh and was extremely generous. If we were out she would always shout a treat – be it lunch or ice creams all round. Maybe I liked her so much because she always pressed several 2 shilling coins into my hand when no one was watching.

The reason I bring up my grandfather at this point in my story is that he had a job as a storeman at a toy factory. He carried, as did all blue-collar workers of that era, a Gladstone bag. This was a sturdy portmanteau with a hinged closure along the top that opened like a hippo's mouth. His bag was embossed crocodile. My grandfather had a rather mean, raggedy, moth-eaten Pekinese dog that lived in this bag most of the time. It would stick its head out of the bag, eyes bulging, tongue drooling, while being transported around from pub to pub.

Many, many toys fell into this portmanteau, which the old Pekinese smuggled past the factory gates by going into a frenzied barking fit, snarling and snapping furiously at anyone who came near it. Sylvie had some grandchildren but I think I was the principal recipient of my grandfather's illegal largesse. I had a whole collection of awful Disney-like cartoon characters that were made out of dense foam and had a memory-wire skeleton so they could be contorted into any shape. (I think they were taken off the market as the memory wire would escape and poke out the occasional child's eye.) I was an ungrateful little prig, though, as I never much liked any of the toys I received.

However, there was one toy that I absolutely loved. Called an Etch A Sketch, it was a drawing device that looked like a little red television. It had two knobs, which, when turned, would draw a line on the screen. The screen was covered with very fine aluminium powder, and a complicated pulley system of finely strung wires connected to the knobs controlled a stylus. The stylus, would scratch away the powder, leaving a fine line. One day I scratched away at the screen until it was completely clear so I could see how it worked. It was filled with tiny balls so that, when it was inverted, they would spread the powder, evenly covering the screen ready for the artist to start again.

With skill and patience you could do drawings from the most simple to the most intricate. Skill I had, but my patience was thin and I would get furious. In fact, my grandfather had to steal me several more Etch A Sketches after I destroyed successive devices. I put my fist through the original when I made a mistake after spending days working on a drawing of a ballerina.

I think the Pekinese died, my grandfather got caught and was subsequently fired, and Auntie Sylvie vanished without explanation. (Whether she kicked him and the rooster out or she succumbed to the sixty-a-day habit, I'll never know.)

When the attraction of the toys and the rooster lost their appeal, I flatly refused to visit my grandfather, probably to mutual relief, and we only saw him at Christmas lunch. When Nanna's Christmas pudding was served and we would be on high alert for sixpences and the endangered thruppence, he would always pretend to choke and would produce a crumpled-up 10 shilling note out of his mouth, much to everyone's amusement.

Although my last Etch A Sketch has long gone, and I didn't give the man a chance, my grandfather is still at least a fond memory of Christmas lunch. He always made me laugh!

47

Pets. What Are They Thinking?

When we lived in Hobbs Street, I had a dachshund whose name was Dashy. He was brown and black and devoted to me. I loved him. But not as passionately as I have loved my more recent dogs – Bonny, Harvey and Tommy. Must be an age thing.

Dashy was a cumbersome creature. The older he got, the fatter he got and the slower his ambulatory progress became. He was never a joyous dog. Except for the first few months when he was a puppy, he wouldn't play ball and frolic around. He was quite stoic – always ten paces behind. I would talk to him, and he would try to sit on me, but you know what dachshunds are like – not easy to arrange on a lap. After a few years, his tummy almost touched the ground, and his poor little legs could barely carry him. We couldn't understand how he got so fat. Then we realised that he was snuffling up the chooks' feed. He would flip up the lid on their feeding trough, stick in his long snout and inhale their chaff. This ruined not only his waistline but eventually his lungs.

One day, my father took him away with no explanation – a strange thing to do to a child. He made absolutely no mention as to what had happened.

My sweet little cat, Ciss Puss, came with us to Hobbs Street and eventually Elizabeth Street. In winter, she always would get into my bed and crawl to the bottom to sleep at my feet. At Hobbs Street, when she was in her prime, she was a prodigious hunter. Unfortunately, she was always depositing her bounty on my doorstep. I would emerge from my bungalow and feel an awful squelch as the guts of a bird, or dismembered rodent, would squish under my (usually bare) foot!

Now, what follows is a terrible story, and I am wracked with guilt about it. One year, for some strange reason, I was going through a butch phase and acquired an air rifle. Ciss Puss and I worked out this marvellous game – she was the cat on heat, and I was on the tin roof. I would position myself on the chook house roof while she would entice sex-crazed tomcats into my range. Then I would pick them off. As one poor tom would catapult through the air, she would look up at me triumphantly before charging off into the night to bring back another victim. She was an absolute minx, beguiling her prey and squirming up the length of the backyard so as to position them in the middle of the lawn where I could get a perfect shot.

If I was out late, she would always wait up for me. She could hear Bluebird chuffing up Williamstown Road when I was miles away. By this stage, though, she was so old that it took her ages to climb up on the back fence by the garage. She would always be there, even in the rain. Of course, she couldn't get down, so I would have to clamber through the jungle and the woodpile to help her.

One day, she disappeared. We searched everywhere. We called out her name and pinned up notes at the school and the milk bar. Sadly, we thought that she had gone away to die. At that time I was sewing for Le Louvre at home in my bungalow. Dad had made me a long cutting table, held up on one end by a deep chest of drawers where I kept all my notions (thread needles, and so on) and fabrics. Ciss Puss had

been missing for about three days when I opened the bottom drawer. There she was. She must have crawled in for a nap, and I had closed the drawer without noticing her. It was the funniest sight – she was completely flat, compressed under the tightly packed fabrics above her. She looked as though she had been run over by a steamroller. For a minute or two, she didn't move. I thought she was dead. Then she got up, had a good stretch and a shake, and emitted a parched little meow. I scooped her up, fluffed her fur, and gave her a drink and a loving squeeze. Life number eight.

She had her daily rituals. Every night after her dinner, she would make her way to the front garden to take her toilet. We had a small front fence that she used to jump over in one bound. One morning, we found her flat on the pavement where she had landed. There was no life number nine. She'd gone to Pussy Heaven.

We had a budgerigar named Chrissy who lived to be a good age as well. When my brother, Edwin, was three or four, he had a wooden horse on wheels, and Chrissy used to sit on its back. He would take the two of them for walks up and down the street.

At Hobbs Street, Chrissy had a cage that looked like a modernist house. It took pride of place, smack in the middle of one wall in the kitchen. Harry Seidler could have designed this cage. It had a yellow feature wall and cantilevered sides in navy and white. Chrissy would fly around the kitchen, land on the edge of my father's beer glass and drink through the froth until he would get drunk and fall off it. My father had taught him to talk. Unfortunately, his vocabulary contained several expletives. My grandmother lived in constant fear that Chrissy would let loose with his colourful language when the vicar dropped in for afternoon tea (which he regularly did). Her worst fears came true one day when Chrissy told him, "Piss off, you silly old bugger."

We had several other budgies over the years, all second-class citizens who lived in far less salubrious surroundings. Several of these met their feathered creator much sooner than Chrissy. I have to admit that I unwittingly helped a couple on their way, probably before they were quite prepared.

One poor creature must have come as a present – because I acquired this large blue wire cage complete with its colour-matched inhabitant. I moved this mobile home around, hanging it on the apple tree on fine days and under the eaves in inclement weather. At night, I brought it inside and put it under a canvas cover. This was my job, along with cleaning the cage and feeding the bird.

My first fatality – an upturned, stiff, little feathered friend – happened when I forgot to bring him in before a late snap frost struck one spring morning. I got a terrible shock when I picked him up from the bottom of the cage and felt how cold he was. Convinced that heat would give back the gift of life, I whacked him in the oven. But then I forgot about him, resulting in my first cremation.

The next victim was the one I have never forgotten nor forgiven myself for. Because of his predecessor's demise, I was particularly vigilant in my care and attention. He had two clear plastic tubular feeders, one for water and the other for seed. Every day, I would change the water and check the level of the seed. In my efforts to keep his home spotless, I was also constantly cleaning. My big mistake was not drying his seed feeder before I filled it up. Unfortunately, a coating of seeds stuck to the tube, giving it the appearance of being packed to the top when it was actually empty. I starved the poor little blighter to death.

To make up for my neglect, I made a supreme effort to send him off in a grand manner. I was just coming into my Egyptian period and decided that embalming was the only fitting way to send this tragic Avis to the other side. In my weekly *Look and Learn* magazines, I had been following the rituals and mysteries of the Egyptian Book of the Dead. Behind the broad beans in the vegetable patch, I made an excavation and built a tomb in the style and manner of the Upper Kingdom.

My tomb had plaster-of-Paris walls painted with hieroglyphics. It had false passages, booby-trapped shafts, sanctums and even inner sanctums. The mummy was a triumph of Cadbury's gold foil. I placed jewels in the bird's eye sockets and painted his beak with "Antique Gold" high-gloss, touch-up paint. I wrapped and wrapped him in the finest cotton gauze the medicine box could provide. (My bloodied gravel knees always ensured an inexhaustible supply of that.) Then, after placing the mummy and a few precious objects that he would need in the afterlife (his mirror bell and a supply of cuttlefish), I filled the chambers with some sand that I had brought home from the sandbox at school. I often wonder what thoughts went through the head of the person who later came across it while planting some lettuce or tomatoes. Or maybe it remains intact to this day!

Having been brought up to believe I was an English prince, it is only natural that I should feel an affinity with Her Majesty's royal choice of dog breeds. When Mark and I decided to get a dog, he let me choose a corgi. We named him Buster or "Basta" (Italian for "enough"). A fluff or longhaired variety, he was a wonderful dog, biting Mark on the bum all the time, trying to show him who was boss! He wasn't allowed on the bed but would sneak up anyway. Starting at the feet end, he would take his time (about half an hour) to slowly creep up the length of the bed until he was above our heads behind the pillows. Not only did he think he was the top banana, he also loved to eat a banana. Every morning, as I made our fruit salad, he would chew one up and then ever so delicately place the little black seed on the floor. Unfortunately, we didn't have the time to train him as we were overwhelmed by the success of our business at the time. As a result, he had no road sense. Being totally disobedient and headstrong, he got out the front door as a guest came in one night. Tragically, no one noticed, and he was hit by a car. We were devastated and swore never to have another dog.

About the same time, we had an amusing little cat named "Mouse" that had mysterious fur; what few distinguishing markings she had would completely vanish when we stroked her. At the Clifton Hill house, I had a cut-out cat that I would place at various spots around the house (as well as a life-size cut-out of Maria Callas standing in the living room!). The first thing Mouse would do when she came inside was to find this cut-out cat and knock it flat. Sadly, Mouse got knocked flat one day as well. That made up our minds.

"No more animals."

By far, my biggest folly was setting up a marine aquarium in the kitchen. It was fabulous except that it was extremely hard to maintain – I had to have it serviced weekly – and most of the costly imported fish proved troublesome. For example, I purchased a beautiful South American fish for about $300. This wrasse was the most vibrant, iridescent emerald green. But when I released it into the tank, it shot straight to the bottom and burrowed into the sand, and I never ever laid eyes on it again.

Another problematic presence in my SeaWorld was a pistol shrimp (so named because of the noise it made when it killed its dinner, like a pistol shot). Although I set many traps for it, I could never catch it. One night, I heard its deadly blast from the bedroom, rushed downstairs and turned on the kitchen light. There it was, devouring yet another expensive gourmet dinner. Enraged, I grabbed some kitchen tongs. As it enjoyed the $60 chef's plate, I took it by surprise and caught it. As I scooped it out, however, it got a terrible shock and carried on a right treat – like the monster out of John Hurt's chest in the film *Alien*. Not knowing what to do with it, I ran around and around the kitchen, screaming like a schoolgirl. Eventually, I popped it down the insinkerator and flipped the switch. In hindsight, I should have cooked and eaten it – the world's most expensive shrimp cocktail!

The tank then took on several incarnations – from saltwater to tropical, tropical to cold water, and finally a home for two goldfish with imitation plants. Nicholas and Alexandra grew into regal beauties like their namesakes, with long glamourous tails three times the length of their bodies. When we were away one year, some guests decided to buy a thank-you gift for us – a small school of iridescent, transparent fish that would serve as maids-in-waiting for the Tsarina. Unfortunately, they had a disease that killed both royal highnesses.

This was the last straw, and I had the tank made into a cocktail cabinet.

Bonny was our first Cairn terrier. She came into Mark's life when I was in Hong Kong. The first time I saw her was as an attached photo in an emailed "résumé" when she was applying for the job. I fell in love with her at first sight. Marilyn, the head of our jewellery business, had rescued her. She was a mess, having been badly neglected and abused. Her puppy collar was so tight that it had to be cut off. Her fur was tangled, and her skin was raw from flea allergies.

Yet, she made the transition to a velvet couch with the greatest of ease. Even though we bought her the best canine sleeping arrangements that money could buy, she decided that was where she wanted to be. I would settle her into her bed but, before I would reach the top of the stairs, you could hear her tiptoeing across the living room towards that velvet sofa. At one stage, when I couldn't sleep, I crept down several times to scold her. "BONNY!" She would go rigid and then either skedaddle back to her bed as fast as she could or crawl there slowly on her belly, trying to be invisible. I eventually gave up the battle and let her have her own way.

I can't believe that the previous owners could have been so cruel to such an adorable animal. Just crazy about her, Mark and I were like proud parents of a newborn baby. Basically a working breed (for hunting), she was adored by all, except the few deliverymen she had an aversion to. When I watched television late at night, she would put her head on my lap and look up at me for hours.

"I wonder what she is thinking," I mused.

Most likely, it was "Get off my bed and let me get to sleep", but her look was so intense and penetrating that I would love to know.

Our next Cairn, Harvey, came into our lives by accident. While walking Bonny in the gardens, we would see a lady who became captivated by her and decided to get a Cairn of her own. One morning, she announced that her Cairn had been born and she would be picking him up in a few weeks. As the conversation evolved, it turned out that the breeder was located next door to friends of ours on the Mornington Peninsula. We were visiting them that weekend and said we would call in to say hello to him.

When we pulled up outside the farm, we could hear a cacophony of yelping, squealing and barking. We had Bonny, so we gathered her up, thinking she would go ballistic. Maybe she thought we were going to leave her there, as she didn't make a sound the entire visit. We met "Jock" and the rest of the litter – a tangled, blurred and hysterical mess of fur. Instantly, we became clucky and wanted one for ourselves. Unfortunately, they had all been sold, and there was a long waiting list for the next litter.

"It's too bad you didn't come yesterday," said Barbara, the breeder. "You could have had that one. A family are picking him up later today." Pointing to the far end of the paddock, she went on to tell his story. He belonged to an old lady who was in and out of hospital so could no longer look after him. I strolled down to say hello. Harvey was a

Wheaten Cairn, named so for the colour. All alone and pressed into the wire fence, he was the saddest dog I ever saw. He looked up into my eyes, and it was love at first sight. I could barely tear myself away.

That night I didn't sleep a wink, not being able to get him out of my thoughts. As soon as I thought it a decent time, I rang Barbara the next morning to ask about him. She said that the family hadn't turned up. He was mine! I think I broke all speed records down to the Peninsular to get him.

Harvey turned out to be quite problematic. Having gone back and forth between Barbara and his owner, the poor thing didn't know whether he was Arthur or Martha. Mark said he would have to go back. I wouldn't have it. He was my soulmate, so I persevered. He wasn't toilet-trained, cried all night and sulked. Gradually, though, he settled, and the house went back to normal. Bonny wasn't mad about him, and showed it, but she eventually accepted him.

Every day, I took Harvey to the office, where he slept under my feet. He had never made a sound – not a bark, a whimper or a sigh— until one day, he started walking around in circles, back and forth, whining and crying, even howling with such intensity that I thought he was turning into a werewolf.

About a week later, we ran into Jock and his new owner. Harvey was Jock's uncle, and they sniffed and seemed to acknowledge their connections. "By the way," said the new mum. "Harvey's former owner died last Wednesday."

That had been the day when Harvey had been so out of sorts. He knew!

From that day on, he settled down. He became quite playful and developed a distinct character. I have to say I have never been as mad about any creature as I was about him. But he wasn't with us to the max, as I had hoped. One year, he suddenly went blind, which mystified our vet and the dozen specialists we consulted. He gradually went downhill over the following twelve months – until our marvellously sympathetic, compassionate vet said it was time to let him go. We knew he was right. Harvey was loved during his short life, and he knew it. I miss him still.

Bonny missed him too.

Twelve months later, we decided to get another dog. Barbara placed us on a waiting list, and several months later our puppy was ready to be viewed. Yes, he was adorable, but I had spotted another one, Tommy, out of the corner of my eye. "What about him?" I enquired.

Once again, I had fallen in love at first sight. He was a few months older than the brood I'd been introduced to. And, sorry, he wasn't available. He was a reject, a dud, too many health issues. Apparently, he had serious trouble with his liver and needed a stent, an operation that was not often successful. His teeth also needed serious attention. Operations were scheduled, but it would be months before an assessment could be made. Could he have a healthy future and a normal life? We decided to wait. Several months later, we were reunited.

The operations were a success. Tommy is ravishingly beautiful, like Harvey was, and he knows it. His teeth are as sharp as needles, capable of shredding a toilet roll in thirty seconds (payback should we leave him alone for more than half an hour). When we first got him, and Mark would return from his morning walk with him, he would bound into the bedroom to assault me, bashing my skull as punishment for my sleeping in. It really hurt! Then he would thunder around the bed, and into and out of the dressing room, at 100 miles an hour, barking like a lunatic. At first, I thought it was just a puppy thing, and he would grow out of it. But it took him more than three years to shed this morning ritual.

A wheaten colour like Harvey when we got him, Tommy has since turned a dark brindle like Bonny. He never ceases to amuse and delight us at every single thing he does. We photograph his every move, expression and gesture, and I'm sure he is constantly thinking of new ways to dazzle us with his beauty and talent. I will never forget Harvey. He remains forever in my heart, as does our precious Bonny, who passed on not long after Harvey did. This new one has filled the huge void they left.

It's not fair that dogs have such short lives; however, a Cairn can live to be seventeen. Hopefully, we have a few more precious years left.

I do know what this one is thinking: "Food!"

48

Lost Paintings

I had a surprise call from an old friend, a somewhat estranged friend. We had been, as the saying goes, "thick as thieves" at one point in our lives. It was nice to chat; the past differences and grudges seemed forgotten. He told me he had seen a painting in a junk/curio shop in Preston that had my signature on it. Preston was becoming gentrified, and trendy shops selling furniture and ephemera from the 1950s, 60s and 70s had sprung up all along the high street.

I asked my friend about the painting. He described a stylised woman. Her blue gown was in a 1930s style, and she was holding flowers, a spray of orchids. It sounded like a painting I had done over thirty years ago. My friend said he didn't know that I painted and I told him that I had just started to paint again and of my plans to study full time. I had done the "after hours" course at the Victorian College of the Arts, and after our end-of-the-year show everyone said that becoming a mature-age student would be a cinch. I had told all my friends, I told everybody I met, strangers in the street and worst of all my staff, that I was going to study at the VCA. It was

very embarrassing when I was flatly rejected and had to go back to work!

I tootled out to Preston and found the shop, and there was my painting in the window. It had a very smart hand-printed card on it – "Gregory Ladner 1973" – as if I was some artist of note. I was delighted to see it, but it wasn't the painting my friend had described; it was another painting I had done in the same period. I was very excited, thinking that my two missing paintings had surfaced. I had done only nine paintings in my life, and I knew where they all were except these two.

I introduced myself to the woman who ran the shop. I asked where the other painting was, the one with the woman holding the orchids, hoping it hadn't been sold in the interim. Orchids? No, she had only ever had this one painting. That was spooky, as my friend had described the other painting in detail. There was no way he could have had knowledge of the other work. I didn't have a photograph of it, and even my recollection of it had faded over time. The shop owner called her husband, who effused over the painting, telling me they had owned it for years, initially putting it in the shop as décor and had just decided to part with it. They asked me to relate the story behind it.

In 1973 my mother belonged to a women's club, Beta Sigma, Phi; they were having their annual art show and, as I had just recently finished two paintings, she asked me to include them in the show. I turned the invitation down. Celia had told all her friends in the club of her brilliant son, the artist.

She begged, she, threatened, she appealed to reason and finally, on condition that they were not for sale, I agreed. However, they had to appear to be for sale, so I put an outrageous sum of $500 on each one. Lo and behold, they sold on the first day. An American woman living here was mad about them and bought them. She wanted to meet the artist, so I arranged to be there when she picked them up; she told me she would keep one and send one to her friend who owned a gallery in Los Angeles. "Honey, you're going to be famous."

I never heard from her again!

So here was one of the paintings more than forty-five years later, for sale at half the price I had sold it for – not a good investment! I bought it, having received a further discount of $50 for being the artist. I was delighted to have it back. Seeing it again, I didn't think it was such a good painting, but it had a certain style even though its flaws and lack of technique were painfully obvious. I have it hanging in my studio and daily ponder how it came full circle and the fate of its sibling.

Did the painting of the woman holding the spray of orchids make it to LA? Did it sell? Was she hanging on some wall in West Hollywood? Or did she go heels up straight into a Beverly Hills dumpster?

Will it turn up one day long after I am dead and be hailed as a masterpiece? I can see the headlines now: "One from his early glamour period", "National Gallery Victoria acquires *White Orchids* for record sum!", "Director exclaims 'She has come home!'"

49

Celia

It must be very clear by now that Celia was the most important woman in my life. She conceived, carried, delivered, nurtured, educated, and (above all) loved me. I am everything I am because of that unconditional love.

I know I have a generous head of hair from her – she hardly had a grey hair well into her eighties – and her strong, elegant nails. Now, unfortunately, I am taking on some of her other physical attributes. Her figure, for one. I get a shock sometimes when I think I see her in the mirror, especially from the back in a foggy bathroom.

"Mum, get out of here!"

I know that her curled-up toes and crippled hands will be my lot in the next decade or so.

My artist bent also stems from her genes. I have a roll of drawings that she did at school from the ages of eleven to fourteen. Some of them are exquisite. She showed masterful skill at drawing, and her sense of colour was pure and subtle. That she loved doing those drawings is quite evident. They are all formal studies of flowers and geometric designs that would have been regulation classroom exercises, but they have that extra something that is hard to define. She might have pursued a career in art had the Second World War not intervened, sending her and thousands of others in directions beyond their immediate control.

When she was sixteen, she wanted to become a nurse but her father forbade it. He didn't want her to go off to the war. He had seen the horror of the battlefront twice and didn't want his little princess to see such a nightmare world. Images and memories of war had never left him. He sported a big moustache that hid where his lip had been shot off at Gallipoli, but his retiring and gentle demeanour hid darker wounds.

Celia was determined to do something towards the war effort. Although she didn't exactly run away, she lied about her age and joined her older sister, Norma, doing the serious wartime work of making bombs in a munitions factory in Melbourne. When she first arrived, she lived with an aunt who worked in the cafeteria at Flinders Street Station. Their dinner was always the leftovers from lunch. My grandfather didn't think they were being looked after properly and moved to Melbourne to make sure she was all right. Later, my grandmother started the business in Wingfield Street so they could all be together.

Munitions work was dangerous, but Celia came through it all to tell many stories. My favourite one is of a male supervisor who would "borrow" lunch from all the girls. A sandwich here, a cake there, a piece of fruit. They were all fed up, but there was nothing they could say. One day they made an apple-and-sultana sandwich and left it (strategically placed) on the lunch table. It looked like the real thing, except it was apple studded with plump, juicy blowflies. He never commandeered as much as a dry cracker again.

Celia kept in touch with many of the girls, and I remember going with her to visit those older women for many years. One of the girls, Cynthia, was in a time warp, frozen in the same style as when her job finished at the cessation of the war. She still curled her hair in a victory roll with a snood and wore the square-shouldered dresses of the day, often in heavy crêpe de chine in musky floral prints. A paste brooch at the neckline, three graduated strings of pearls and lace-up shoes with sensible heels accessorised the look. It was like morphing into a wartime film with Greer Garson.

Invariably, Cynthia would tell the story of the blowfly sandwich, and we would all laugh as if hearing it for the first time. She was a straight-laced and genteel lady, and I would always have to be on my best behaviour. It was not until she had passed away that Celia told me a story about her. One night, she had gone out with an American soldier. In the morning, she had been surprised to see a little blue butterfly tattooed on her inner thigh, quite a few inches above her knee. She couldn't remember how it had got there! Celia said Cynthia was always thought to be the dangerous spark in the heavily bunkered underground munitions shed where they worked. If anything was going to blow up, they thought it would be her.

My mother put her wage packet on the table every week, and my grandmother gave her back £1 to live on. In contrast, Norma didn't pay board or make any other contribution, as she was saving for her trousseau. It was always a delicate point with my mother. My grandmother never put any of her earnings away for *her*; instead, they went into paying off the milk bar business, where Celia worked as well.

From those early years in Melbourne, my mother never stopped working. All the years of my growing up, she often had two jobs. Sometimes, she would do night shift. For years, she worked nights and Saturdays at the TAB when the trotting or greyhound races were on. She didn't stop, even when she was expecting my younger brother and when he was little. As my grandmother always lived with us, maybe Celia was getting a little back via unpaid babysitting.

Although I tell people that my grandmother brought me up, my mother was always there. She was there when I came home from school, she often cooked dinner, and we always sat down to eat as a family. Although my grandmother cooked good English food, my mother was the first in our street to cook "cuisine". Such innovations as tinned pineapple rings on thick ham steaks and spaghetti Bolognese with

Parmesan cheese in a handy green cardboard tube were breakthrough gastronomy in those days. Steak Diane was a specialty; the fillet steak was beaten to the thickness of heavy paper and marinated for hours in lemon juice, "garlic", a dash of Tabasco and olive oil, then it was flashed in a pan for hardly a minute or two. I think Celia must have had this at the Silver Grill, served à table, as it was not an any-night-of-the-week dish, just for special occasions.

Over time, she had all sorts of jobs. One was working for a firm in the city in a role that would be called "PA" today. Required to look the part, she was particularly elegant during that period. I can remember all of the outfits. My favourite winter one was a knobbly tweed suit with a long pencil skirt that had a little pleat so she could walk. It was in one of my favourite colours – "donkey". The jacket was very fitted through the waist and flared into a short peplum. It wrapped over and fastened asymmetrically with three large buttons that looked like swirled toffees. The bracelet-length sleeves had turn-back cuffs of dark-brown mink matching the collar. The shoes were very, very high, and I regularly fell over when wearing them.

My favourite summer outfit was an embroidered pale-blue Irish linen dress that swirled and danced as she walked. I was always embarassed when she picked me up from school as all the other mums were drab by comparison.

My mother led a busy life, entertaining and going to parties and balls, but she never failed to bring me home something, be it a helium balloon or a party favour off the table. I especially liked a menu. She always aspired to something better in life and certainly instilled that desire in me.

I vividly recall seeing *High Society*. The song *Who Wants to Be a Millionaire?* struck a particular chord. We must have been singing it one day. When I sang "I do" instead of "I don't", she came back with, "YOU CAN." She worked hard and saved. When Hobbs Street was sold, Nanna also finally came good and gave Celia a share of the proceeds. With this money, she bought the big, solid, triple-fronted "Former Doctor's House" in Elizabeth Street, Newport.

I think most of my mother's disappointments in life stemmed from her adoration of her father. No man ever lived up to him; my father certainly didn't. Her father had told her she was a princess, and I think she was typical of many, many women who want that knight in shining armour to sweep them onto the saddle and ride off into the sunset. No one could do anything as well as her daddy. Sometimes, even *I* felt annoyed about this shining example of humanity that no one could equal. I guess my father eventually gave up trying. I never met my maternal grandfather and only had the myth to relate to. I am sure he was wonderful, and I hope that he imparted some of his genes to me. However, what's frightening about that statement is that it could equally apply to my paternal grandfather's genes. My father's father was a horror story!

Celia did eventually find her knight in shining armour in the form of a dashing Indian former fighter pilot who literally swept her off her feet and negated her disappointment in men. Duncan was her saviour (and mine). He was a devoted husband, and they had a wonderful life together. They travelled, and for a few years they lived in Bahrain, where Duncan worked for a sheik who was developing a wildlife sanctuary. The stories from those years are numerous. I gather that their home was a refuge for many fellow ex-pats. I can imagine Celia as the mother hen, cooking and fussing over all the lonely young men living there at that time. Everyone was welcome for dinner, and the door was always open.

She used to buy chicken livers to make pâté. Because she was the only customer buying them, the store manager asked what she did with them. So, one day, she brought him in some pâté and found herself with a little business on the side. Her pâté was highly sought after in the ex-pat community. That was Celia: always on the lookout for an opportunity and something more to do.

The first real dress I made was for her (not that Teddy's frocks weren't real). Having purchased the Elna with my holiday wrecking money, I bought some bright cotton and made her a sundress to wear in Torquay. One year, I saved up and bought a length of bouclé tweed to make my first Chanel-style suit for her. It was in pale pink, beige and caramel colours, and I gave it the full-shebang Chanel treatment, including the heavy gold chain to weight the facings, so the jacket always hung correctly. It was, of course, edge to edge with matching braid trim.

During my years at Le Louvre, I had access to cupboards of vintage fabrics that had gone out of mode. I made Celia dozens of fabulous gowns from this treasure trove. I paid little or nothing for fabulous Bianchini organdies, chiffons and pure-silk crêpe de chines. Georgina would give me most of them, as we couldn't use them.

My later contributions to Celia's wardrobe would be the occasional kaftan from our resort-wear range. They were easy to slip over her head – due to deteriorating health, her days with buttons were well and truly over. I visited one day, which happened to be her thirty-fourth wedding anniversary. In her hair, she was wearing the little, hand-painted flowers I had made to match her wedding dress. The colour had darkened a bit over the years, but they looked very pretty – as she did – Celia had to go into a nursing home because Duncan couldn't care for her at home as her health deteriorated. I don't know how she had managed to hold a lipstick, but she had done her own make-up that day. Her face lit up as she saw me, and my heart nearly broke as I thought about that happy day more than three decades before.

Not many sons get the opportunity to plan a wedding for their mother – but, as mentioned, I did just that when Celia and Duncan had decided to marry. Apart from Miss Wightman's black chandelier with the pink rock-crystal drops, I wanted flowers to be the dominant element. I planned one massive display on the mantelpiece and another in my antique armoire, the backdrop for the ceremony. It was February, one of those months that get hotter and hotter, and flowers were scarce. I had managed to secure every available tall white gladiolus, oriental lily and tuberose in town but had nothing for the bouquet.

Georgina was in charge of the catering, and we were having roast chickens, a tower of freshly steamed prawns, and salads. The wedding cake was the classic croquembouche, which I ordered from Le Croissant in Armadale. At five in the morning, I got up to start roasting the chickens. About 8 am, Georgina and I set off for the Queen Victoria Market to get the salad ingredients and prawns. We were driving past Melbourne University when she screamed, "Stop the car!" I got such a shock that I slammed on the brakes, nearly causing an accident.

"Stop the car," she repeated "pull in there."

In the grounds of the university, a magnificent *Magnolia grandiflora* was in full bloom.

"There's Celia's bouquet."

What followed was a hilarious scene that could have been lifted from the Buster Keaton archives or the *Keystone Cops*. With Georgina on my shoulders, I wobbled around, not being able to see where I was going, while she tried to grab a branch so we could break off a magnolia. Eventually, she broke off a bough with a few blooms, and we collapsed in a heap of laughter on the grass.

Georgina had conned Marisa Sillitto to help in the kitchen. They chopped and sliced and made bowls and bowls of various exotic salads for the wedding reception. I think they were still making them as the wedding was taking place and they had to get dressed in a hurry for the party.

I made Celia a bias-cut dress in the palest apricot georgette. Its three-tiered cascade was scalloped all around, the scallops being hand-painted in pearl. With long ropes of baroque pearls borrowed from Miss Wightman completing the effect, she looked lovely.

Minutes before the wedding, I couldn't find the bouquet I had made after the morning's gymnastics. I had assembled it at the last moment to keep it fresh, as the temperature was soaring towards 46 degrees. It was just a single bloom and a bud, but it looked perfect. I searched everywhere. Finally deciding to go ahead without it, I gathered the guests and was about to snip something from the flowers over the mantelpiece when Rose Crowder got up from where she had been sitting in the cool hall, revealing the bouquet slightly squashed but still presentable.

I had saved up for Charles Heidsieck Champagne on Miss Wightman's recommendation, and it was a very successful party – apart from the fact that no one ate any of the superb salads that Georgina had slaved over for hours. A cool change swept through. We opened all the windows, the silver curtains billowed through the room, and the pink rock crystals chinked and sparkled. Celia left for India in a trousseau I had made, and thus started a wonderful new life with her knight in shining armour.

I know you will find this a strange and shocking admission after reading this memoir so far, but I dreamt and planned how to kill my mother at the end because I couldn't bear to see her in such a deteriorated state. When I was a little boy, about ten, she would draw me into her arms, cuddle me and whisper a plea. She made me promise that if she ever got really old and sick, I would take a gun and shoot her. I don't know what I felt at the time, but I always hugged her back and promised that I would. That time came. Indeed, it was well overdue, and I felt I had let her down.

I wish I could have, and I *would* have if I had thought I could get away with it. I plotted many ways of carrying out her request, although the promised gun was out of the question. Too loud and messy, and I wouldn't have known how to get my hands on one. My schemes and plans were meticulously thought out, but I knew that I would get caught, no matter where I parked the car or which disguise I wore. After watching so many forensic dramas on television, my mind had become finely attuned to how criminals and police think, and I could always pick who "dun it" only minutes into the show. But all that training meant that I could also see how I would slip up. A new career as a hitman for the Mob may have been on the cards, but I am grateful that the perfect crime was beyond me.

It was sad to see Celia at the end. I know that she hated being ensnared by the very thing that had frightened her all those years before. She had always been so dynamic. I thought she was more beautiful than any other mother. She was glamorous and vivacious, always a whirlwind of style and fragrance on her way somewhere. She would pull up my chin, draw my face to hers and plant a big kiss goodbye. Then off she'd go. She never stopped.

It is a cruel twist of fate that the body wears out, and the mind gets exhausted. But there was something in her eyes, that same twinkle shining through the struggle to tell me what she was thinking. On my last visit, she reached out to me and touched me on the face.

"YOU CAN."

Warning

As you have apparently read this far, I don't want you to be disillusioned and I would rather you continue to think that I am a lovely, kind and almost saintly person.

If you answer YES to ANY THREE of the following questions, it is seriously suggested that you read no further.

1. Are you a happy clapper?

2. Are you under the age of fifteen?

3. Would you consider yourself homophobic?

4. Are you offended by naughty words?

5. Are you horrified at the prospect that there is such a thing as pre-pubescent sexuality?

6. Do you often use the expression "Too much information"?

7. Do you find absolutely shocking what others may see as "Who's been a naughty boy then?"

8. Have you ever stalked, or been stalked by, an ex?

9. Are you sure you're older than fifteen?

10. Were you still a virgin at twenty-five?

11. Are you still a virgin now?

50

Gayer than Laughter

Younger than springtime are you, softer than starlight are you
Warmer than the winds of June are the gentle lips you gave me
Gayer than laughter are you, sweeter than music are you
Angel and lover, heaven and earth are you to me.

It took these lyrics from *Younger Than Springtime* in Rodgers and Hammerstein's smash hit musical *South Pacific* to ignite the gay flame of my being. I was aged eight or nine, and the movies proved pivotal in my life.

In a steaming tropical jungle set, handsome Lieutenant Cable embraces Liat, the young, innocent and nubile daughter of Bloody Mary. One of the lead roles, Bloody Mary, is the lovable but conniving matriarch of the local village; she is out to fleece the interloping American Army reconnoitring in the South Pacific. She pins great hope on her daughter, Liat, marrying an American. From the clouds of rising steam and the pulsating colours on the Technicolor screen – not to mention the state of Liat's hair – it is fair to surmise that Bloody Mary will get her way.

Her daughter has just been ravished. And Lieutenant Cable is expressing undying devotion. (Surprising, given such a brief encounter.)

Lieutenant Cable is naked to the waist, adorned with only a silver chain and army dog tags. The silver discs catch the light as if touched by Tinkerbell's wand. Liat's tiny frame is cradled in his powerful arms, her innocent naivety reflected in his glowing, tanned, trim, taut and terrific torso. He tears himself away when the departing boat's hooter summons him back to the main island. She races down the mountain with his forgotten shirt, past luminous, sparkling waterfalls, catching up to him on a bamboo bridge. In that split second, when Liat hurls herself into his arms, I knew that it should have been me.

As children, our first sexual awakenings emerged in innocent (or innocent-enough) games of Doctors and Nurses.

"I'll show you mine if you show me yours."

When I moved to the bungalow at 13 Hobbs Street, my bungalow immediately became the local hospital. The waiting room was the old Dodge in the adjacent garage. One of the older girls played chief matron, bossing everyone else around. She always had my pants down around my ankles, examining my bits. She would tickle and play with my little willie until it stood on end and involuntarily sprinkled a small stream of hot golden wee into a specimen (Vegemite) jar. She would also make me bend over and then pretend to take my temperature by sticking up my bottom something pretending to be a thermometer (often a stick).

I thoroughly enjoyed all the things she did to me, but she always kept her own cottontails firmly in place, never letting me carry out an exploratory on her. However, she was very good at instructing me on what to do to the next victim. It usually involved peculiar surgical implements, scratchy hairbrushes or kitchen utensils. I was only too happy to carry out her wishes and to give her detailed medical reports.

Kids don't play in street gangs today. They tweet, text and sext. After school, they go to ballet, Kung Fu, Mandarin or golf lessons, and then come home and go straight on the computer. There, predators lurk. The internet is so bombarded with sexual images and potential dangers that parental control systems cannot protect our vulnerable young completely.

In our street gang, some of the older boys' medical studies had advanced beyond twigs up the bottom. One day, they were giving one of the younger girls a very comprehensive check-up on the operating table (my bed) when my mother came home unexpectedly and discovered them. She screamed like a banshee, lashing out and beating them as they pulled up their hospital blues and fled in all directions.

Today, the parents would be suing each other. It would be on all the current affairs television programs and in all the scandal rags. Probably thirteen at most, the boys would be dragged through the courts and sent off to juvenile detention and rehabilitation. Poor little Raylene would spend the rest of her life in therapy.

Maybe our Raylene did have therapy back then. From what I heard later, she turned out okay, with a husband and kids. As for the boys, I never kept in touch. I think I was more psychologically scarred by the incident than anyone. Not that I am judging my mother, nor looking for excuses as to how things turned out. But, whenever I was with a girl (during those years when I was still working out my sexuality), I was always expecting Celia to come into the room screaming and wielding a broom – like that day in the surgical ward of the Hobbs Street Bungalow Hospital.

I think it's too late for me to find Raylene's therapist!

Anyway, HSBH was closed for good, and my sexual adventures moved a couple of doors up the street with a boy a couple of years older. I would sneak out at night into his bedroom, where he would expand on what I had experienced at the clinic with Nurse Pam.

My first orgasm happened one night after leaving him. My poor cock was still hard as a rock and quite swollen from being twisted, sucked, rubbed and generally fiddled with. The cool sheets at home made it feel better, but it still wouldn't go down. I lay there quietly, not quite knowing what had just gone on. The soothing top sheet looked like a circus tent in the moonlight. After a while, I started to do to myself what Gary had done. He had achieved no end result, but I managed to inflict my first orgasm within a few minutes.

Primal desire – the biological urge designed with procreation as its purpose – drives our life force just as much as the need for air and sustenance. That night, it was awakened in me, and I couldn't wait to explore it again. Since time immemorial, recreation versus procreation has been problematic.

Confused with notions of love and happiness, sex is often mistaken for life's raison d'être. It has enriched and motivated many of our religious, philosophical and spiritual treasures. It has inspired artists,

musicians and writers. On the darker side, however, hungering for it has caused so much trouble – wars, murder, treachery, lust, debauchery and DIVORCE.

"If only they could put something in the water!"

So that was my beginning. I lost contact with Gary, the boy up the road, although I do know that he got married and had offspring. But let me tell you another story about him before moving on.

There was a playground on the other side of the railway line in Yarraville.

It had a slide, swings, see-saws, that kind of thing, and sat on a bare little hillock about 10 minutes' walk away. This boy and I used to go there late at night, get undressed, and reclothe ourselves in dresses made out of rough hessian sugar bags. (His design and idea, I can assure you.) Then we would get on the swings and work up as much momentum as we could. We would swing so high that the chain would go slack for a moment; it felt like you were suspended mid-air. The hessian was very rough on the dick, but the gush of cold air up the frock was refreshing and exhilarating. Looking back, I think it was quite a peculiar activity, but I thought nothing of it at the time. (A fashion note here – Teddy never wore anything more textured than raw silk!) I often wonder what sort of tricks and costumes Gary inflicted upon his poor wife.

We all know about the scourge of paedophilia. Uncles, neighbours, priests and teachers have sexually abused so many poor children and it is reprehensible. But my experience was not at all satisfactory, and because it was something I actually wanted I felt terribly cheated. I only had one teacher who was so inclined, a Mr Aldwych.

Constantly bailing me up in the school toilets for some fabricated misdemeanour, he would press me up against the brick wall and rest his arm above my head so that my eyes were at the same level as his crotch. He was a very tall, thin young man who dressed in a style that was more 1940s than of the day. His high-waisted trousers were quite voluminous, with lots of pleats at the waist. Among these folds, I could see his little sergeant saluting. He must have had quite a small dick, but it would go up and then down, up and then down. Nothing ever came of these reprimands, nor when he kept me back in class on some other feeble excuse. He would squeeze us into a tiny desk, overshadowing me with his lanky frame. Again, the little sergeant would salute up and down. Maybe he was waiting for me to make the first move and grab it, but I didn't think it was up to me, despite the fact that I was gagging for it – as the expression so tastelessly puts it – being fully cognisant from an early age as to what it was that I wanted.

Somehow, I naturally gravitated to just what I wanted. Summer offered all sorts of opportunities during the six weeks my family spent "camping" at Torquay. The communal showers presented my first experience. When the man in the adjacent shower dropped his soap, and it slid into my stall, his manoeuvres to retrieve it resulted in his lathering quite a froth with that cake of Imperial Leather.

Although they may have disappeared from the landscape today, back then, a "beat" was a public toilet that provided gay men with a meeting place, social club and recreational facility. Several were dotted around the beachfront and parks in Torquay, and they were very popular during the high summer. Guys would advertise on the back of the doors, leaving statistics (age, predilections and fulsome attractions) to arrange assignations. Never one to waste words, my tag line was straightforward: Age 14, 7 inches. It seemed to do the trick, and I enjoyed a very popular summer.

One particular beat toilet had a TARDIS quality about it – Time And Relative Dimension in Space. It was in the middle of nowhere, deep in the heavily tea-treed no man's land on the walk from the main beach to the surf beach. A wooden construction had been shoddily built in the sand by the local authorities. With a nasty tilt to the left, it consisted of two toilets side by side. One of the planks in the wall between them was missing. In gay terminology, this was called a "glory hole"!

There always seemed to be a couple of guys, if not more, nonchalantly standing in line, waiting to make use of the clubrooms. A lot of butch posturing went on, everyone pretending to be cut short while on a bushwalk, no one making eye contact. In fact, sometimes, there was an undeniable air of animosity. I always felt it an odd thing about gay and closeted men and denial. They were all there for the same thing but had to put up a pretence. Often when I arrived, I would be permitted to jump the queue because a pretty fourteen-year-old would relax the tension, and barriers would drop as quickly as my bathers. I often look at the children of our friends, especially the ones about that age, and think to myself, "No, they couldn't possibly."

I was terribly promiscuous. Thank God, it was a different time. I could have been murdered, dismembered or kept tied up on a mattress in a basement for years. It was before we had ever heard of the term "safe sex". Luckily, though, I never caught any nasty diseases. I didn't even get a case of the "crabs" until I was in my mid-twenties.

That was an amusing incident that must interrupt the chronology of this chapter. I was working at Le Louvre when I was afflicted by the symptoms of the dreaded "crab lice". I had no idea what was wrong, except that something was. I told Miss Wightman that I needed an hour off to see a doctor. She asked what was wrong. I could hardly tell her. So, I said I was feeling off-colour, tired and generally rundown.

"Oh, you must see Mr Williams."

Her doctor was so highly qualified that he wasn't "Dr" but "Mr". All the doctors would consult Mr Williams when they reached a brick wall. He was a consultant's consultant.

She got on the phone directly and, within two minutes, I found myself at his rooms a few doors up Collins Street, just next to the venerable premises of The Melbourne Club. The rooms were high Victorian and very gloomy. It was like stepping back a hundred years. There was no sound and almost no light. "Nurse" greeted me, having spoken to Miss Wightman only minutes before. Nurse (that's how you addressed her) ushered me into Mr Williams's hallowed inner sanctum. Mr Williams must have been ninety-five if he was a day. He was dressed in full morning suit with a starched wing collar polished like the finest marble. Having shrunk several sizes since he first wore this suit, he looked like a character from a Tim Burton film.

"Now, young man, what seems to be the problem? Miss Wightman tells me you are somewhat out of sorts."

At that precise moment, the party going on in my knickers turned fervent. I told him my symptoms. He told me to drop my pants, adjusted his pince-nez, and had a close look. Maybe, in his rarified world, he had never come across a case such as mine. As I rearranged myself, he gruffly gave me the following advice: "Take a brisk walk by the sea several mornings a week and take some iron tablets. Good morning!"

When I asked for an account, Nurse assured me there would be no charge. As I turned to leave, she slipped a folded note into my hand and suggested that I discreetly hand it to a male pharmacist. She must have been eavesdropping on the consultation, as the pharmacist supplied me with a lotion and some different advice, which did the trick.

Back in town after a summer of earthly delights, I had to expand my horizons beyond visiting Gary up the road because his family moved away, so that option disappeared. I soon discovered that Seddon railway station was a "beat". It was in a very dilapidated state – again a timber and corrugated-iron hodgepodge of buildings. The men's toilets faced each other, and again a missing plank (which would go missing again the moment it was replaced) facilitated a steady stream of after-dark activity. I soon figured out that sitting up in the peppercorn trees gave me an excellent vantage point to watch what was going on. Sometimes the to-and-fro was amusement enough.

I was considering going professional at this stage, and, by chance, I found my first regular paying customer. One night, the moon was full. It was so bright that there was no traffic at the beat. I was feeling the effects of that moon, growing hair on the backs of my hand, and getting restless and desperate. An old man who looked like the understudy in *Waiting for Godot* approached me, took my hand gently and told me to follow him. At the end of the station, he unlocked a bolt and led me into a small service yard that I didn't know existed. In the moonlight, he completely undressed me. I just stood there, and he just looked, turning me around and looking some more. This went on for ages.

Meanwhile, he engaged in various activities that seemed to give him great pleasure. It was quite a departure from the "wham bam, thank you ma'm" that typified the furtive couplings I had experienced in the sand dunes. He didn't remove anything from his own body except his woollen gloves. And when he had finished with me, he insisted on dressing me.

I was quite pleased to be getting back into my clothes by this time, as it was the beginning of winter. It was very erotic – the full moon, the steamy breath, the woollen gloves on the ground next to my pile of clothes. As we left, he gave me five 2 shilling coins. I was a working boy! This was the life for me!

I saw him about a dozen times, then he vanished. I watched out for him as I lurked in those peppercorn trees over the next few years. As I said, I always liked an older man! But he was very old, and I guess he had passed away. I like to think that I brought some joy to his latter days.

Gay men generally have an obsession with appearance, seeking perfect bodies and handsome faces. And yet some of my best casual sexual experiences have been with people far from the idealised model, which has never been important to me, and some of the dullest bashes I have ever had were with handsome gods with celestial bodies.

For the next few years, I romped around the various traps. I had lots of what is referred to in the gay lexicon as "fuck buddies" – non-committal, casual and occasional relationships, the foundation of which was sex. I had one with an ambulance driver, the venue being the back of his ambulance. I thought it was hilarious – not a lot of room on the stretcher bed and all those drips and oxygen tanks!

Once, I was involved in a threesome with two fuddy-duddy suburban queens, guys in their mid-forties. They were a hoot. They would spread out a picnic blanket in their living room. I never once saw the bedroom. When I arrived, they would be naked but still fussing around. One was vacuuming on one visit. They would put on highly inappropriate music (such as the *William Tell Overture*), which would dictate the tempo for the action! For a fly on the wall, the scene must have looked like an early black-and-white Chaplin film. You know, all jerky and fast, like the cameraman was on crack!

One oddball used to pretend that his mother was in her bedroom, the door being slightly ajar and light spilling into the darkened hall. He was another one who preferred the open kitchen or living room floor to a comfortable bed. We would tiptoe around, never making a noise, not even during or after sex. I knew he lived alone, as I peeked into the "mother's room" once when he went to have a pee. I played along with the game for a while. Then one night, when I had become bored with him, I screamed out as I was leaving, "Goodnight, Mum. Sleep well."

The most famous beat was underground in the middle of a busy roundabout in Footscray that was full of activity at all times of the day and night. Once, I descended the stairs and found the place under about 4 inches of water. This didn't deter the silly poofs in denial. Pretending that they were having a wee, they were all lined up at the urinal while ankle-deep in water! I didn't go there regularly as it was dangerous. Gay bashers would occasionally entrap and lay waste to any victims unlucky enough to be there at the time. Having seen the aftermath of one such bloodbath, I never went there again.

Not all beats are public conveniences. The most popular in Melbourne was Toorak Road, South Yarra. From Punt Road to Chapel Street, men would cruise up and down as soon the sun went down, "window shopping" for those in denial. Cruisers in cars would cruise the cruisers on foot! They would play cat-and-mouse games, with people hopping in and out of cars, all looking for Mr Right (for the night). A wants B. C wants A. B fancies C. C is appalled. In comes D, who will have anyone but annoys everyone.

When I first moved in to Avoca Street, almost on the corner of "Toorak Road", this beat was in its heyday. One night, I had my mother over for dinner, showing her the new flat. The bay window looked out over the very epicentre of Cruise Central. Taking in the view, Mum commented on how cosmopolitan the area was and how nice it was to see people out and about so late at night. All the shop windows must have been on timers – they all blacked out simultaneously – but the window shoppers were undeterred!

I met my first boyfriend on Toorak Road long before I moved to South Yarra. The Regent Theatre was still operating back then, and it would show early Hollywood classics on Friday nights. Although I knew the films by heart from my lunchtime TV, it was something else to see idols like Greta Garbo on a giant cinema screen. I would go every Friday night and soon became aware of the cat-and-mouse cruising games as I walked a couple of blocks to the railway station. I hopped in quite a few cars.

I met Aden on one of these Friday-night passeggiatas. By this stage, I had installed the hide-a-man, walk-in wardrobe in the bungalow at Hobbs Street. I didn't entertain men frequently – only when I thought the risk was worth it. Aden *was* worth it, and I became infatuated. He was a newsreader on television and also managed a couple of up-and-coming pop singers. I discovered that one of those pop stars who had been under his wing was still entertaining. He must be on a Zimmer frame by now.

Aden was twenty-four and said that any good journalist worth his salt should be dead by twenty-five. This made me nervous, especially when I couldn't track him down. He flew to New Zealand to cover the Wahine disaster, the helicopter he was in crashed, almost fulfilling his destiny. Beside myself, I thrashed around on the living room floor, following the news coverage on TV. My mother was quite surprised, as it was the first time I had ever shown the slightest interest in the news. And the last time!

I continued sneaking out to meet him. Feigning tiredness one night while watching Graham Kennedy's *In Melbourne Tonight*, I excused myself and went off to bed. I changed into my brand-new trench coat, a pale camel colour, and walked to the phone booth at Seddon station to arrange our liaison. But he couldn't meet me, so I went home. I changed back into pyjamas and roughed up my hair. Because it was still early, I came back into the living room, yawning and stretching and saying that I couldn't sleep. I was stopped dead in my tracks – not only by the look on my parents' faces but also by the sight of the open Venetian blinds on the picture window. Before I had left, I had made sure they were closed. SPRUNG!

I was sprung several times – once when walking home from the Thumpin' Tum discotheque at 4 am. On New Footscray Road, a car pulled over, and I thought, "Good. The night's not over yet." Imagine my

surprise to find the driver was my father coming home from night shift!
I loved the Thumpin' Tum and went there whenever I could afford it.
One night, my father was part of a sweep that police made through the
various clubs in the city. There I was dancing away when I saw him in his
navy serge uniform. Being quick and slim, I was able to hide behind the
cigarette machine.

The Rose Bowl was another underground activity centre that
I frequented. It was so named as it was underground, surrounded by a
garden of roses. I was driving my mother's little Bluebird by this stage.
Cars also figured in the mating game, and an old, beaten-up Morris
Minor didn't exude much allure, so I would park it around the corner.
I had more success hopping into someone else's car than luring anyone
into that poor little, rattling rust-trap on wheels.

I met my next boyfriend at the Rose Bowl. He drove the latest flashy
white MG, a surrogate appendage for qualities he lacked, hair being one
of them. He was in his fifties and small and nervous. I used to watch
him trying to hook up with someone. He would get knocked back time
after time, but he was persistent and always finished up either driving
away with a passenger or with someone following the racy little MG into
the night. He never approached me. Maybe it was the car. One night,
though, as a last resort, he did approach me. Feeling sorry for him,
I agreed to go back to his apartment. As it turned out, he owned one
of the first penthouses in the city. And – true to form – the short,
nervous, bald doctor was a terrific lover.

As with Aden, I couldn't separate sex and love. The doctor was very
promiscuous and made no promises of fidelity, but I became infatuated
and got myself in a twist emotionally. Sometimes, he would call me
into his rooms in Collins Street. Unlike Mr Williams's Pre-Raphaelite
mausoleum, his rooms were sleek and modern. Without any more of a
to-do than "G'day Mate", he would ask me to roll up a sleeve and then
give me an injection. He could have been giving me anything. I never
thought to ask. But I figured he was protecting me from any minor
sexually transmitted infections that he might have picked up.

After becoming obsessed with him, I turned into a demented stalker. One night, he fobbed me off with a weak excuse that he was working back late, but I had binoculars trained on his kitchen window, so I knew it was a fib. I followed him to the Rose Bowl, where he picked someone up immediately. I took myself off to the Windsor Hotel and had a few drinks, dripping wet tears into a dry martini. Later that night, I continued my stalking and saw him score another hit at the Rose Bowl. This flipped me over the edge. After a few more martinis, I was quite drunk and decided to go home with the first guy that asked. That was a big mistake. My guard was down. I was emotional and drunk.

Although I lived to tell this tale, it was the closest I ever came to a sticky end. I had gone off with a wiry, dark, quite handsome Yugoslav (or central European). Years before it was fashionable, he had a rugged, unshaven face. I soon felt uncomfortable and very sober. Usually, several opportunities arise to get out of a situation like the one I found myself in. But nothing could deflect this rendezvous from its dire direction. He became agitated and started to get rough, ripping the buttons off my beautiful Agnona coat as he tried to undress me. He talked like a mad man about what he liked to do and what he wanted to do to me. He flung open a wardrobe covered with pages and pages of pornography, pinned in layers on the backs of the doors.

I was getting desperate. If he got any more of my clothes off, I was a goner, I thought. So, I tried to engage him in any sort of conversation. Noting that most of the pornography was straight porn – with graphic close-ups of vaginas, puckered-up bottoms, enormous breasts and big purple penises, all glistening with eager anticipation – I started to talk like a rangy old sailor. It was dirty talk so vile that its memory makes me want to wash my mouth out with soapy water to this day. He became quite animated. All at once, I could see myself gaining the advantage. During this banter, somehow, my mother came into play.

"You like to fuck your mother?" he asked.

His face lit up like a beacon.

"Yes," I said. "All the time. She loves it. Would you like to fuck her?"

In a flash, he had my coat back on me, and we were out the door and in his car. Well, at least I was out of his lair. My mind was going at 100 miles an hour, almost as fast as my mouth. I devised an escape plan and directed him towards the underground beat in Footscray. He knew it well, and I suggested picking up another team member as my mother was tireless. This would be a night to remember.

There was a footbridge crossing the railway line next to a set of traffic lights on the way. My plan was to leap out, whether the lights were red or green. The lights were green as we approached, and he was going very fast. But, thankfully, they changed to red, and we stopped. Just as they were about to switch back to green, I leapt out and charged towards the overpass. He couldn't do anything but drive on. I could hear the cars behind him blasting their horns as I made my way home. The most damage the evening had done was to tarnish the image of my mother and remove a few buttons on an Italian coat.

The Rose Bowl was also where I met the first real love of my life. He was extremely handsome and a wonderful lover. Our affair lasted about six years plus a small encore but it ended badly with my heart being broken. My inability to see the difference between love and sex proved fatal. We shared a passion, but he was cerebral, and I wasn't. I suppose I suffered a mini-breakdown and wasn't thinking clearly for a while.

Georgina was about to go away on a trip. I assured her I would be fine. Trying to carry on, as usual, I packed her clothes for her six-week trip. When she arrived in Paris in the middle of a sweltering heatwave, she opened her suitcase to find I had packed it full of her dirty winter clothes. She sent them home and bought out the entire Sonia Rykiel boutique in Saint-Germain-des-Prés.

I got over my broken heart, although I didn't have sex with anyone for two years. I still hit the dance floor but lived my sex life vicariously through my best friend, who was extremely energetic. Everyone was a "prince", with the best body, the best this, the best that. From what I could gather, the best thing about them was that they all vanished into thin air in the morning. I still had many admirers, but I couldn't commit to anything after the last dance. I remember Monday night was the Hotel Chevron's "Gay Night", and this gorgeous guy with a mass of curly hair like Louis XIV would ask me every week, "Dy'a wanna dance or what?" I never did find out what the "or what" was.

The spell was finally broken one night by a very persistent young man from Brisbane. I was at a club, sitting at the bar, giving off my best frosty Garbo "I vant to be alone" impression. He was so annoying and would not leave me in peace. He was tall, dark and handsome, if someone so young could be categorised in that way. Maybe it would be better to say that he was extremely cute and cheeky. When my favourite Human League song came on, he mimed "Don't *you want me, baby*" at me from across the bar. That cracked me up, and I eventually gave in.

Donald and I had a wonderful affair, which continued by correspondence after he returned to Brisbane. He would write to me every day. He was extremely artistic, and his letters were works of art. Sometimes, the envelope would explode with a thousand little drawings. Or the letter would unfold and unfold and fill a room. I kept them for years until Mark destroyed most of them in a fit of pique one night. I still have some somewhere, and I still have him as a friend. Donald fell in love with someone in Brisbane as I fell in love with Mark, and we were both happy for each other.

I am still friends with all of my ex-boyfriends, including the doctor. (I was invited to his ninety-fifth birthday celebration!) Mark has always been quite understanding. Unfortunately, I have been cursed with the dreaded green dragon, so I would never have put up with that had the shoe been on the other foot.

⁓

Many of my female friends have expressed dismay at the idea of my writing candidly about sex in this chapter.

"Would a girl be able to read it?"

Other female friends hope for a shocking exposé, down the "I always wanted to know what gay men do" lane.

I have given a great deal of thought to whether or not to include this chapter. After reading this memoir, there won't be much you don't know about me. I wanted to make this chapter optional, so you could choose to know my secrets, or not.

The image of the totally promiscuous gay male is a stereotype, and I hope this glimpse into my world will counteract that perception. Although I can't deny that promiscuity was part of my life before I met Mark, I finally figured out the sex–love conundrum, and life promptly fell into place.

Gideon Sundback, the inventor of the zipper, has a lot to answer for. I am sure many articles of clothing over the centuries – from the toga to the silk-lined opera cape to the kilt – have made it very easy for a man to quickly access the equipment, have a quick grope and instantly satisfy his primal urge. Still, I think the zipper takes the prize. It makes the mission so uncomplicated!

With "gaydar" – that allegedly inbuilt radar system that gay men have to tell when other gay men are in the vicinity – sex is only a fleeting look away. In my previous life, this radar system never proved wrong. I have had anonymous encounters in all sorts of strange places. I had an amazing encounter with a guy in my carriage on a train between Rome and Florence. He didn't even let go of the newspaper he was reading. Once in Rome, while sightseeing the ruins, a sideways glance from a dark, handsome Roman found us completely naked behind an arch in quite a busy tourist attraction in less than a few minutes. I remember glimpsing the hems of nuns' habits, hearing the clicks of cameras, and feeling contempt for a tour guide expounding utter nonsense to a group of exhausted Japanese. Once, when I was in Sydney on my reconnaissance for Le Louvre at the Wentworth Hotel, I had finished my morning appointments and had two and a half hours to wait for my 2 pm fitting. I went downstairs for a spot of lunch on the terrace. Approaching the lift to return to my room, there were two handsome cowboys in sharp, shiny suits, wearing huge white Stetson hats. Entering the lift, they pushed the button to their floor and asked me what floor I was going. Gaydar

kicked in, and I replied, "What floor are you on?" We frolicked around and had a swell time until I needed to go and check the hem on a French two-piece suit. One of the Texans (they were in town for a conference) kept his Stetson on.

I suppose the element of danger played an integral part in these adventures. There are as many dark corners in gay sex as in heterosexual quarters – areas that don't interest me. One high-profile gay icon has expressed the opinion that he would just as well have a cup of tea as have sex. Well, I wouldn't go that far. But sex, to me, isn't the prime source of happiness. Maybe I burnt out early.

As in any marriage, with the passage of time, love eclipses sex and becomes the most important aspect of a relationship. At this stage of my life, I am fortunate to have love in abundance. Have I had the best of both love and sex? I've certainly been reckless with my self-indulgences. I never thought about the issues that worry young gay men today. No one did in those days.

As mentioned already, Miss Wightman had a saying about many of the women who graced the copper doors of her haute couture salon: "The wind never touched" them. Sometimes, I feel like I have lived a breeze-free existence. My sex life has never been a source of angst. It's been fun, varied and colourful.

I've loved a few girls and a lot of boys. I've met some great people along the way, some of whom are still in my life and still loved. I have always had Teddy, a constant in my life, the poor little bugger still tortured with pins when it's time for a new frock. The long pearl hatpin has long gone but not the joy and silliness of a boy and his bear sharing a life well lived. I have alluded to the movies when opening and closing many chapters in this memoir. What movie should I call on now?

My choice, a bit twee but entirely appropriate, is *Love Is a Many Splendored Thing*, in which Nat King Cole sings:

> *Love is nature's way of giving a reason to be living,*
> *The golden crown that makes a man a king.*

It was the answer to the conundrum that had confused me for so long. If only the world watched more movies, they might cotton on!

Coda

It's not over yet. I want to show my father that I really can paint; house painter indeed!

Acknowledgements

I wish to acknowledge the following:
Courtney Nicholls and Hannah Louey at Hardie Grant, who
have been a delight to work with. Kara Baker, who introduced
me to Julie Pinkham at Hardie Grant, who set the ball rolling.
Kate Slattery for finding the right balance and placing of
the illustrations. Morgan Williams for his encouragement
and introducing me to my primary editor, Rell Hannah,
who managed my ramblings, cut me in half and somehow
made sense of it all. Sally Moss, my in-house editor,
for her direction, dedication and discretion. Teddy.
My husband, Mark, for everything else.